Market New Products Successfully

Market New Products Successfully

KEVIN J. CLANCY
PETER C. KRIEG
MARIANNE McGARRY WOLF

LEXINGTON BOOKS

A Division of
ROWMAN & LITTLEFIELD PUBLISHERS, INC.
Lanham • *Boulder* • *New York* • *Toronto* • *Oxford*

LEXINGTON BOOKS

A division of Rowman & Littlefield Publishers, Inc.
A wholly owned subsidiary of The Rowman & Littlefield Publishing Group, Inc.
4501 Forbes Boulevard, Suite 200
Lanham, Maryland 20706

PO Box 317
Oxford
OX2 9RU, UK

British Library Cataloguing in Publication Information Available

Library of Congress Cataloging-in-Publication Data

Clancy, Kevin J., 1942–
  Market new products successfully : using simulated test marketing technology / by
  Kevin J. Clancy, Peter C. Krieg, Marianne McGarry Wolf.
        p. cm.
  Includes bibliographical references and index.
  ISBN-10: 0-7391-1179-5 (cloth : alk. paper)
  ISBN-13: 978-0-7391-1179-6
        1. Marketing—Computer simulation. 2. New products—Marketing. 3. Test
  marketing. I. Krieg, Peter C., 1951– II. Wolf, Marianne McGarry, 1952– III. Title.
  HF5415.125.C578 2005
  658.8'00285—dc22   2005011852

Printed in the United States of America

∞™ The paper used in this publication meets the minimum requirements of American
National Standard for Information Sciences—Permanence of Paper for Printed Library
Materials, ANSI/NISO Z39.48-1992.

Contents

List of Figures

Acknowledgments

We are especially pleased to acknowledge the early contributions of Dr. David Learner and James K. DeVoe at BBDO Advertising; their consultants, Professors Abraham Charnes and William Cooper of Carnegie Mellon University and their successors at BBDO; and Dr. Lewis Pringle, Dr. Larry Light, and Edward Brody for their magnificent contributions to marketing and management science, particularly new product forecasting technology. BBDO's DEMON (Decision Mapping via Optimal GO-NO Networks), published in *Management Science* in 1966 and NEWS (New Product Early Warning System) published in *Management Science* 16 years later, represented path-breaking efforts to model the new product introduction process.

We are equally pleased to acknowledge the seminal contributions of Florence Skelly and Bob Goldberg of the Yankelovich organization who were the creators and champions of The Laboratory Test Market, the first and in many ways the most interesting of the early simulated test marketing methodologies. Their pioneering work for packaged goods clients such as Procter & Gamble and Pillsbury revolutionized the way that marketers introduced new products.

Special thanks also go to their protégé, the brilliant Robert Shulman, our former partner at Yankelovich Clancy Shulman and, later, Copernicus, and now CEO of Markitecture, as well as coauthor of our earlier volume on this topic, who, as a visionary and proselytizer, encouraged the development of the Litmus model and introduced it to consumer products and services marketers throughout the United States and Canada.

We also acknowledge the strong contribution to simulated test marketing made by Professors Glen L. Urban, John R. Hauser, and Alvin J. Silk, and their colleagues at Management Decision Systems, for their work on the Assessor model, which represented a more theoretically grounded and methodologically sophisticated variant of Yankelovich's Laboratory Test Market.

We would also like to recognize the contributions Jacques Blanchard, Lisa Carter, Gerald Eskin, Louis Forte, Russ and Doug Haley, Philip Kotler, Lynn Lin, John Malek, Dudley Ruch, Robert Wachsler, Gerry Wind, and Joseph Woodlock for their many contributions to the field and our thinking.

We are especially indebted to Dr. Steve Tipps of Copernicus, Professor Joseph Blackburn of the Owen School of Management at Vanderbilt University, Professor Paul Berger of the Boston University School of Management, and Professor Dale Wilson of the Eli Broad Graduate School of Management at Michigan State University, who have consulted to us on this topic for many years and for their many contributions to the LITMUS and Discovery models and this book.

The client companies that used our services at one time or another over the years for simulated test marketing purposes deserve a special note of recognition. The CEOs, marketing directors, and research directors who saw promise in the emerging technology and sought our assistance in employing it to assess and improve a new product/new service marketing plan often contributed to our thinking and led to model refinements for which they received little formal recognition. These companies include (but are not limited to) American Express, Bristol-Myers Squibb, Campbell Soup Co., Citicorp, Clorox, Colgate-Palmolive, ConAgra, Gillette, H. J. Heinz, Kraft, Lever Bros., McDonald's, Merck, Norelco, Ore-Ida, Ortho-McNeil, Pfizer, Ralston Purina, Pepsi-Cola, and Visa.

Finally, we would like to thank Wally Wood, an extremely talented business writer, editor, novelist, authority on all things Japanese, and friend, whose skills and spirit throughout five difficult books continue to impress us; the very creative Ami Bowen of Copernicus Marketing Consulting, who served as project manager for this book from initiation to publication; Dana Gee and Sam Dennis of Spot Design: and Jason Hallman and Audrey Babkirk at Rowman & Littlefield for their support on this project.

Any errors in the manuscript are entirely our own which will be corrected in future printings of this book.

1

Why New Products Fail

Watching the game films on Monday after Sunday's loss, any knowledgeable fan can spot the quarterback's mistakes and explain what he might have done to win the game.

Once a new product or service has failed, any knowledgeable marketing executive can spot the company's mistakes and suggest what it might have done to introduce a winner. The challenge, of course, is not in spotting the mistakes after the product has bombed, but avoiding them in the first place, which is what this book is designed to help you do.

New and repositioned products and services, both consumer and business-to-business, fail for many reasons, and this chapter will talk about some of them to sketch the landscape in which most new products fail. Indeed, let's start with a little Monday-morning quarterbacking of Cottonelle Fresh Rollwipes.

Kimberly-Clark introduced Cottonelle Fresh Rollwipes as "America's first and only dispersible, pre-moistened wipe on a roll." This "breakthrough product" was, according to the corporation's press release, "the most significant category innovation since toilet paper first appeared in roll form in 1890." Cottonelle Fresh Rollwipes "deliver the cleaning and freshening of pre-moistened wipes with the convenience and disposability of toilet paper."

Kimberly-Clark was certain a large market existed for the product. Its research had established that 63 percent of the American population—or something like 144 million people—had experimented with a wet "cleansing method." Even better, one of four use a moist wipe daily. Virtually all of these prospects use a baby wipe, but baby wipes should not be flushed down the toilet because they clog septic systems and municipal water treatment plants; thus the advantage of a "dispersible" wipe that breaks up in water.

Kimberly-Clark had been selling tubs containing sheets of "dispersible" moistened toilet paper for years, which *could* be flushed, and the growth of this product convinced the corporation to invest research money into finding a more convenient and consumer-friendly delivery mechanism.

The folks in research and development came up with a refillable beige plastic dispenser that clipped to a standard toilet paper spindle and held both a roll of dry toilet paper and the wet Fresh Rollwipes. The dispenser with four starter rolls was to sell for $8.99; a refill pack of four rolls was $3.99. Kimberly-Clark, which says it spent $100 million in research on the project, protected the product and its dispenser with 30 patents.

In making the January 2001 announcement, the corporation said that the U.S. toilet paper market was $4.8 billion a year, and it expected first-year Fresh Rollwipes sales to reach at least $150 million. Kimberly-Clark expected Fresh Rollwipes sales to be $500 million within six years. Even better, those sales would expand the total U.S. toilet paper market because moistened toilet paper tends to supplement dry toilet paper rather than replace it, so Fresh Rollwipes would not severely cannibalize ordinary Cottonelle sales.

But by October, ten months later, Cottonelle Fresh Rollwipes sales were about a third of the forecast $150 million according to Information Resources Inc. Kimberly-Clark blamed the economy for poor sales, but in our experience, if consumers are really interested in a new product, a weak economy will not have a dramatic effect on sales of a product with a sticker price of $25 or less. Something was wrong with Kimberly-Clark's marketing, and the *Wall Street Journal* has reported some of the corporation's missteps.[1]

WHAT WENT WRONG WITH ROLLWIPES
Start with the premature announcement. Although Kimberly-Clark rolled out the publicity and advertising in January, it was not ready to ship the product to stores until July. This is like turning the air conditioning on full blast in winter to cool the house in midsummer. True, the late arrival of manufacturing equipment was responsible for "a good part" of the delay, but by July, most

shoppers had forgotten about the hype. Rob Almond purchases paper goods as director of housekeeping services for Richfield Nursing Center, in Salem, Virginia—one of the markets where Rollwipes was available. He told the *Journal*, "I know I've heard something about it. I can't recall if it was a commercial or a comedian making fun of it."

Not only was the advertising ill-timed, but it was also ineffective. Granted, Kimberly-Clark was trying to promote a product and its benefits in solving a problem few people can talk about without embarrassment, but the advertising and promotion never explained to consumers what the product does. Fresh Rollwipes advertising agency WPP Group's J. Walter Thompson created a fun image, with shots of people from behind, splashing in the water. The $35 million advertising campaign carried the slogan, "Sometimes wetter is better." A print ad was an extreme close-up of a sumo wrestler's behind. Analysts criticized the ads for not clearly explaining the product's benefit—or helping create demand.

Finally, Kimberly-Clark ran the ads nationally when a) the product was not available at all and b) when it was finally available only in certain southern markets.

The product had yet another problem that research should have identified. Unlike the wet wipes in boxes that bashful consumers can hide in a bathroom's vanity, Cottonelle Fresh Rollwipes came in a very visible plastic dispenser. The dispenser was about the size of two rolls of toilet paper on top of one other. Not every bathroom has space for such a dispenser, and not every consumer wants beige plastic. As Tom Vierhile, president of Marketing Intelligence Service Ltd., told the *Wall Street Journal*, "You do not want to have to ask someone to redecorate their bathroom."[2]

If ever a product was suitable for a sampling campaign, Cottonelle Fresh Rollwipes was it. (And Kimberly-Clark could have produced a ton of samples with a piece of the $35 million advertising and promotion budget.) But it did not design Rollwipes in small trial sizes, which meant it could not pass out free samples. Rather, it scheduled a van, outfitted with a mobile restroom and Fresh Rollwipes, to stop at public places in the Southeast in mid-September 2001. It was pure bad luck the road trip got canceled after September 11th.

Something else the corporation could not control, of course, was the competition. Shortly after Kimberly-Clark announced Fresh Rollwipes, a small California company, Moist Mates LLC, claimed that John J. Marino, a Boston entrepreneur, had invented wet toilet paper on a roll and brought it to market in 1996. Aside from the intellectual property issue, the Moist Mates sales history might have given Kimberly-Clark pause. Five years after the product's introduction, it was being sold through only eight retail outlets representing 528 stores in the entire United States.

Nevertheless, Procter & Gamble Co. (P&G), listening to the buzz Kimberly-Clark's announcement generated, wanted a "me-too" product and bought Moist Mates. P&G repackaged Moist Mates under the name Charmin Fresh Mates, shipped it to the same markets as Fresh Rollwipes, and started TV advertising the same day. A Fresh Mates starter kit dispenser with one refill roll of 99 sheets was expected to sell for $2.49 to $2.99 (versus Rollwipes' $8.99).

A year and a half after Kimberly-Clark's big announcement, Fresh Rollwipes were in one regional market and corporate executives said sales were so disappointing they were not financially material. At P&G a spokeswoman said the company was happy with Fresh Mates but declined to discuss any expansion plans for "competitive" reasons.

THE HIGH FREQUENCY OF MARKETING FAILURE

Like the executives at Kimberly-Clark, corporate managements around the globe believe new and improved products lead to growth and profitability. In 2004, package goods marketers introduced more than 33,185 new food and nonfood products, 1.5 percent below 2003, according to Productscan Online.[3]

Of course, not all of these (or even most of them) are "new" products in the sense that the world has never seen anything like them before. Most of these are "me-too" products, different versions of the same product other companies offer according to Productscan Online.[4] About 13 percent are seasonal products, and 6 percent are line extensions such as the recently introduced Betty Crocker Pour & Frost Pourable Frosting, Budweiser B-to-the-E Beer, Kleenex Anti-Viral Facial Tissue, or the Swiffer Carpet Flick. Only 1.5 percent of new food products are "classically innovative," and most of these fail as well. What percentage succeeds?

Regrettably, companies do not report their product and service failures with the same eagerness they report their product successes. Although there is no definitive answer, the consensus among marketing executives is that at most only 10 percent succeed while denying their own companies suffer such a pitiful rate.

A recent Nielsen Bases (Booz Allen Sales Estimating System) and Ernst & Young study put the failure rate of new U.S. consumer products at 95 percent.[5]

These results, of course, are not limited to consumer products. Our own experience with both consumer services and business-to-business products and services suggests a failure rate of at least 90 percent. Today, based on our experience and research, we believe that no more than 10 percent of all new products or services are successful—that is, still on the market and profitable after three years. This is true for virtually any category you consider: consumer durables, pharmaceuticals, financial services, business-to-business products and services (think of the dot com debacle), and more. Even television programs and movies. Consider the highly publicized recent movies that bombed at the box office—*Stealth, The Island, Kingdom of Heaven, Bad News Bears.* The exact figures may vary by category, but not as much as one might think.

Marketing executives understand that far more products fail than succeed, yet they also know companies have to maintain a steady stream of new products to grow—or to maintain pace with competitors. In one sense, that is absolutely true. Technological advances, changing consumer tastes, and competition all mean that companies must continue to innovate to avoid being run over by the wheels of change.

Yet, as Robert M. McMath and Thom Forbes title their book *What Were They Thinking?*[6], what were marketers thinking when they introduced Frito-Lay Lemonade? Bengay Aspirin? Louis Sherry No Sugar Added Gorgonzola Cheese Dressing? Cracker Jack Cereal? Smucker's Premium Ketchup? Fruit of the Loom Laundry Detergent?

What were the marketers at 3Com thinking when they announced Audrey? Designed to be "the nerve center for the home," Audrey offered one-touch access to e-mail, Web channels, a household calendar, address book, and Palm HotSync technology. It had a wireless keyboard, touch screen, and a microphone so users could send voice messages.

Five months after introducing the device, 3Com discontinued marketing it. Aside from 3Com's internal problems (it wanted to cut $1 billion out of its operating costs in that fiscal year), Audrey had her own problems. The thing cost $499, and it could not connect through America Online, which meant all prospects that used AOL had to subscribe to another Internet service provider to use Audrey.

Gateway solved that problem by introduced the Connected Touch Pad, its version of Audrey, which worked *only* with AOL. It, however, was $600 and flopped. Compaq introduced its iPAQ IA-1, which worked only with the MSN network and cost $99 to $599 depending on how long the customer committed to MSN Internet. But as Milosz Skrzypczak, an analyst with The Yankee Group, observed, "The average consumer looks at an Internet appliance and asks, 'Why am I going to buy it? What's the purpose of this device?'"[7]

Financial services are rife with failure. The evidence we've been quietly collecting for years suggests a failure rate of 90 percent or greater for new products and services introduced by banks, brokerage houses, credit card companies, and credit unions. In the fast food industry, only one in a hundred new products introduced regionally or nationally is considered to be a success.

Business-to-business products and services also routinely fail. One spectacular example of a business-to-business service failure was Sprint's Integrated On-Demand Network (ION). The service was designed to give small businesses and high-end residential customers local and long-distance voice and high-speed Internet service. Sprint began rolling out the service in Kansas City, Missouri, Denver, and Seattle in the fall of 1999. The basic package included 2,200 minutes of domestic calling time per month, regardless of where the calls went, and unlimited Internet access at speeds in excess of 1 megabit per second. The service was $160 a month, and required buying a $250 customer-premises terminal and paying a $150 installation fee.

A Sprint spokesman said that the monthly package fee represented a $40 savings over what small-business customers typically pay for separate services, and "it offers the convenience of one bill." At first, Sprint offered the service only to existing customers, and then began marketing to other prospects; then, six months after ION's launch, Sprint announced a new feature to the service—Distance Free Voice. This was a long-distance and local voice package geared to companies with a large number of telecommuters or branch offices.

Clearly Sprint misjudged the market. In the fall of 2001, it announced that it was discontinuing ION, firing 6,000 employees, and eliminating 1,500 contract positions. ION was never profitable, and shutting it down with the attendant layoffs contributed largely to a $1.23 billion fourth quarter loss.[8]

BRANDS ARE BECOMING COMMODITIES

There is no question it is growing more difficult to introduce a successful new product or service. For 20 years or so after World War II, more than half of all new products introduced succeeded (by succeeded we mean the product was still on the shelf and profitable 3 years after introduction). Products that did succeed could expect to be around 50 years or more.

Even 25 years ago, perhaps a quarter of the products companies launched succeeded. Markets for many product categories were less penetrated and less saturated than they are today. A large part of a new product's sales came from category growth, rather than from consumer brand switching, and companies were pioneering new categories.

Today, almost all consumer markets are mature. Any real growth comes from population increases, which never exceed 1 to 2 percent a year. To survive at all, a new product must wrench market share away from other, established brands, or create a new category, or both. Red Bull, as an illustration, for a time the fastest-growing soft drink in America, accomplished both.

In the 2000s, many brands are in decline because there has been an industry shift from brand-building advertising to promotional programs, a shift from information-oriented to entertainment-oriented advertising, and a shift from communications that convey a distinctive positioning strategy to communications that focus on brand essence or imagery. As a result, many brands are becoming commodities in consumers' minds, as shown by four published studies on this topic, including one done by Copernicus/Synovate, an abstract of which was recently published in the *Harvard Business Review*.[9]

Our study found that consumers perceive the leading brands becoming more similar than different in categories as diverse as hair care products and rental cars. Of the 48 categories we evaluated, consumers see the leading brands in 39 of them becoming more similar over time. In 4 categories, the leading brands are maintaining their level of differentiation, and in only 4 categories do consumers see the leading brands becoming more different—and 2 of these are political parties (Democrats/Republicans) and religious denominations (Protestant/Catholic). See figure 1.1 for the top 30 categories in terms of increasing commoditization.

As brands become more similar in the consumer's mind, a low price becomes more important than a brand name. In 28 of 37 product categories in which we queried respondents about price, consumers indicated low price was more important than brand name when making a purchase. In only three categories (automobiles, liquor, and beer) is brand name more important than price—and this by a modest margin.[10] All this suggests that

Similarity Scores For Leading Brands
in 30 Product Categories

From: *Brand Confusion*, Clancy and Trout, *Harvard Business Review*, March 2002

Pairs of Leading Brands	Similarity Score
Credit Cards: Visa/Mastercard	90
Office Supply Stores: Staples/Office Depot	80
Hair Care Products: L Oreal/Clairol	74
Online Reference Sites: Maps.com/MapQuest.com	74
Catalog Clothing Brands: L.L. Bean/Land s End	72
Pet Supply Stores: PetsMart/PetCo	68
Gas Stations: Mobil/Shell	68
Bookstores: Barnes & Noble/Borders	68
Bottled Water: Aquafina/Evian	64
Major Household Appliances: Whirlpool/GE	60
Banks: Citibank/Bank of America	60
Cookies: Chips Ahoy/Chips Deluxe	56
Airlines: United/American	56
Health & Fitness Clubs: Bally s/Gold s Gym	56
Athletic Shoes: Nike/Adidas	54
Long-Distance Telephone Service: AT&T/MCI	54
Online Toy Stores: ToysRUs.com/eToys.com	50
Cars: Toyota/Honda	46
Weight Loss Programs: Jenny Craig/Weight Watchers	44
Internet Service Providers: America On-Line/AT&T WorldNet	44
Online Bookstores: Amazon.com/Barnes&Noble.com	42
Personal Computers: IBM/Compaq	42
TV Networks: NBC/CBS	40
Cosmetics: Revlon/Cover Girl	36
Rental Cars: Enterprise/Hertz	36
Brokerages: Merrill Lynch/Fidelity	34
Internet Search Engines: Yahoo/MSN	34
Potato Chips: Lay s/Ruffles	32
Diapers: Huggies/Pampers	32
Toothpaste: Colgate/Crest	30

* More positive values indicate increasing similarity between brands.
A score of 200 indicates that the brands have become redundant
(e.g., a commodity with no difference between them)

FIGURE 1.1.

companies introducing a new product or service should focus on a distinctive positioning strategy so that consumers do not immediately regard the new entry as just another commodity, which—usually—costs more than the existing commodities.

Adding to the marketing complexity, the retail trade is now a marketplace power. As recently as the early 1980s, retailers tended to be passive channels for product distribution. Today, retailers are an active, powerful marketing element (just ask any Wal-Mart, Costco, Best Buy, Circuit City, Home Depot, Office Max, or Staples supplier). They have provoked price competition among manufacturers. They insist on slotting allowances (money to put the product on their shelves), promotional allowances, and exit fees (money to take the product off the shelves, money that makes up what they would have earned if the product had sold properly). The last time we looked, Wal-Mart received $75 million just in penalty fees alone. These tend to insure retailers against the flood of new product failures and raise the manufacturers' cost of entry.

Add these costs to the price of making yourself heard through advertising in an increasingly cacophonous marketplace. Consider the growth in video, audio, and print vehicles over the last 35 years. Figure 1.2 is based on media options available in Burlington, Vermont, and Plattsburgh, New York, in 1960 and 2002, two neighboring cities connected by ferry across Lake Champlain.

While Burlingtonites and Plattsburghers could watch only 2 full-power broadcast television stations in 1960, they can now choose among 10 full-power and 6 low-power broadcast TV stations, not to mention more than 150 cable channels and more than 300 channels for those with satellite TV.

In print, they could choose among at least 750 national weekly and monthly magazines in 1960. Today they can choose from approximately 4,500 national weekly and monthly magazines and at least 18 local monthly magazines.

With this explosion in media options, marketers have watched advertising's productivity decline in the past decade, particularly network television's. When the three networks reached 96 percent of all American homes, network TV was critically important in building brand awareness and in telling consumers that new products were desirable and available. It was also a time of 60-second commercials in which it was possible to tell a story. Today, commercials are 30-, 20-, 10-, and even 5-seconds long.

An Explosion in Media on
Two Sides of Lake Champlain

Media options	1960	2002
Video	2 full-power broadcast TV stations Movies	10 full-power, 6 low-power broadcast TV stations Cable TV: 150+ channels Satellite: 300+ channels Streaming Internet video Movies, DVDs, VCRs
Audio	15 full-power broadcast radio stations Record albums	35 full-power broadcast radio stations 100+ satellite radio channels Streaming Internet audio CDs, MP3s, cassettes
Print	2 metropolitan daily newspapers Approximately 5 neighborhood/ suburban local weekly newspapers 1 national newspaper At least 750 national weekly and monthly magazines	2 metropolitan daily newspapers At least 20 neighborhood/suburban local weekly newspapers At least 20 national and international newspapers Approximately 4,500 national weekly and monthly magazines At least 18 local monthly magazines

Source: NBS, Viacom, and Fox networks/*Boston Herald*, January 13, 2003, p.019

FIGURE 1.2.

As figure 1.2 suggests, traditional marketing communications have lost much of their effect through media fragmentation, splintered communications budgets, and the prevalence of promotional pricing. It is difficult—often impossible—for new product marketers to generate an adequate margin, one that will pay for the marketing program and return a profit in any reasonable time. If Kimberly-Clark spent, as it said, $100 million to develop and another $35 million to introduce Cottonelle Fresh Rollwipes, how long would it take for the $3.99 product to show a profit even if it had been successful?

THE PROBLEMS WITH LINE EXTENSIONS

If new products are so difficult to introduce, what about line extensions? Many marketing executives believe that line extensions are less risky than new products or services. Or they believe that because line extensions are easier to develop and introduce than completely new brands, they are the most profitable. They are often mistaken. Consider the experience of Kraft Foods.

Betsy Holden, as co–chief executive of Kraft Foods Inc., led the corporation through the launch of dozens of line extensions, slightly different versions of Kraft's core brands including Jell-O, Chips Ahoy!, and Kraft Macaroni and Cheese. Advertising, for the most part, focused on promoting the latest extension of the old favorite. It worked for a while, but without a successful totally new brand launch (DiGiorno frozen pizza hit stores in the the mid-1990s), along with dwindling shelf space and declining customer interest in yet another version of Oreos, Kraft's sales began to flatten.

The response from Kraft? More line extensions, some only marginally successful, others disastrous (e.g., Ooey Gooey Warm 'N Chewy Chips Ahoy! for which analysts estimate Kraft took a $17 million hit when it had to take the cookies back). With sales growth flat, and no new offerings in emerging categories such as organic and soy, Kraft's old brands were out of sync with consumer concerns about transfats and general nutrition. As the *Wall Street Journal* commented, "Years of failing to develop new categories and products has given Kraft a lineup that seems stuck in a time warp."[11] Kraft's owners finally decided to move Holden to a "global leadership position," and named her co-CEO, Roger Deromedi, as the sole CEO.

Sergio Zyman, the former marketing chief of Coca-Cola, once condemned what he called "lazy marketing"—the idea that when the going gets tough for your core brands and it seems too hard to grow them, you're better off filling the channel with line extensions and niche products to build the bottom line. We agree that line extensions and niche products are often lazy marketing. They can also be even more risky than developing a new brand. And yet this is exactly what Coke has done in recent years with its disastrous Surge (a niche product designed to compete with Pepsi's Mountain Dew) and recent Vanilla Coke and C2 introductions.

We first tried Vanilla Coke by accident. Eric Paquette in our Boston R&D office likes a Coca-Cola in the morning. We were on a coffee run, and grabbed a can of Vanilla Coke at the local convenience store by accident. We did not know it was Vanilla Coke until we delivered it to Eric. Indeed, the Vanilla Coke packaging was so remarkably similar to Coke Classic, we could not believe the resemblance was accidental. We suspect it was part of Coca-Cola's sampling program to get people to buy Vanilla Coke when they thought they were buying something else.

Once we realized what we had, we then bought some for ourselves. We remember drinking Vanilla Coke in soda fountains as kids, and thought we would try it. However, the new version's flavor was horrendous, with an aftertaste that lasted for hours. The taste was so bad that we questioned our senses, so we bought a six-pack and held a blind taste test in our office. Thirteen people sampled the stuff—to universal disdain, including Eric, a Coke aficionado. A week or two later we saw our first Vanilla Coke commercial and found it to be uninspiring. Not, in our judgment, an auspicious introduction.

Six months later we saw our first Pepsi commercial for Pepsi Vanilla. In it, a Coke truck driver turns up REO Speedwagon's "Ridin' the Storm Out" on his dashboard radio while waiting at a traffic light. Moments later, a Pepsi driver pulls his truck alongside at the light. He nods to the Coke driver, then pushes a button on his dash that turns his truck into a giant, bouncing music machine. We thought the commercial was exciting, funny, and clearly positions Pepsi as different from Coke.

Inspired, we bought some Pepsi Vanilla and noted the product name— Pepsi Vanilla versus Vanilla Coke. Pepsi is not diluting its brand by putting the variety in front of the name. The beverage is Pepsi, which happens to be vanilla flavored. Also, the packaging is distinctive; it would be hard to mistake Pepsi Vanilla for Pepsi Cola.

In the interest of marketing research, we ran a double blind product taste test in the office, sampling Pepsi Vanilla and Vanilla Coke. Only 1 of the 13 people thought the Coke product tasted better. Even with a sample size that small and no pretense of scientific rigor, the chance that Coke was comparable to Pepsi in taste is modest. So, on a packaging dimension, a product dimension, an advertising dimension, and a name dimension, the Pepsi effort is a superior vanilla effort and this is reflected in sales.

LINE EXTENSIONS CAN UNDERMINE CORE BRANDS

Many companies cling to the belief that because an existing brand name lends instant consumer recognition to an extension, the money saved on advertising and promotion represents less financial risk to the company. It is true that in certain special situations, line extensions can reinvigorate an aging brand with more contemporary features and can thereby bring more profits to the company (not every one of Kraft's line extensions failed). We would be the last to say that line extensions are never a good tactic.

But line extensions can also undermine the equity and reputation of the original core brand—a cost much greater than any savings on advertising or promotions. When do line extensions go wrong?

1. *When an existing brand name is attached to a disappointing product.*

New Coke was perhaps the quintessential example of a product taking a perfectly good brand name and damaging it. More recently, World Wrestling Entertainment's failed foray into football with the circus-like XFL jeopardized the WWE brand. Ziploc TableTops, a line of semi-disposable plates, cups, and bowls, only hurt the Ziploc storage bag brand among retailers.

SC Johnson & Son launched Ziploc TableTops with $65 million in marketing support. Priced at $22.99 for a four-place setting, they were more than what Wal-Mart and Target charge for some four-place settings in regular tableware. Rather than merchandise Ziploc TableTops with housewares or plastic kitchen storage ware, SC Johnson paid higher slotting fees to have the line displayed with paper plates and cups that retail in some cases for less than a penny apiece.

A few months later, Clorox Co. launched Store 'N Eat, a similar product that sells for $2.59 for three plates, versus Ziploc TableTops $5.99 for four plates— or as unit shelf pricing shows the most naïve customer, 86¢ for one Clorox plate versus $1.50 for one Ziploc. One disgusted retailer told *Advertising Age*, "If they don't delist [TableTops], we'll do it for them come first of the year."[12]

2. *When an existing brand name is added to an inappropriate product.*

Cool Mint Listerine Toothpaste failed because consumers think of Listerine as having a bad taste, something they don't want in their toothpaste. They have accepted Listerine mouthwash's medicinal taste because advertising has convinced them that "Listerine kills the germs that cause bad breath." If it didn't taste so terrible, goes the thinking, it wouldn't be so effective. But a toothpaste is supposed to prevent cavities and gum disease, not—primarily—to stop bad breath. Toothpaste doesn't have to taste bad to be effective, and Cool Mint Listerine Toothpaste bombed.

So, we suspect, will Citrus Listerine Mouthwash, the company's latest introduction, which is positioned as tasting better than the original. But America has gotten to know and appreciate the taste of Listerine—it tastes bad, we believe, because it's killing germs. Citrus Listerine just tastes bad.

3. *When an existing brand name is overused and its positioning gets watered down in the consumer's mind.*

The company is left with a bunch of products, with only the appearance of being in the same general category.

Healthy Choice was a major success when it began life as a line of frozen entrees. We were very proud at the time to be part of the brand's success—we did the original simulated test markets work that forecast a triumph. With that success, however, ConAgra Foods, the marketer, began slapping the brand on all kinds of products—both disappointing and inappropriate—and within a relatively short time had managed to damage whatever the brand had stood for originally.

P&G extended the Olay brand (after dropping the "Oil of") not only to all products moisturizing, but also to cleansing products and even to makeup. What was Olay's positioning with this diverse line of products? "Provides superior moisture" or "improves overall appearance"? Consumers could not figure it out either, and Olay scrapped the cosmetics line.

For over two decades, companies have been going wild with line extensions. While some have been able to inject at least subtle differences into line extension—Tropicana's line of orange juice ranges from vitamin-enhanced to pulpy to regular to premium regular to less acidic, for example—many companies succeed only in confusing customers rather than producing growth.

Take Colgate toothpaste, for example. How do you decide between Colgate Sparkling White toothpaste "For Sparkling White Teeth" and Colgate Tartar Control Plus Whitening toothpaste "For Clean, White Teeth," or one of their other six or seven other similarly named and positioned toothpastes?

Clancy recently had the annoying experience of going to a local CVS to buy Colgate's Total. He could not find it on the shelf amidst a sea of facings for Colgate line extensions and competitive offerings. So he grumpily picked up the old standby, Crest, a brand he had not used in years.

Rather than adding more to the bottom line and building loyalty to the brand, line extensions often convert consumer from brand shoppers into feature shoppers. They buy a product for a certain feature such as "has baking soda," "provides longer coverage," or "available anywhere 24 hours a day." In 1980, Kotex offered Maxi Pads for feminine protection. Today there are Maxi Regular; Super Maxi; Thin Maxi; Thin Super Maxi; Ultra Thin Maxi; Ultra Thin Long Maxi; Shaped Maxi; Overnites; Curved Maxi; Curved Super Maxi; and god knows what else. Will Canine Maxi be next?

From a competitive perspective, most of these new features are easy to replicate, so they offer a point of differentiation for only a limited time. When Arm & Hammer extended its baking soda brand to toothpaste, it enjoyed only temporary success as better-funded competitors (i.e., P&G and Colgate) quickly brought their own baking soda toothpaste products to market.

When a big single brand becomes a portfolio of smaller pieces, the company's management task becomes much more complex. Such product proliferation means that more and more products are chasing a relatively stable amount of shelf space. As we learned in Economics 101, when demand increases and supply remains constant, prices rise.

Companies take a hit to profits when they have to pay higher prices for shelf space for their larger product portfolios. In addition, line extensions within the same category tend to cannibalize the sales of the core product or service. Marketers, eager for quick success, introduce the line extension to a major brand. The "line extension manager" introduces the new entry, diverting resources away from its parent. The extension may achieve its sales objective and the manager is rewarded. The parent brand, however, has begun its slow decline and the diagnosis is cannibalism.

Net incremental profits (NIP)—not sales—should be the criterion for evaluating line extensions. And when a company takes NIP into account, line extensions often prove to be far less attractive than most marketers have been led to believe. This is true of products like laundry detergent and toothpaste as well as services. Merrill Lynch's online trading extension of its traditional service took away sales and commissions from its staff of highly trained brokers, one of the defining features of its brand. Achieving growth with line extensions, while always possible, is far more risky than it may seem, and companies considering a line extension should consider NIP rather than sales as a measure of success.

THE HIGH COST OF MARKETING FAILURE

The key issue here, whether discussing new products or services, is the cost of marketing failure. How much money do American companies waste introducing products that do not deliver what they promise, that are not positioned clearly, that are not supported adequately, that are too similar to existing products?

One way might be to calculate that figure is to take the average cost to introduce a new product and multiply it by the number of failures.

The difficulty is deciding on cost. It probably costs $1 million in advertising, promotions, sales effort, public relations, and other marketing activities to introduce a new credit card in Cleveland and $50,000 to introduce a new ice cream flavor in St. Paul. Somewhere in between is a worthless "average" cost to introduce a new product.

Another way is to look at figures we do know.

In 2004, companies spent approximately $250 billion in measured media. Promotion spending is often equal to (or greater than) advertising spending, and the sales efforts, public relations, direct marketing, the Internet, and other marketing costs often in total equal the advertising campaign. Assume, therefore, that advertising represents about one third of all marketing costs. Three times $250 billion equals $750 billion, an estimate of the total amount companies spent on *all* marketing costs in 2004.

Most of that, of course, went for existing products and services. Assume that $150 billion, or about 20 percent—and some of our clients think this is much too low—went for advertising, promotion, and marketing costs for new products and services.

Yet, as we suggested at the beginning of this chapter, only 10 percent at best of all new products and services succeed; the $15 billion spent on them returned a profit to their companies. This, however, implies that the rest of the investment, or around $135 billion, was wasted in 2004.

To reduce the huge cost and effort on products that are likely to fail, companies have tried to minimize the risk by testing their new ideas before rolling them out nationally. But as we'll see in a moment, traditional test marketing—the way most firms go about evaluating new products prior to a national introduction—may be more hindrance than help.

NOTES

1. Emily Nelson "How One Toilet Paper Product Wiped Out After Its Launch: Problems with a Portable Potty," *Wall Street Journal*, April 15, 2002, B1.

2. Nelson, "One Toilet Paper Product," B1.

3. "'Build a Better Mousetrap': 2004 New Product Innovations of the Year," December 27, 2004, www.productscan.com

4. Ibid.

5. See Deloitte and Touche, "Vision in Manufacturing Study," Deloitte Consulting and Kenan-Flager Business School, March 6, 1998; and ACNielsen, "New Product Introduction— Successful Innovation/Failure: Fragile Boundary," ACNielsen Bases and Ernst & Young Global Client Consulting, June 24, 1999.

6. Robert M. McMath, and Thom Forbes, *What Were They Thinking?* (New York: Times Books, 1998).

7. Furger, Roberta, "So long, Audrey," Family PC, June 2001, 62.

8. Adapted from John Rendleman, "Sprint's ION to Reach Smaller Businesses," *PC Week,* June 28, 1999, p.55; Fred Dawson, "Sprint's ION Launches Hit Cable, Telcos," *Multichannel News,* November 29, 1999, p.75; Chuck Moozakis, "Sprint Ups the Ante for ION," *TechWeb,* May 11, 2000; "Sprint Discharges ION," *Information Week,* October 23, 2001, p.24; Shawn Young, "Sprint Posts Loss of $1.23 Billion amid Charges, Failed Web Effort," *Wall Street Journal,* February 5, 2002.

9. Kevin J. Clancy and Jack Trout, "Brand Confusion," *Harvard Business Review,* March 2002.

10. Copernicus/Synovate. *The Commoditization of Brands and Its Implications for Marketers,* December 2000.

11. Sarah Ellison, "Endless Extensions of Oreos, Chips Ahoy! and Jell-O Brands Created a New-Product Void," *Wall Street Journal,* December 18, 2003.

12. Jack Neff, "Ziploc 'Disposable' Tableware a $65 Million Marketing Flop." *Advertising Age,* November 25, 2002.

2

Why Test Marketing Fails

Test marketing does not occur in a vacuum. Marketers do not wake up one morning and decide because the sun is shining that today is a good day to introduce a new product or service into the marketplace. This sometimes happens, of course, but it's not common.

Before sophisticated marketers introduce a new product, they have done serious thinking and lots of research. They generally go through a process that begins with understanding the marketplace as it exists today, consumer trends in the marketplace, consumer problems in the marketplace—that is, gaps between what people are looking for and what they're getting right now—technological improvements, new materials, everything.

Following this, they often undertake qualitative research. They may hold 6 to 12 or, as we've seen in one recent case, as many as 40 focus group interviews as part of "skunk works" project designed to generate some really new ideas. This work is often followed by day-long creativity sessions, where key company people come together along with outside experts and sometimes buyers in the product category, that is, the consumers who might be prospects for the new products.

Following the ideation session and based on the knowledge of the market, the company creates new product concepts. The more concepts that evolve from this work, we think, the better. Some companies tend to focus on 1 or 2; others might go for 15 or 20 different ideas. Sometimes, marketers do more qualitative research to flesh out those ideas. And then the companies move into a screening phase.

In a screening phase, surveys are undertaken among 200 to 600 buyers in the product category, whether the category be toothpaste or business software. Each of these buyers are exposed to five or more alternative concepts, generally unbranded (branding tends to diminish discrimination between the concepts), and measured in terms of purchase probability, uniqueness, whether the product represents a solution to their problems, fit with the company's image, fit with the corporate brand, and more. Figure 2.1 illustrates this process.

New Product Development Process

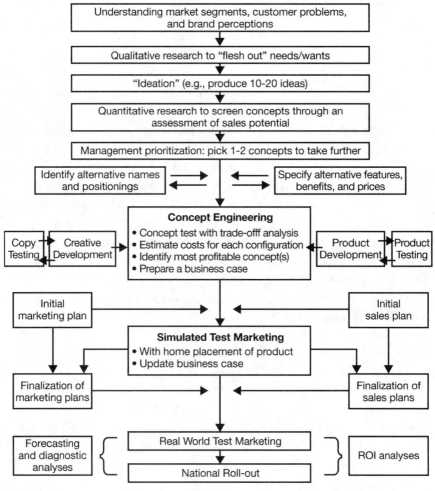

FIGURE 2.1.

Really sophisticated companies will take one or two of these concepts into concept optimization work, the kind we discuss later in this book. For example, Dunkin' Donuts, a national quick service restaurant brand best known for brewing "the best coffee in America," has approached the design of new product and service concepts, using a hybrid variant of choice modeling technology (also known as concept engineering) to evaluate over two billion different configurations for new product and service ideas. They test these among large, representative groups of Dunkin' Donuts customers and prospects; they employ modeling to create demand and cost functions for each configuration. This process leads to the discovery of financially optimal concepts.

These are turned over to food technologists and operations specialists who are charged with creating the actual product or service. These are formally tested in terms of taste, appearance, and so on (for a new product), customer satisfaction, speed of service, and so on (for the delivery time of a new food product in quick service), and their likely effect on incremental revenue and profit. At the same time, the advertising agency is developing and testing alternative ad concepts. Finally, after all this work, work that might take a year and a half or two (although the process can be accelerated), management decides to take the restaurant concept into test market.

THE NEED FOR TEST MARKETS

At one time, a company that wanted to test the market for a new product or service did so by conducting a real-world experiment. Indeed, 20 years ago, the authors of a standard text on new product development wrote, "In terms of providing a realistic evaluation of a marketing program, there is no substitute for conducting an experiment in which the marketing program (or perhaps several versions of it) are implemented in a limited but carefully selected part of the market."[1]

We do not disagree with this idea, but we believe that the real-world test should come late in the process, *after* the company has run a simulated market test. We also agree there may be situations when no test at all is appropriate. A Revlon executive pointed out that "in our field—primarily higher-priced cosmetics not geared for mass distribution—it would be unnecessary for us to market test. When we develop a new product, say an improved liquid makeup, we know it's going to sell because we're familiar with the field. And we've got 1,500 demonstrators in department stores to promote it."[2]

We should put that observation in context, however. It is unlikely that a failed liquid makeup product—even an improved liquid makeup—would threaten Revlon's financial stability. The cost of a full-blown market test might well be larger than Revlon's total profit on such a line extension. In many situations, it may be less expensive to introduce a marginally successful product or even a total failure than to test it and its marketing programs to ensure success. Sometimes a cheap failure makes better business sense than an expensive victory.

When a company's new product development costs and marketing investment is significant—Kimberly-Clark's Fresh Rollwipes and Sprint's Integrated On-Demand Network are two likely examples from the last chapter—it *does* make sense to test, and the traditional test has been in the real world. The underlying assumption is that through such an experiment a company can determine a marketing program's impact with all its interdependencies in actual market circumstances. This is more valid and reliable than the artificial context of concept tests and virtually all product tests.

A company employs a test market for two basic reasons:

1. To gain information and experience with the marketing program before totally committing to it
2. To predict the outcome when the company implements the marketing program in the national marketplace

Yet, some chief executives and top managers still seem to have trouble with this concept. Take our experience with what we will call The Poor Person's Pantry.[3]

LET'S SEE WHO SALUTES

Not long ago, the founder of a Boston nonprofit that successfully provides housing assistance to low-income families called us. Andrew, as we will call him, told us that his organization had been doing some good things, and he wanted to expand its mission. Would we meet with him? We said that as it happened, we were going to be in Boston for a meeting, and would arrange our schedule to meet with him and his team.

A week later, we met with Andrew, his chief operating officer, his chief financial officer, and the head of this new organization we will call The Poor Person's Pantry to protect the reputations of those involved.

Their opening question was, in essence, How would you go about finding out whether the idea of offering reduced-cost groceries to low-income, working families would be appealing?

We asked for more details, and they told us that their plan—which they'd already explored in two focus groups—was to develop a network of super-markets and chain drug stores that would accept a card that gives the con-sumer a 30 percent discount on their grocery bill. Present the card at checkout, and receive the benefit. The Poor Person's Pantry would pay the dif-ference to the retailer in a deal to be negotiated. People who applied for the card would have to pay a monthly subscription fee, but that would be mini-mal and based on family income.

Andrew and his team wanted to offer The Poor Person's Pantry card to an a priori-determined market target—people who met an income requirement (it would vary by the size of the family and location of residence) and who did not have food stamps. "We want to offer many, many more American families the opportunity to buy good, healthy food," said Andrew. "So what would you do?"

We proposed a simulation study (something we'll describe later as a souped-up concept test market). We explained that in a concept test, you show prospective consumers the concept, get their reaction, and use norms to con-vert what they say they will do into what they will actually do. The marketing plan and the model provide a forecast.

We said not only could we test one concept, but we could test different ele-ments of the concept—the name, the price, the offer, collateral material, virtu-ally everything about the offering—to learn what turned people on and what turned them off. As we described this to the group, Andrew seemed to be less and less interested. For a moment, we thought he was going to fall asleep.

He told us once again he had a group of investors who wanted to do some-thing about the nutritional needs of low-income Americans. Andrew said this group was very concerned about the risk of this new business. They were think-ing of offering it throughout the nation, particularly where a lot of the target market resides—inner cities, Indian reservations, Appalachia, and rural areas.

As the meeting was winding down, Andrew asked us to write up a proposal. We said we could, but we also requested that they send us the concept they'd discussed in the focus groups. We received it a few days later.

The three-page concept plus appendices read like a long entry in the *Federal Record*. It went on and on and on. And on. It was not clear who was eligible for the card, what you could actually use the card for (it excluded not only things like tobacco and alcoholic beverages, but also soft drinks, processed cookies, frozen entrees—but not frozen bagged vegetables—"and certain other items at the retailer's discretion"), and what happened to your eligibility if your income rose above the maximum.

We called Andrew to say, "There's no analog to this concept in the real world. You're talking about using television. You've got thirty seconds to communicate a story. This is a sixty-minute infomercial."

Nevertheless, we wrote a proposal based on the meeting, outlining exactly what we felt the organization needed. A six-month-long study would take virtually all the risk out of marketing the idea. It would tell them whether the concept would fly or not, what needed to be fixed to make it fly (we personally thought some prospects might have problems with the card's name), and where it would fly.

Andrew's COO called back. "We've got to do this quickly. We need the results by middle of next month. No later than the end of the month." We said, You can't get the results that quickly. You need to take the time to get it right rather than do it over and over." She said she'd get back to us.

A month later, Andrew's assistant called to say thanks so much for the help but they were going ahead and developing commercials. In essence they'd rather be wrong on time than right late. They were going to run the commercials in three different markets to see who salutes.

We said, "Nobody's going to salute because you haven't figured out what the concept is, never mind how to communicate it efficiently. You don't know how to describe it or what media to use. You don't know the right media budget to get this thing across. People aren't going to salute and you're going to walk away concluding the idea is bad. The idea may be bad, or it may be good, but it's certainly bad marketing."

He said, "Well, that's what we want to do because Andrew just doesn't want to wait any longer."

A spot TV campaign ran, time and money were wasted, and the idea died, not to be revived. We call this The Testosterone Rush.

GAINING INFORMATION AND EXPERIENCE

The test market acts as a pilot operation for the national (or regional) marketing program, just as a pilot production facility might serve to debug a manufacturing process. In fact, business-to-business (B-to-B) marketers call their test market research a pilot test.

In a pilot test, the company tries new processes, new go-to-market strategies, in isolated areas to see what effects emerge. Typically the company establishes a set of metrics—the most important being the return on investment (ROI)—to evaluate whether the program is operating successfully or not.

Unlike consumer marketing, B-to-B marketing typically does not evaluate media strategies or marketing expenditures as much as changes in process (how the sales process works, for example) or strategies for interacting with customers. At one client, we fundamentally changed the entire sales process, and pilot-tested to see if the process had the effects we anticipated. (It did.)

Compared with consumer marketing, many B-to-B marketers deal with relatively few customers. Five hundred target companies with three decision-makers each is not uncommon. Customer needs are fairly straightforward: is the new offering going to help make more money, save money, or both? Also, regional/geographic differences tend to be less important than industry differences. For example, pharmaceutical salespeople who call on individual doctors in Maine and Texas have a more similar marketing challenge than those who call on individual doctors and those who call on hospitals in the same state.

In one recent engagement for an industrial electronics company, the client insisted on talking to fewer than 75 industry decision-makers in two cities about a new service. They wanted to see if they could change behavior—so we wanted to work with individuals we believed could change, and what would be the market's response to the change.

This firm, like many B-to-B marketers today, is trying to wrap itself in services to broaden their approach so they become solutions providers. That's the emerging strategy. The way a company sells products to other companies these days is to make sure the customer's experience is very favorable relative to any other alternative—not only provide a product, but also "engineer" precisely all the services and the buying experience surrounding that product to generate an optimal level of profitability.

Although in both consumer and B-to-B marketing, a real-world test may provide a realistic measure of the marketing program's impact, it has methodological problems that make market prediction difficult—and sometimes impossible.

A traditional test market has at least four steps:

1. The company selects test cities or corporate sites.
2. Marketers establish the length of the test effort.
3. The company implements and controls the marketing program in each test city/site.
4. It evaluates the program and forecasts how the new product or service will perform in a national effort.

Problems start immediately with the test city selection. A test city (or in the case of B-to-B, the companies and decision makers included in the research) should represent the country as a whole in terms of characteristics that will affect the test outcome, product usage, consumer attitudes, and demographics. If the researchers know the idiosyncrasies of a market, of course, they can adjust the results to compensate. For example, southerners eat more biscuits than Americans on average; teenagers drink more soda than adults; older people buy more pharmaceutical products than younger people; and big companies buy more of everything.

For consumer products, the company must have access to data to evaluate a test, which means retail cooperation. Store audit information provides sales data adjusted for inventory changes and gives other useful information, such as shelf facings and in-store promotions. To obtain store audit data, of course, the company must select test cities that contain retailers who will cooperate with store audits.

The test market communities should be isolated from contaminating media that "spills in" from nearby cities. For example, half the advertising reaching the Springfield-Holyoke, Massachusetts, area originates elsewhere. On the other hand, too much media spilling out of the test market into surrounding areas is wasteful and increases the test's cost.

It may be desirable to use test market cities that do not have much "product spillage" outside the area so that it is possible to measure sales within the market. Columbus, Ohio, for example, has considerable spillage; Phoenix-Tucson has little.

After choosing the test market cities, the second major consideration is time. If possible, a test market normally should operate for one to two years to give the marketer solid data on trial, repeat, and seasonal variations. Even if the company takes the program national after a year it should continue to monitor the test market to detect the impact of changes in the environment.

A market test requires an extended time for several reasons. Researchers can observe important seasonal factors only if the test continues for a full year. In addition, initial consumer interest often cannot predict a program's staying power. Finally, it is useful to allow the competition and other market factors to react to see what likely impact they will have on the new brand's performance.

The third major consideration is how the company carries out and controls the marketing program in each test city. Obviously the company wants the test cities to reflect the national program, but as we have already noted this is never easy. The company may not have defined the national program precisely enough, or it may not be easy to apply the marketing program in selected test markets. For example, the company may not be able to translate the national advertising budget to a local level, or the test market may not be well-defined in terms of scheduling television commercials. The company's sales people and retailers may give the test product special consideration—care that the product would not have in the national market.

We regularly see this in B-to-B engagements where the sales force courts customers and prospects when a test is underway in a way that bears no relationship to what they do day to day.

Then again, competitors may sabotage the test, usually deliberately, but sometimes by accident. Robert M. McMath, who founded the New Products Showcase and Learning Center, says in his book *What Were They Thinking?* that by purchasing sample products on behalf of clients, he has screwed up more than one market test. "Many years ago, for example, a shampoo called Wash & Comb hit test markets. It promised to eliminate tangles. Competitors were extremely interested and bought thousands of samples. My consulting firm alone purchased 3,000 bottles in the Atlanta market. As a result, Wash & Comb looked like a sure winner. But real people weren't buying it; other marketers were. It bombed when it rolled out nationally."[4] After that experience, McMath resolved to notify a company whenever he bought an inordinate amount of product.

The fourth major consideration is how to monitor the test results. The traditional measure was sales based on manufacturer shipments or warehouse withdrawals. Since inventory fluctuations can badly distort the sales pattern, and manufacturer shipments and warehouse withdrawals are not a sensitive measure of consumer response, they have been abandoned for store audit data—actual sales figures not sensitive to inventory fluctuations. Store audits also provide information about such variables as distribution, shelf facings, and in-store promotional activity—all factors that affect the product's sales.

Unfortunately, manufacturer shipments, warehouse withdrawals, and even consumer sales data tell very little about the impact of the marketing program in building and maintaining a successful new product or service. What's required is intelligence based on interviewing a cross section of prospective and actual buyers.

The company has to obtain measures such as consumer brand awareness, attitudes, trial, and repeat purchase either from consumer panels or surveys. Brand awareness and consumer attitudes serve as leading edge indicators for evaluating the marketing program and can help in interpreting sales data. The most useful information a company may obtain from consumers, however, is whether they bought the product, whether they were satisfied with it, and whether they bought it again or plan to do so.

Early in his career, Kevin Clancy, one of this book's authors, worked on a "convertible cigarette," a seemingly ordinary filter cigarette with a break-through, magical property. The filter contained micro-encapsulated menthol that the smoker could activate by squeezing the filter. Early returns from test markets indicated the company was enjoying tremendous success; smokers appeared to love the idea because sales during the first eight weeks rose faster than a July 4th rocket.

Unfortunately, sales fell almost as quickly. Once smokers tried the product, they hated it. Sometimes a light squeeze gave a blast of menthol that was like a fist in the throat; other times it took a karate chop to release any menthol taste at all. The product enjoyed virtually no repeat sales, a fact that a tracking study clearly revealed. Without such a tracking study, the manufacturer might have mistakenly believed that it had a clear winner and geared up accordingly.

TEST MARKETING TRENDS

Companies have not changed the type of data they collect or the key measures they use to evaluate it. What *has* changed are the methods for capturing the data and disseminating messages. UPC scanners at the checkout, consumer data cards and individual hand-held scanners (to link individual consumers to specific product sales), and individually targetable cable television has improved test market execution and design capability. These have also led to increased experimentation with marketing variables for both new and established products.

The basics of an in-market test on a "things-we-need-to-know" basis have not changed. But the go/no-go decision has become far more difficult as companies learn more and more about market dynamics. To understand them adequately, the company must understand historical trends, market nuances, variable responsiveness, and more.

A number of forces are at work on marketing research. For example, response rates for telephone surveys dropped from 40 percent in 1990 to 14 percent in 2000 to less than 10 percent today. The reasons include the proliferation of telephone numbers dedicated exclusively to fax machines, computers, or both; widespread access to the Internet using nondedicated phone lines; and the spread of call-screening devices and the extent to which potential respondents use them to avoid unwanted calls.[5]

Simultaneously, consumers became less cooperative in shopping malls. ACNielsen reports that "mall traffic, the source of consumer input to the Bases models, plummeted from an average of 30 completed questionnaires per location per day in the 1970s to a mere five a day in the 1990s. Eighty percent of shoppers diligently avoided recruitment and fully one third of those who did qualify refused to participate, boosting administrative costs and causing timing delays. When queried, it turned out that time-stressed consumers wanted to participate in the research, but on their own terms and in their own time."[6]

Research companies have responded to these two challenges by forming consumer Internet panels. Many marketers don't realize there are two broad methods of Internet data collection: panels and databases. A panel represents a large group of respondents who agree to participate in the Internet survey on multiple occasions. This is comparable to the mail panels made popular by market researcher firms Market Facts (now Synovate) and NFO in the 1960s and 1970s.

When a company does a survey among a panel, it talks to the same people each time. In contrast, a database is simply a large group of e-mail addresses that a company can contact for a survey. The probability that the same respondents will be in two different surveys over a relatively short period of time is relatively small.

The reliability of panel data is very high. If a company is measuring advertising performance, for example, the research company can call panel members who agreed to participate, and three months later, after the campaign launch, call the same people. The company does not have to adjust for sampling error.

According to Greg McMahon, a senior vice president at Synovate, making this distinction between the methods is critical: "Only research firms with true Internet panels maintain detailed demographic (and other) information about their panel members and balance their samples so they match U.S. Census statistics. Without this balance, there is a very high risk survey results will not measure what they are supposed to and lack study-to-study consistency" (G. McMahon, pers. comm.). Also, the average response rate to a Web survey is less than 1 percent, making it even less likely to get a reliable read on the potential of a new product.

A company called BetaSphere says that "by leveraging its experience with previous customer feedback programs, and drawing on its proprietary database of 65,000 product evaluators, BetaSphere assisted Palm with profiling and recruiting candidates for the Palm VII beta program. 'Any beta program can "get feedback,"' maintained May Tsoi, product marketing manager for Palm. 'Our real challenge is to target exactly the right demographic for our market, so we have high confidence in the type of feedback we receive. The right participants absolutely determine the success of the process.'"[7]

Finding the right participants can be a problem. Not everyone has Internet access, so that automatically affects the kinds of products and services that can use the Web. A major brewer recently asked us to undertake a study among Hispanic beer drinkers in America. Because the CEO wanted to save money, he asked whether the work could be done over the Internet. Our research established that many companies are using the Internet to probe the perceptions and behavior of Hispanics, but recent research found that Hispanics with Internet access are very different than those without. For example, Hispanics with Internet access are better educated and tend to live in the Southeast, as opposed to California and the Southwest.

At present, it is impossible to use random-digit dialing to e-mail people who *do* have Internet access, since those addresses are not published in the same way phone numbers are. Moreover, some marketers worry about the security of images, product designs, and other proprietary information contained in online research; they are afraid hackers and competitors will be able to filch their information from the Web.

THE TROUBLE WITH TRADITIONAL TEST MARKETS

Test markets are fraught with problems. Often the company selects a test market because it's easy to manage, or because a retailer in the market will cooperate with the test, and not because the market represents the target the company in fact wants to reach.

Traditional test marketing has five major defects:

1. *Traditional test markets are expensive.*

They can cost as little as $1 million or $2 million, but typically run more. A $20 million test is not uncommon. Green Mountain Energy spent $35 million testing various programs for their new and highly successful energy brand in California alone. Marketing executives have complained that when they add up the research, the media, the effort throughout the organization to control it, and check the test market, the costs are hard to swallow.

2. *Traditional test markets take too long.*

Waiting 6 months to a year, 18 months, or longer for results is simply not competitive in an environment where the pace of change has picked up as much as it has in many product categories.

3. *Traditional test markets give away ideas.*

Marketers routinely gripe, "They're not secure, and as a result we're giving our competitors free marketing intelligence."

4. *Competitors can sabotage the results.*

Even modest efforts by competitors can spoil the company's ability to read the test market results as McMath pointed out. Competitors have sabotaged tests by having their sales people pull the new products off retail shelves, turn them sideways, or move them to other shelves where shoppers will not notice them. (Fortunately, what competitors do in a test market to affect a brand's performance is not what they're likely to do in the national market, which is too big and unmanageable.)

As a more extreme example—but by no means unique—take the experience we had with what we call The Case of the Annihilated Brand. This food product's advertising and promotion budget, projected nationally, was $70 million. The company assumed that the competition, faced with the prospect of battling a new brand, might increase its advertising and promotional spending by as much as 80 percent over the base period. Using this assumption, a model was employed that forecast the new brand would obtain a profitable 3.6 percent market share by the end of Year 1.

The company introduced the brand in test markets—where the brand failed miserably. By the end of Year 1, the brand's market share was 0.7 percent—a clear disaster. Was the research and the modeling flawed? Didn't the company support the brand adequately with advertising and promotion?

An autopsy revealed that the company's advertising and promotional spending were in line with what it had said it would spend. The competition's spending, however, had not increased 80 percent in the test markets. It had increased *630 percent.* Projected nationally, this amounted to $1 billion. In effect, the competitive program "gave away" the existing product to regular buyers at a heavily discounted price. Consumers wisely responded by stocking up, which took them out of the market for months. The move overwhelmed and annihilated the new brand.

Of course a competitor that increased its spending 630 percent could not have sustained the expense for very long and not nationally. At that rate, the corporation was losing money—certainly in the test markets. But this was not a national introduction, and the competitive management obviously felt it was worthwhile to lose money in the test markets to prevent the new brand from establishing itself.

5. *Traditional test markets usually fail to tell marketers what they need to know to achieve success.*

While a product failing in a test market isn't as painful as failing in the national rollout, it's often difficult to determine why. Was the problem with the way the company executed the idea or was the idea simply too small? Was the problem with the marketing program or with the competitive response? Typically, marketing managers test too few plans before introducing a new (or repositioned) product into the real world. Most do not even realize how many plans they could test. Consider The Case of the Escalating Sevens.

Assume we are managing the introduction of a new IBM solutions consulting service for business. Assume further that we have to make a dozen key marketing decisions and that we have only seven choices for each—seven names, seven outsourcing levels, seven service frequencies, seven types of service, seven performance guarantees, and so on.

For example, service response times could be

1. Less than 1 hour,
2. 1 to 3 hours,
3. 3 to 6 hours,
4. 6 to 12 hours,
5. 12 to 24 hours,
6. 1 to 3 days, or
7. 4 to 7 days.

If there are 12 ingredients in the marketing mix and exactly 7 options for each, how many different plans might a marketing manager develop?

Not 12 times seven, but 12 to the seventh power: almost 14 billion (in fact, 13,841,000,000).

Given such a staggering number of possibilities, how do modern marketing managers handle the problem? Most companies do some research—usually focus groups, some concept, product, and copy testing. And then management uses its experience and best judgment to pick the best options from the different possibilities and puts together the best plan it can. This is the plan it takes into the traditional test market. But what are the odds of picking the best plan out of 14 billion when the company does so little research? Not one in a billion.

Our example is based on the assumption of a dozen marketing mix ingredients and exactly seven options for each. In the real world there may be many more than this or fewer, but our point is the same. Managers seem to select the marketing plans they take into test markets impulsively, and as a result, marketplace failure abounds. Worse, little information flows back to the manager on how the marketing program could be improved. If a company actually tested 3 or 30 or 300 of the plans it might develop, managers would have a wonderful basis to discover the factors that led to success or failure. Yet, traditional test marketing is simply too complex, too time-consuming, and too expensive to permit such an analysis.

A BRIEF FOR SIMULATED TEST MARKETING

To improve the odds of new product success in an age of unprecedented competitive response levels, marketers can employ simulated test marketing. A well-done simulated test market reduces risks that include not only lost marketing and sales dollars but also corporate capital—the expense of installing production lines or building a new factory to manufacture the product. Why would a company spend $2 million or $3 million and wait a year and half to learn of a failure about which it can do little, when it can spend $150,000 or $200,000 and take three to six months to learn how to fix any problems?

A simulated test market (STM) study increases efficiency. If a company has, say, three new-product development projects underway, and one seems to offer more volume and greater margins, sagacious management would promote that project rather than the others. The STM can indicate the project offering the greatest return. An STM can also optimize the company's marketing efficiency in a new product it does go ahead with—to see the effect, say, of shifting a budgeted $1 million from television advertising to a coupon or vice versa. (We discuss optimization in detail in chapter 11.)

An STM study maintains security. As soon as a company puts a product into a real-world test, everyone who cares knows about it, starting with the competition's sales people. Often the competition can come up with a "me-too" (if not a "me-better") product. McMath says that "Procter & Gamble took about three years to test a toilet-bowl cleaner called Brigade that slowly released its contents from the tank into the water as you flushed. Meanwhile, the leading toilet-bowl-cleaner companies asked their chemists to knock off the Brigade concept. By the time Procter & Gamble (P&G) had fine-tuned Brigade, Vanish and Ty-D-Bol were already well established in the marketplace."[8]

A simulated test market can save the company time. The STM can give you results in three to six months where you may have to wait more than a year for the same results from an in-market test.

Time, as an element of competitive advantage, is only beginning to gain currency. But as a strategic weapon, time is the equivalent of money, productivity, quality, even innovation. George Stalk, Jr., a vice president of the Boston Consulting Group, writes in *Competing Against Time,* "The ways leading companies manage time—in production, in new product development and introduction, in sales and distribution—represent the most powerful new sources of competitive advantage. While time is a basic performance variable, management seldom monitors its consumption explicitly—almost never with the same precision accorded sales and costs. Yet time is a more critical competitive yardstick than traditional financial measurements."[9]

Jim Findley, an executive vice president at Information Resources Inc., says that his company's research shows that being first to market means shelf space

("Retailers want number one and often need number two—to avoid a monopoly situation—but subsequent entries have to fight for shelf space"), publicity ("First brands get it; subsequent brands don't"), and consumer loyalty.[10]

Yet Findley also points out that being first is no guarantee of dominance. Healthy Choice Bowl Creations was the first "bowl" product, a frozen, microwaveable package of pasta or rice with sauce and meat or chicken. Introduced in July 1998, Bowl Creations annual U.S. grocery sales rose to $80 million in 1999 (IRI InfoScan sales data), then drifted down to $72 million in 2000, and to $60 million in 2001. Uncle Ben's Rice Bowls were introduced in May 1999, ten months after Healthy Choice. Annual sales of the Uncle Ben's original versions and flankers were $65 million in 1999, $135 million in 2000, and $194 million in 2001.[11]

A company that builds its strategy on flexible manufacturing and rapid-response systems is a more powerful competitor than one with a traditional strategy based on low wages or manufacturing cost efficiencies. "These older, cost-based strategies require managers to do whatever is necessary to drive down costs," Stalk writes, "move production to or source from a low-wage country; build new facilities or consolidate old plants to gain economies of scale."[12] These all do reduce costs, but at the expense of responsiveness—and today, many customers are more interested in quick response than in price.

Time-based marketing allows companies to serve key customer needs quickly, which in turn creates more value. The total time required to produce a product or service—not cost—defines a firm's competitive advantage. "Early adopters report that actions modeled on just-in-time—simplified flows, waste reduction, reduced setup times and batch sizes—can also dramatically reduce time in product development, engineering, and customer service," says Professor Joseph Blackburn, of the Owen School of Management at Vanderbilt University and a long-time friend and consultant to the authors. "Firms able to achieve faster response times have reported growth rates over three times the industry average and double the profitability. Thus the payoff is market dominance" (J. Blackburn, pers. comm.).

SIMULATED TEST MARKETING IMPROVES EFFICIENCY

Today's better STMs capture every important component in the marketing mix and assess the effect of any plan on product awareness, trial, repeat rates, market share, profitability, and more. These STMs test any plan the marketer wants to consider—even a competitor's. The marketer simply enters the plan into the computer and the model forecasts what is likely to occur month by month in the real world.

Some simulated test marketing methodologies are even smart enough to help recommend a plan and we have never seen a plan a sophisticated STM recommends that does not beat the one submitted by the product manager. Sometimes the margin is modest; sometimes the difference is overwhelming.

Simulated test marketing is the single best validated tool in all of marketing research. For new packaged goods, the better STMs can forecast what will happen in the real world, plus or minus 15 percent.

This is not to say, however, there are no cases when an STM result goes awry. The biggest failures come about, however, because the assumptions on which the model made its forecast were flawed. If a company estimates a distribution level of 90 percent and obtains only 60 percent in the national introduction, the volume forecast can be off substantially because, in some product categories, distribution corresponds almost one-to-one with volume.

Not only may the assumptions be mistaken, but the market's dynamics may also change between the STM and the actual test market. The company may have a new competitor, one it did not know existed when it did the STM. Did Coke know that Pepsi Edge would soon follow C2?

Sometimes the company's commitment changes between the STM and the real-world market test. Or, to put it another way, in most STMs, companies assume adequate marketing support, support that may dry up by the time the firm begins the product's national introduction. For an STM study, it's easy to say that you're going to spend $24 million on advertising because no one has to write a check. It's something else to spend real money.

Discrepancies also arise between the STM performance and the actual test market because the real world is messier than an STM. But discrepancies also arise between a real-world market test and the national introduction. Companies routinely obtain test market distribution levels that are much higher than they ever see again because the sales force is excited by the new product and the salespeople work harder than usual to put the product on the shelves and make sure it is properly displayed. This sensitivity to the product's success brings results the company never repeats.

But when real-world test results are significantly worse than the STM research results, we ask the client, "What's happening in the test market? What are the shelf facings . . . the distribution? What is the trade activity . . . consumer promotion . . . your share of voice? What is the competition doing?" With these new inputs, an STM can virtually always match what's going on in the market.

At that point we can ask different questions: "Given what's happening, is there anything we can do, anything we can learn from the simulation that would produce a better plan? Given that the competition has increased its promotional spending in our test markets by 630 percent, can we add markets until it becomes just too expensive for them to continue?"

Today the goal of simulated test marketing research is not to obtain a simple volume forecast on which top management makes a go/no-go decision. The objective is to provide diagnostic insights that will help improve product success odds. Telling marketers they will obtain a 5 percent share or a 10 percent share is not adequate. Sophisticated marketing executives want insights that will help them build—or modify—plans that improve the odds of profitable growth.

A good STM will tell you not only how you're doing but also what to do differently. A sophisticated decision support system combines simulated test marketing with mathematical modeling of the marketing mix. Such a system goes beyond forecasting first-year volume potential to providing insights into improving the advertising, the concept, the product and packaging, and the marketing plan itself.

Marketers can ask a state-of-the-science STM model to evaluate every ingredient in the marketing plan in terms of effects on sales or profits or both. The model will run hundreds—in some cases thousands—of simulations to identify those factors that contribute most to marketing success.

MANAGEMENT IMPLICATIONS

This chapter has discussed the need to test before introducing a new product. Our experience in the last decade is that it's more likely that corporate management—particularly new product managers—are imprudent rather than prudent in their test market decisions. Most seem eager to race into the market, betting the ranch that the product will be successful.

We've pointed out the problems with traditional test markets—they are expensive, take a long time, give away ideas, can be sabotaged, and are difficult to analyze. And we've made a strong case for STM studies, which overcome these problems.

But simulated test marketing is not a panacea. There are many instances where management needs to be cautious.

One instance is the pharmaceutical industry where corporations routinely set ROI requirements at 300 to 400 percent—and have good reasons for doing so. If an STM for a new medication projects an ROI of 200, it falls on the cusp of whether to introduce the product or not. It makes sense to err on the side of caution and go into a test market first, which could be an individual market or it could be a set of test markets. In either event, it should be reliable enough to give you decent feedback before an expensive national introduction.

Another instance is where the introduction's cost could injure the company's financial health. We have seen situations where a $1 billion company wants to spend $200 million on a national introduction. It's a very expensive package goods effort, but everybody in the company is excited; they want to play with the P&Gs and the Coca-Colas and the McDonald's of the world. They request $200 million to launch the product and $70,000 for an STM to say whether the product will be successful or not.

If the STM forecasts success at all—and it usually doesn't—it is going to project an ROI in the neighborhood of, say, 30 percent. A 30 percent return on investment is better than putting the company's money in a certificate of deposit, but it's also incredibly risky.

What if this is one of the outlier cases? All STM models promise a forecasting accuracy of about 90 percent, plus or minus. That is, in 90 out of 100 cases, the forecast is accurate within 15 percent. But what if the company is one of the 10 cases where the forecast is very wrong? What if someone along the line has misread the data? Or if the sampling error works in the product's favor?

All these things can happen, so the greater the financial risk to the company, the greater the need for caution. We do not encourage managers to take major risks based solely on a simulated test marketing study.

But what is the source of STM research? How did this methodology get its start and what is its status today?

NOTES

1. David A. Aaker and George S. Day, *Marketing Research*, (New York: John Wiley & Sons, 1983), 680. This section draws upon Aaker and Day's overview, which in turn

draws on Alvin A. Achenbaum's "Market Testing: Using the Marketplace as a Laboratory," in *Handbook of Marketing Research*, ed. Robert Ferber (New York: McGraw-Hill, 1974).

2. Philip Kotler, *Marketing Management* (Upper Saddle River, NJ: Prentice Hall, 2003), 368.

3. While this case is true we have disguised both the details and the name; our "People's Pantry" has no connection with any organization with a similar name.

4. Robert M. McMath and Thom Forbes, *What Were They Thinking?* (New York: Times Books, 1998), 87.

5. Peter Tuckel and Harry O'Neill, "The Vanishing Respondent in Telephone Surveys," *Journal of Advertising Research* (September/October 2002), 26.

6. Jim Miller and Sheila Lundy, "Test Marketing Plugs Into the Internet," *Consumer Insight Magazine*, acnielsenbases.com/news/Test Marketing Plugs into the Internet.pdf.

7. Betasphere, Inc. "Palm, Inc., and BetaSphere Partner to Assure Quality, Ease-of-Use and Stability of the Palm VII Organizer," www.betasphere.com/customers/case_study_palm.html.

8. McMath, *Thinking*, 53.

9. George Stalk Jr., *Competing Against Time: How Time-Based Competition Is Reshaping Global Markets* (New York: The Free Press, 1990), 21.

10. Jim Findley, "How to Beat the New Product Odds" (presentation at the American Marketing Association, Connecticut Chapter, Norwalk, CT, June 11, 2002).

11. Findley, "How to Beat the New Product Odds."

12. Stalk, George Jr. *Competing Against Time: How Time-Based Competition is Reshaping Global Markets*, New York: The Free Press, 1990, 21.

3

The Origins of Simulated Test Marketing

Given the issues of cost, time, and security connected with traditional in-market tests and the development of new research tools (which allowed researchers to collect and manipulate vast amounts of data inexpensively), marketers began looking into simulated test marketing close to 40 years ago. Many of the marketing research ideas (such as research design and measurement issues) later incorporated into simulated test marketing studies were first developed in the mid-to-late-1960s.

At the beginning, these efforts followed two separate paths that eventually converged. The first was the "mathematical modeling" path; the second the "laboratory experiment" path. The first started with the idea that researchers could use historic data—advertising and promotional spending, distribution, market share, and much, much more—to build a series of equations that would forecast new product sales.

The second path started with the idea that if researchers could "simulate" in a laboratory setting the process by which consumers learn about and buy a new product, it would be possible to forecast real-world sales based on the experiment's results.

By the 1970s, simulated test marketing research models had become a major force in the marketplace. The 1980s saw a number of major refinements in the simulated test market (STM) procedures themselves and saw literally thousands of applications. During this decade, the major STMs underwent quite a bit of evolution and convergence—that is, they are far more similar today than

they were a generation ago—and now may resemble their original specifica-
tions only slightly.

MATHEMATICALLY MODELING NEW PRODUCT PERFORMANCE

The origins of serious mathematical modeling of new product performance can
be traced to the Batten, Barton, Durstine & Osborn Advertising Agency (now
known as BBDO) in the early 1960s. By 1966, Dr. David Learner, who was research director of BBDO, and James DeVoe, an associate research director at
BBDO, and two world-renowned Carnegie-Mellon professors, Abraham Charnes
and William Cooper, had done a considerable amount of work on the topic cul-
minating with the publication of a pioneering paper titled "DEMON: Decision
Mapping via Optimal GO-NO Networks—A Model for Marketing New Products."[1] They described a very sophisticated mathematical model of the new product marketing process that BBDO was testing with several clients at the time.

The Demon model examined very complex relationships for the first time,
including those between advertising spending and consumer awareness and
between promotion and new product trial. With Demon, a researcher could
forecast brand awareness, trial, repeat purchase, and sales using techniques
that were at the cutting edge of the new and emerging discipline of management science.

Unfortunately, the Demon model could estimate none of the model parameters such as the attention-getting power of the advertising, awareness-to-
trial conversion, and trial-to-repeat conversion *prior* to an actual test market.
Typically, in a Demon application, a marketer would introduce a new product
into test markets; collect data on awareness, trial, repeat, usage rate, and other
factors by telephone at three or more points in time soon after the product's
introduction (typically within three months); and then use this data to estimate the model's parameters. Demon would then be used to tell the marketer
how the product would perform at the end of the first, second, and third years
following introduction.

This meant a marketer could for the first time use a mathematical model
to make national projections from the test market experience and could, theoretically, use Demon to improve the marketing plan before going national—
a revolutionary concept at the time.

After three years of experimentation, which was accompanied by growing ex-
citement in the industry concerning this new technology, the model fell into dis-

use. It was simply too complicated and too sophisticated. There were too many input parameters, the computing technology at the time was slow, and management found it difficult to understand what DEMON could do for them. DEMON's future was not helped when David Learner, its developer and champion, left BBDO to become president of a high technology firm in Pittsburgh.

Edward I. Brody, at one time a senior vice president at BBDO New York, has pointed out that other advertising agencies such as Leo Burnett, DDB Needham, and NW Ayer, in addition to BBDO, were also pioneering the development of new product forecasting models during the 1960s.[2] But BBDO clearly had the lead in model development and academic acceptance.

By 1970, two young BBDO management scientists, Drs. Larry Light (now executive vice president, global chief marketing officer at McDonald's) and Lewis Pringle (now professor of marketing at the University of Miami of Ohio) followed up on Learner's work at BBDO. They took the best of DEMON to create a newer, simpler, stochastic model of the new product introduction process, a model called NEWS, an acronym for New Product Early Warning System.[3] NEWS, however, like its predecessor, was also limited by its inability to make valid predictions *before* an actual new product test market experience.

Companies initially used NEWS only with early test market data (typically obtained from the first two or three months of an in-market test) to provide a forecast and certain diagnostic information for the remainder of the test market period. By the late 1970s, however, NEWS had been calibrated to feed off concept and product testing data so that actual test market insights were no longer necessary to make a forecast.

LABORATORY TESTING NEW PRODUCT PERFORMANCE

Learner and his associates were barely aware at the time of what Yankelovich, Skelly & White (YSW) was doing fewer than ten blocks away on Madison Avenue to create the Laboratory Test Market (LTM) that YSW introduced in 1968—an example of independent, almost simultaneous inventions with funding coming from Pillsbury and Procter & Gamble. The LTM measured consumer trial in a laboratory environment by making prospects aware of the new product through advertising and distribution, followed by an actual in-home experience to estimate the likelihood of repeat purchases.

YSW exposed a group of about 500 consumers to advertising for a new product and its competitors. They then brought these people into mini-stores set up for study purposes in different research facilities around the country. Often this store was a large shelf display featuring all the brands for the product category under investigation that a consumer might see in a supermarket. The consumers had an opportunity to buy anything they wanted (at a discount), but clearly the store's focal point was the new product. People who bought the product took it home and used it. Later—the time varying by product and purchase cycle—YSW researchers phoned the consumers who had bought the product, asked their reactions, and asked if they'd like to reorder. Their responses gave YSW the probability that a consumer would repurchase the product if she found it in a store.

Based on the answers to these and other questions, and tempered by normative insights, LTM researchers produced an estimate of trial (or, more technically, an estimate of awareness-to-trial conversion, given distribution), an estimate of trial-to-repeat conversion, and the usage rate. If consumers were to purchase the new product just as frequently as other products in the category, YSW would assign a usage rate index of 1. On the other hand, if heavy users were going to buy this product or if consumers were going to buy it more frequently than other brands in the category its usage index would be greater than 1, which could be 1.1, 1.2, 1.3, or more.

The YSW researchers would then apply a factor they called "clout." YSW used this variable to account for the effects of advertising spending, sampling, couponing, and the manufacturer's overall marketing power. A small, obscure, weak manufacturer had less clout than a large, well-known, powerful corporation. A YSW committee based its judgmental estimate of clout figure on historical experience, and these estimates—and they *were* simply estimates—ranged from 0 to 100.

To develop a final forecast, YSW would take the consumer trial figure, multiply it by the client's estimated distribution at the end of the year, multiply that by the estimated clout, multiply that by repeat purchase, multiply that by the index of usage rate, and the final result was an estimate of what YSW called "on-going market share" in units.

As a simple example: Say that 40 percent of the prospects bought the new product in the laboratory store. YSW, recognizing that people's behavior in the laboratory was generally overstated, developed norms by which they reduced the 40 percent to a number the firm felt more closely reflected what people would do in the real world. Assume that in this case the researchers felt that only three quarters of those who bought in the laboratory store would actually buy in a real store. YSW therefore multiplied the 40 percent by 0.75, so the trial figure becomes 30 percent.

The 30 percent is affected by product distribution (with 100 percent distribution, every one of the 30 percent could find and buy the product; less distribution, and not everyone who would buy it can buy it). Assume for the sake of simplicity the manufacturer estimated the product would have 67 percent distribution at the end of the year. Multiply the 30 percent by 0.67 to obtain 20 percent.

YSW now multiplied the 20 percent by the clout factor. Assume the marketer had average advertising clout, or a clout of 50. Multiply the 20 percent by 0.5 and the trial figure becomes 10 percent.

YSW further reduced the trial rate by repeat purchase, and let's assume that half the people who originally bought the product will buy it again. Multiplying the 10 percent by 0.5 reduces the repeat figure to 5 percent. Finally, assume that the people who were buying this product were either light users—80 percent of average—or they were going to be using this product to fill 80 percent of their normal requirements. In either event, YSW multiplied the 5 percent by 0.8, which yields a 4 percent on-going share of market.

The system, though primitive in many respects—what's often referred to today as a back-of-the-envelope methodology—worked (and still works) remarkably well. Over its first ten years, the LTM proved to be accurate plus or minus 10 to 15 percent about 90 percent of the time in forecasting a new product's first year sales.

THE PILLSBURY SCHOOL OF SIMULATED TEST MARKETING

The work that ultimately led to today's Bases simulated test marketing system began at the Pillsbury Company in the early 1960s. Gerald J. Eskin, who became one of the founders of Information Resources Inc. (IRI) but was then at Pillsbury, has said that his marketing research mentor, Dudley Ruch—in our view, one of the most brilliant, innovative, and supportive people in the marketing research profession—asked him to work on the following problem.

Suppose the company has three to six months of data from a test market. Suppose the data included some diagnostic information on purchasing patterns—who's buying the new product and how many times they buy it. From this information, said Ruch, forecast the product's first year sales and the likelihood that the product will grow or decline thereafter.[4]

Eskin says that he started with trial/repeat modeling. He went back to work that Joseph Woodlock had done at MRCA in the 1950s with Louis Fourt. "I took the Fourt Woodlock Model and expanded it," says Eskin. "I studied each repeat level separately. First repeat. Second repeat. Third repeat, etc. I also looked at repeat in a new way, one that took account of the amount of time that a person had to make a repeat purchase. These, we called 'true repeat curves.'"[5]

These curves described both the probability that an individual would repurchase a product and the distribution of time until the next purchase. The Pillsbury researchers called the finished model PanPro for Panel Projection.

In one sense, as Eskin freely acknowledges, PanPro was a kind of sales accounting model. It described how people go through the process of first buying a new product, waiting a time, deciding to buy the product again, then perhaps waiting a time again, and if they decide to repurchase, to make a third purchase, and so on. Note that PanPro was not a model that would forecast results from test market data. It was *not* a pretest market simulator.

When Gerald Eskin finished the PanPro project at Pillsbury, John Malec visited Pillsbury and asked Eskin if he were interested in developing a model that would work *prior* to the test market—a simulator. At the time Malec was working at the NPD Group, Port Washington, New York. Eskin reports that he did develop such a model, but not by building it from scratch. Rather, he collected concept test data and product test data for a wide range of products and tied these measures into the PanPro model, which produced the ESP (for Estimating Sales Potential) model.[6] The NPD Group has been marketing the ESP model since 1975. The company introduced versions of the model designed specifically for line extensions and for product restagings in 1980 and 1983, respectively, and the model is known now as Simulator ESP.

Eskin says that shortly after ESP was developed, Lin Y. S. Lynn, who was also working at Pillsbury, was inspired by the same Dudley Ruch (and indirectly by the YSW LTM—because Ruch and Pillsbury were major clients of the Yankelovich firm), and developed an interest in simulated test marketing research. "Lynn was exposed to my early work at Pillsbury and had knowledge of the PanPro model and the NPD work for that matter," Eskin reports.[7] After leaving Pillsbury to go to Burke Marketing Research, in Covington, Kentucky, Lynn developed a simulator model along lines similar to the ESP model. This became the Bases model, which Burke introduced in 1978, a model which went on to become the most widely used laboratory simulation model in the world.

It's interesting to note that Bases became so successful despite its modeling simplicity and attitudinal rather than behavioral foundations. In the YSW LTM, as we've said, consumers were exposed to advertising for the new and for competitive products in a laboratory environment; they were brought into a store where they used their own money to buy the product; and after trying it at home, they were asked if they wanted to reorder it. The Bases approach simply called for presenting the new product in concept form to consumers and asking them how likely they would be to buy. Their answers went on a five-point purchase probability scale, from "Definitely would buy" to "Definitely would not buy." Each of the five points on the scale is multiplied by a "conversion probability"—90 percent, 75 percent, 50 percent, 10 percent, 0 percent—to generate an estimate of awareness-to-trial.

Following a period of in-home use, Bases gave consumers the same rating scale and asked them how likely they would be to buy the product again. Bases then applied a second set of weights and multiplied a string of figures to estimate the market share at the end of the first year following launch: the client-provided, year-end awareness figure, times the projected trial number, times distribution, times Nielsen all commodity volume (ACV) distribution estimates, times the forecast repeat purchase figure, times the purchase rate. For more than 25 years this very simple but enormously successful model has demonstrated a satisfactory level of validity and has gone on to become the market leader in terms of the number of new products tested and revenues.

ACADEMICALLY GROUNDED LABORATORY STM SYSTEMS

Management Decision Systems, Inc. (MDS) introduced the Assessor model in 1973 after initial development work by Professors Alvin J. Silk and Glen L. Urban of the Sloan School at MIT. (Silk went on to become a chair at Harvard Business School while Urban became the dean of Sloan.) Unlike all previous laboratory methods, Assessor received an academic imprimatur when two seminal papers based on the model were published in the *Journal of Marketing Research* and presented at numerous academic and professional conferences.

The Assessor model conceptualized awareness (a common concept today, but revolutionary at the time—remember it was assumed in LTM's "clout" factor), in the same way that BBDO researchers did in their Demon and News models. It based the awareness figure on estimates developed between the client and the client's ad agency. The Assessor researchers measured trial in the laboratory setting, much like YSW LTM, but instead of measuring trial by buying behavior—the Yankelovich approach—Assessor researchers gave prospects vouchers they could use to buy any product they wanted in a model store; the coupon-induced trial behavior coupled with a sophisticated constant sum-based preference model were the Assessor analogs to Yankelovich laboratory buying behavior and the Bases five-point purchase probability scale.

Like its predecessor, the LTM, the Assessor model called for contacting "buyers" of the test product a few weeks after the purchase to gather information about attitudes toward the new product and repurchase intentions and plans. In addition, the Assessor model used the same constant sum model employed to estimate trial, to estimate what proportion of on-going sales a brand could obtain. They told prospects, "If you could divide ten chips among the leading brands in the category, how many chips would you give to the different brands?" In other words, they employed two different approaches for estimating trial and repeat, one was behavioral, the other was attitudinal.

As a consequence, Assessor had an awareness-to-trial conversion estimate, just as Yankelovich had its clout-to-trial conversion estimate. Assessor multiplied that figure by year-end distribution, multiplied that by an estimate of repeat purchase and by a usage rate, and that gave them a year-end share estimate.

Any comparison of the leading laboratory STMs cannot help but give high marks to the original—the LTM, in contrast to Assessor, ESP, or Bases—because a) it was based on actual buying behavior as opposed to coupon redemption methodologies or self-reported inclinations to buy responses (or both), and because b) YSW consultants had more experience in estimating clout than Assessor or Bases researchers had in working with the awareness numbers provided by clients and their ad agencies.

In fact, clients and their ad agencies almost always inflated the awareness numbers by a considerable margin. Given that a linear relationship exists in all these models between where they start and where they end, to the extent that someone exaggerates an awareness estimate, every other figure will also be exaggerated—most significantly the year-end share estimate. Marketers praise the modeling intricacies of Assessor, however, and the simplicity and relatively low cost of a Bases study, thus explaining in part the strong success of these methods.

In 1979, Malec and Eskin started IRI, which acquired MDS in the mid-1980s. "As you might expect," says Eskin, "we couldn't resist the temptation to try to improve on our earlier work. But as you might also expect, the Assessor model also has some of the flavor of those earlier PanPro-based models."[8] Assessor's preference structure models were merged with IRI's FASTRAC in-store scanning system database; and the model became known as Assessor-FT in 1985.

The M/A/R/C Group of Irving, Texas, bought the rights to the Assessor model in July 1989. Before that, M/A/R/C had ENTRO, its own simulated test marketing system, with which it had been successful. M/A/R/C established a new subsidiary company, MACRO Strategies Inc., to provide marketing consulting and modeling services, including STM research studies. In November 1999, Omnicom acquired M/A/R/C Group, which became part of Omnicom's Diversified Agency Services division. M/A/R/C continues to offer the Assessor system.

AN ASSESSOR SPIN-OFF—THE FRANCO-AMERICAN LABORATORY STM

In the early 1970s, Jacques Blanchard, a native of France, was sent to MIT's Sloan School of Management by a major European management consulting firm. The firm wanted him to develop a market modeling business in Europe, and he worked as an MBA student of Glen Urban's. Blanchard worked with Urban on SPRINTER (an early model similar to DEMON in design that made predictions on the basis of early in-market tests) and on Perceptor, which was introduced in Europe in 1972.

Perceptor is a tool to understand consumer preferences for different products as a function of their competitive positioning and buyer perceptions. It relates preferences to buying behavior. Blanchard says, in fact, that some of the findings of Assessor came from earlier work done on Perceptor. "There already was a trial and repeat mechanism in Perceptor which was a new concept for Assessor. We already had a lot of experience in the evaluation of concepts and how people react to perception before launch, and we also had a lot of work using market response modeling on in-market data for new products, both in the U.S. and in Europe."[9]

Then Assessor was developed, and Blanchard and his associates tested Assessor's microstructure in Europe before it was released there in 1975 (and in Japan shortly afterwards). At the time they were using the Perceptor technology to evaluate concept-use placement tests and make projections. Blanchard did some microstructure validation of the trial and repeat model in Assessor that they had used in developing Perceptor. In 1979, his firm, Novaction, headquartered in Paris, introduced the Perceptor/Concept Test System based on Assessor, and in 1983 introduced several new modules covering line extensions, relaunches, price elasticity, and experience database.

Novaction introduced Designor in 1986, in which the emphasis was heavily on improving the marketing plan, rather than simply volume forecasting. Designor was a combination of Perceptor, Assessor, and several new modeling tools, including an awareness forecasting subsystem, designed to make forecasts in a unique way not available through MDS in the United States.

Today's Designor forecasts trial using a combination of the coupon methodology and the sophisticated preference model that made Assessor famous, integrated with repeat purchase, usage rate, and awareness forecasting approaches that are entirely its own. These tools are coupled with a third forecasting methodology, an analog model. This model forecasts new product performance based on the IDQV (impact, differentiation, quality, and value) of the new product compared to the IDQV of other products with similar market structures whose sales performance is known.

Interestingly, the work on Designor, Assessor, Bases, and the LTM coincided with the work at BBDO on new product forecasting and marketing mix models, starting with Demon and ending with News. The mathematical models required real world data to make valid forecasts while the laboratory models lacked a sophisticated marketing mix component to do more accurate forecasts and diagnostics.

MATHEMATICAL MODELING MEETS LABORATORY TESTS

In 1977 Florence Skelly, one of the YSW principals and a pioneer in the field of marketing research, met Kevin Clancy, who she knew was interested in mathematical models. She also knew that he had worked on the News model at BBDO Advertising. Concerned that Assessor was having a negative impact on the LTM business, Skelly asked Clancy if he could combine the LTM technology and 10 years of normative data with a mathematical model of the new product process to refine the forecasts and improve the LTM system's capabilities. Clancy thought he could, and he and Professor Joseph Blackburn spent the next year working on a model they eventually called LITMUS.

To test the LITMUS model, Skelly and Robert Goldberg, a YSW new products guru who had been working on the LTM from its beginnings, gave Clancy and Blackburn 20 new product marketing plans for which YSW already knew the real world results. They asked Clancy and Blackburn to run a forecast through the LITMUS model so they could compare the forecast to what had actually happened.

At the meeting to discuss the results, each group had 20 envelopes. Clancy's envelopes contained the forecast of what the product would do based on the marketing plan input, laboratory response, and LITMUS's calculations; the LTM veterans' envelopes held the products' actual results. The veterans expected major differences between the forecasts and the actual results because they could not believe a mathematical model could equal the intelligence and expertise of a group that had been making new product forecasts for a decade.

In fact, the LITMUS model's forecasts were virtually identical to the actual results in 17 of the 20 cases. The results were so close that Clancy and Blackburn decided to write up the results for publication[10] and YSW began to market the LITMUS program in 1981.

One of the three cases in which LITMUS produced a result that was quite different from the real world experience was for a new peanut chip (a peanut equivalent of the chocolate chip). LITMUS factored its trial estimates by expected Nielsen ACV[11] estimates and produced a sales forecast which was just about half what the manufacturer actually achieved in the real world.

In analyzing the differences between the model and the actual experience, Clancy and Blackburn found that the model didn't take account for the fact that many housewives, pushing their carts down supermarket aisles, would reach out to grab a package of chocolate chips to quiet a restless child. They would see the new peanut chip product beside chocolate chips on the shelf and take it for the novelty or—in some cases—by mistake. As a result, the usual effect of product distribution was considerably different (and greater) for this product than for most others. Real world sales were terrific.

LITMUS had a number of properties that were unique at the time. Its sub-model for forecasting awareness, as an illustration, contained 13 different determinants of what awareness should be for a new product—including advertising impact and gross rating points by time period, media impact, and forgetting coefficients. This differentiated LITMUS from the original LTM, which didn't have a formal awareness function at all, and from the Assessor model and other simulated test marketing models introduced later, which called for advertising agencies and clients to estimate awareness.

In addition to the awareness submodel, the evolving LITMUS enjoyed some other technological innovations. Among them that the model did not assume (as all models did at the time) a linear relationship between distribution and sales—an innovation inspired by the peanut chip case. Research had discovered that the more involved consumers are in the product category, the more likely they are to shop in several stores to find the product. One can imagine a situation where consumers are so involved that they will go from store to store to store to find a new entry until they do find it.

For that reason, in those categories, and for those consumers, a 10 percent distribution level might act in the same way that an 80 or 90 percent distribution level might perform for a very low involvement product. LITMUS took this into account by estimating each consumer's involvement level and correcting distribution by that knowledge to estimate the real distribution effect.

Among the differences between LITMUS and other models at the time, we should mention a third. For the first time in an STM model, LITMUS took into account the product's purchase cycle, differentiating between a product that a consumer might buy once or twice a year and one a consumer would buy weekly. Because LITMUS was able to provide weekly or monthly estimated sales and accumulate them over time, the model needed to know in what month the company was advertising the product and what distribution occurred in what month. Other models, ignoring these issues altogether, could not differentiate between time periods when a corporation might have very high advertising spending levels and no distribution or periods when the firm had high distribution and no advertising.

IMPROVEMENTS IN THE DISCOVERY MODEL

In 1992, Clancy and Shulman left the Yankelovich firm and 18 months later started a new organization called Copernicus Marketing Consulting. Almost immediately Clancy and his protégé, Dr. Steve Tipps, began working on a new simulated test marketing model, one that, like LITMUS, would combine the best of marketing mix model and laboratory testing. The result, launched for the first time in 1995, was called Discovery.

The Discovery model was able to improve and extend LITMUS's capabilities. For example, the Discovery model was able to take into account new ways to generate awareness, such as new forms of Internet formats, public relations campaigns, outdoor advertising, and word of mouth.

Also, no STM model before Discovery had taken into account the decay of consumer memory even after someone has purchased the new product. Marketers assumed that awareness stayed in effect after consumers had tried a product. In other words, once someone has become a trier, she (or he) is forever aware, and she no longer needs to be hit by media. Yet people forget, and she may not be aware at the time she makes her next purchase. We have learned that regular media messages, especially for frequently purchased products, are significant.

Discovery was also the first model to explicitly consider the interaction between the four major drivers of awareness: advertising, promotion, sampling, and distribution. In previous models, the effects of these factors were treated separately and aggregated. The Discovery model considers the possibility of statistical interactions taking place where one variable is able to intensify or attenuate the effects of others.

By looking at tracking data of current purchases, Discovery is also able to understand and develop a measure of how gross rating points (GRPs) continue to add to the current franchise, especially in product categories where customers tend to buy multiple brands. This is particularly significant when companies want to evaluate a variety of media plans. They want to know which ones will produce the best first-year sales.

Previous STM models all favored front-loaded campaigns because the advertisers and their agencies assumed that if they could create as much awareness as possible at the product's introduction, if they could obtain as many triers as possible, these people would be aware of the brand for the rest of the year. Applications of the model find that, in fact, depending on the product category, the marketer may have to advertise continuously to ensure that people remember the brand throughout the year.

At the same time, once someone has tried a new product, she tends to be more sensitive to media. Current brand users can be 1.5 to 3 times more receptive than average to the brand's advertising. The same GRPs will have a 1.5 to 3 times greater effect on current brand users than they have on the average person.

A very important distinction between Discovery and earlier models is that Discovery is able to project results for campaigns for restaged products where there has been a level of brand awareness—and perhaps trial and usage—established. In this situation, the awareness criteria is not brand awareness, but campaign awareness (also known as campaign penetration).

Campaign awareness is important for restaged campaigns because the marketer hopes to see a change in customer purchase habits due to the new message. It is not enough that consumers know the brand's name or have once seen and recalled brand advertising. If the customer did not process the new message, there's no chance it will change her behavior (unless some corroborating merchandising sparks memory once she is in the store).

Campaign awareness is even more important for direct-to-consumer (DTC) campaigns than for restaged campaigns. Because the consumer has to internalize the product message, carry it around until her doctor's appointment, and then remember to ask the doctor about the medication. (There is usually no in-examining-room merchandising to spark memory.)

For established campaigns, restaged campaigns, and for DTC products an advertiser's GRPs have to work so much harder than for a new product because they must get prospects to a level where they are able to play back the ad. Our research has found that less than half the people who claim that they saw an ad are able to play back something—anything—about the ad. Yet that is the measure a marketer must understand, and it is where some tracking companies make a mistake. They report high awareness numbers, but the numbers are high only because people have seen ads from years past and recall having seen them.

The Discovery model also takes into account not only ACV distribution (the percentage or number of stores that carry the product weighted by the volume the stores represent), but also a measure of shelf presence. Sometimes this can make a significant difference, particularly where an aggressive competitor dominates a store's shelves.

The methods and models discussed here are, of course, not the only simulated test marketing approaches available today. The published academic literature discusses two other STM research programs: Elrick & Lavidge's Comp[12] and BBDO Worldwide's News/Planner.[13] In addition to the STMs that the academic literature has examined, a variety of other STM research services are available commercially. Because the literature does not explain them in detail, however, it is impossible to know from the outside how these models work.

There are also services that call themselves simulated test marketing, but fall outside the scope of this book. For example, one service claimed it "helps you evaluate and prioritize business development ideas." A study is based on a questionnaire that includes questions like, "How will customers initially perceive the price of your product or service in the absolute?" "How do you believe customers will perceive the value received for the money spent when purchasing your product or service?" "How unique would the average customer perceive your idea to be?" Considering that this service has no direct consumer input and therefore does not simulate a test market, it is not a simulated test marketing study as we would define one.

We have observed over time both the evolution and the convergence of the different major systems. They have been improved, in terms of their capabilities, and they have converged in the sense that they have become more similar to one another. Today, for example, all of the services appear to be taking a similar approach to the problem of evaluating many different marketing plans prior to an actual test market introduction such that there is now a blurring of the distinctions between the commercially available technologies. Which raises the question: how do the major simulated test marketing models compare in their methodologies and outputs? The next chapter covers them in depth.

NOTES

1. Abraham Charnes, William W. Cooper, James K. DeVoe, and David B. Learner, "Demon: Decision Mapping via Optimal GO-NO Networks—A Model for Marketing New Products," *Management Science.* July 12, 1966, 865–88.

2. Edward I. Brody, "When and How to Use New Product Models: General Issues and a Personal View" (paper presented to the ARF Pre Test Market Research Workshop, Chicago, June 2, 1988).

3. Lewis G. Pringle, R. Dale Wilson, and Edward I Brody, "News: A Decision-Oriented Model for New Product Analysis and Forecasting," *Marketing Science* 1 (Winter, 1982), 1–29.

4. Gerald J. Eskin, "Setting a Forward Agenda for Test Market Modeling" (paper presented at the ARF Pre Test Market Research Workshop, Chicago, June 2, 1988).

5. For a description of the model, see Gerald J. Eskin, "Dynamic Forecasts of New Product Demand Using a Depth of Repeat Model," *Journal of Marketing Research* 10 (May 1973), 115–29.

6. Eskin, "Forward Agenda."

7. Eskin, "Forward Agenda."

8. Eskin, "Forward Agenda."

9. Eskin, "Forward Agenda."

10. Joseph D. Blackburn and Kevin J. Clancy, "Litmus: A New Product Planning Model," in *Proceedings: Market Measurement and Analysis*, ed. Robert P. Leone, Providence, R.I. (The Institute of Management Sciences, 1983), 182–193.

11. ACV, or all commodity volume, is the percentage of all sales for that product category captured by the stores in which the new product is distributed. Assume a new soft drink is distributed only in Kroger Stores. The manufacturer failed to get distribution anyplace else. As it turns out, that's not that bad because—to make up a number—16 percent of all U.S. soft drink sales are in Kroger supermarkets. So the marketer is in stores that represent 16 percent of all the sales. In other words, a 16 percent ACV.

12. Philip C. Burger, Howard Gundee, and Robert Lavidge, "COMP: A Comprehensive System for the Evaluation of New Products," in *New Product Forecasting: Models and Applications*, ed. Yoram Wind, Vijay Mahajan, and Richard N. Cardozo (Lexington, Mass.: Lexington Books), 1981, 269–83.

13. Lewis G. Pringle, R. Dale Wilson, and Edward I Brody, "News: A Decision-Oriented Model for New Product Analysis and Forecasting," *Marketing Science* 1 (Winter 1982), 1–29.

4

How the Major STM Systems Compare

A decade ago when we undertook our first serious evaluation of alternative simulated test marketing systems, we made the observation that there are far more similarities than differences. Basically all of the models at that time employed the same basic concepts—brand awareness, trial, repeat purchase, revenues, and sales—and by and large the same input parameters.

Today, as we examine the results of our latest investigation we find there is even more convergence between these systems than at that time. All the major simulated test market (STM) research models—Assessor, Bases, Discovery, MarkeTest, MicroTest, NFO FYI, and Novaction—are similar enough that they exhibit some of the same common strengths and weaknesses.

One of the things that they do best is to quantify topics that were mostly qualitative before the models were invented. A decade ago, companies routinely undertook concept tests, package tests, advertising copy tests, and product tests without the capability of embedding the results in a "big picture model" of how they contribute to marketing success or failure.

A product marketer now has more to work with than, say, a 3.2 score on a "probability of buying" scale or an attention-getting index of 123. Today, through modeling, we routinely combine knowledge of the outcome of such tests with actual behavior and other data (such as retail distribution and marketing plans) to develop sales estimates with reasonable levels of predictive validity.

The models allow marketers to take more factors into consideration when making forecasts. The earliest models focused primarily on the product itself. Over time, researchers paid more and more attention to such marketing variables as distribution, advertising, trade, and consumer promotion, and as a result, models today include most marketing factors.

Basically, however, all simulated test marketing models have buyer inputs and marketing assumptions that the research company feeds into the "model." The models use sophisticated mathematics (we'll show some in the technical appendix at the end of the book) with judgment and logic checks to produce the output. While the inputs are quantitative in themselves, the experience of the research professionals often leads to changes in the inputs to ensure accuracy and reality.

Similarities aside in terms of concepts employed, marketing inputs and outputs, there are some radical differences in the various modeling approaches that we will discuss in this chapter. Some models, as we'll see, are relatively simple in their mathematical sophistication, while others are extremely sophisticated and are grounded in the latest developments in the marketing science literature.

Although all the models require inputs such as consumer reaction to a new product or service, some do this by asking a relatively simple question on a five-point scale, while others include as many as 14 different measures calibrated for different levels of consumer involvement in the product category in order to translate what people say they will do into estimates of what they will really do.

While all models include standard marketing plan inputs such as gross rating points per month and Nielson all commodity volume (ACV) distribution, only a few of them go so far as to include parameters dealing with the Web, public relations, and word-of-mouth. Thus the expression "the devil is in the details" clearly applies to simulated test marketing. Superficially the models are the same; but when you understand the underlying dynamics of what is being measured and how it's being modeled, there are notable differences.

This chapter explores some of the features of STM research methodology and discusses the marketing research procedures different companies use to collect the data that serves as STM input.

We focus on the simulated test marketing research programs that are the most popular in the commercial marketplace and present some of the major features of these methodologies, emphasizing their similarities and differences. This discussion focuses on eight elements:

1. The major players in the field
2. The unique features of the models
3. How the researchers collect data
4. Typical sample sizes
5. Product and concept exposure
6. Types of forecasts and number of marketing plans
7. The additional diagnostics the models can supply
8. Validation rates of the models

We compare each research methodology's approach, and focus on the specific details of each.

THE MAJOR PLAYERS IN THE FIELD

The marketing research industry experienced much change during the late 1990s and into the new millennium. While the profitability of consumer brands have improved globally through the use of marketing research and custom research methodologies, such as simulated test marketing models, the methodologies themselves have become global brands.

Research provided by Todd Kaiser of Synovate, Steve Tipps of Copernicus, and discussions with the users of the major models suggests that the global STM market is roughly $220 million in revenues and companies test over 6,000 concepts or repositionings each year. Most of the concepts tested, we should add, do not include an actual formulation. The purpose of these tests is to generate estimates of customer trial or, at best, sales, given assumptions of repeat product usage and buying behavior.

ACNielsen's Bases, with $90 million[1] in sales, represents approximately 50 percent of the market. ACNielsen purchased Bases in 1998; the model has been used to evaluate more than 28,000 product ideas in more than 50 countries. While the Bases model was originally designed for fast-moving package goods, variants of it have been developed for consumer services and durables.

Research International's MicroTest, with $35 million sales, is approximately 18 percent of the market. MicroTest has been used to test over 17,500 new product ideas in 60 countries since 1971, with much experience in Europe.

Ipsos has another 18 percent of the market, broken down between Novaction, $22 million; Vantis, $10 million; and NPD, $3 million.[2] Ipsos, the global research firm, purchased Novaction with its Designor model in 2001 and Vantis with its Market Simulator model from ACNielsen in 2002. Novaction has been used in 55 countries on over 250 product categories. While the past experience of Vantis has been primarily in North America, Ipsos is using its global markets to expand Vantis worldwide. Ipsos also owns NPD's Simulator ESP and ForecastReid simulated test marketing models.

NFO WorldGroup, Aegis Group, and Omnicom are three other significant players in this category offering unique models. NFO FYI is owned by NFO WorldGroup, which has operations in 40 countries, and which purchased FYI Worldwide, the provider of new product forecasts, in 2002. Much of the global new product forecasting generated by NFO is through Bases. FYI generates most of its forecasts for product launches in North America.

Aegis Group plc, which includes Synovate and Copernicus, operates in 60 countries. Aegis purchased Market Facts with its MarkeTest in 2000 and Copernicus with its Discovery model in 2001. MarkeTest is now marketed by Synovate, which is positioning MarkeTest as a global brand through its 77 custom market research agency offices in 46 countries, while Copernicus's Discovery model has been used for package goods, direct-to-consumer simulations, financial services, and consumer durables in the U.S. and South America.

Omnicom, the advertising agency network, purchased the M/A/R/C Group Inc. in 1999. M/A/R/C Research is the owner of the pioneering Assessor model that has been applied to new product forecasts worldwide.

The information provided here is based on in-depth interviews with the senior research officers of the systems detailed.

UNIQUE FEATURES OF THE MODELS

Each of these systems offers unique features. The services the various forecasting systems provide range from the basics for valid forecasts to custom diagnostics.

ACNielsen's Bases model is the most widely used simulated test marketing model in the world today with a rich heritage going back three decades. Given the model's longevity and size, the company has undertaken a large number of validation studies. Its large database allows for forecasts in many consumer package goods categories and across many countries. Its access to the ACNielsen database provides the forecasters with current data about product launches in the category. The focus of the Bases system is the forecast. Compared to some other systems, it does not provide rich diagnostics.

Research International considers MicroTest unique in its treatment of individual categories. The model is calibrated to reflect the level of inertia in the category. The level of inertia reflects an individual consumer's unwillingness to change because of extraneous factors in the category. In higher risk categories consumers are less willing to change and try a new product. MicroTest forecasts based on individuals, not at the macro level, and the level of inertia in individual categories. Since MicroTest is calibrated differently for individual categories, the model is not limited to package goods. MicroTest is used to generate forecasts for financial services, other services such as air travel and entertainment, and pharmaceuticals. In addition to the forecast, Research International provides additional diagnostics that improve the marketing plan.

NFO FYI says that it is the market leader in return-on-investment analysis of direct-to-consumer marketing for the prescription drug category. Although we can't confirm that claim, it is clear that this firm, led by talented marketing scientists and pharmaceutical industry consultants, is a pioneer in forecasting the effectiveness of direct-to-consumer campaigns. In addition to pharmaceutical sales, the NFO FYI group generates forecasts for consumer package goods, financial services, and durable goods.

Ipsos-Novaction has worldwide experience in consumer package goods, high tech products, financial services, and durable goods. Its alliance with Vantis through Ipsos will allow Ipsos-Novaction to focus on consumer package goods while Ipsos-Vantis applies its expertise to financial services and durable goods. The Ipsos-Vantis model, Market Simulator, was developed to adjust for consumer overstatement and closely represents the buy/sell process in many product categories, including business-to-business applications. The model will be calibrated differently when testing the sales of a new alcoholic beverage, a new mobile phone, or a new dental test kit.

Synovate's MarkeTest model has focused on early stage forecasting of concepts. In addition to examining the market response to traditional consumer package goods, MarkeTest examines response to other products such as new toys, board games, and magazine concepts. Synovate has now redirected its focus from primarily concept testing to tests that include the product itself. It does this through measures of product performance on attributes in, say, food products such as sweetness, saltiness, and texture. Synovate's global expansion of MarkeTest is being executed by establishing in-country forecasting groups to ensure that analytical professionals who have knowledge of the local culture and market do the forecasting. In addition to generating forecasts, Synovate provides a profile of the target market and other diagnostics.

Marketers employ Copernicus's Discovery system to evaluate and improve in-market performance of new products or new campaigns for established brands. It may be utilized at every stage of product development and may be applied for any consumer or business-to-business product or service category: consumer package goods, financial services, other services, durables, and pharmaceuticals. The model is calibrated differently by product category based on an innovative assessment of buyer involvement in the category. Copernicus provides diagnostics and recommendations concerning the target market and the positioning of the new or relaunched product or service, media type, weight, pricing, and so on to help optimize the marketing plan.

M/A/R/C Research's Assessor model employs versatility and logic for all categories when forecasting, according to the company. All evaluations are based on the individual respondent's competitive set. The custom nature of the forecasting model allows Assessor to be used in a variety of categories for both consumer and business-to-business products such as financial services, other services, and high tech products. The Assessor model is employed to evaluate consumer package goods, financial services, other services, high tech products, durable goods, and prescription and over-the-counter pharmaceuticals.

HOW THE RESEARCHERS COLLECT DATA

Marketing response data collection has evolved significantly. In the United States the dominant methodology to expose consumers to a new product or concept through the 1990s was via mall intercept or recruitment to a central location. With a drop in the rate of completed questionnaires at malls, however, and the growth of the Internet, the Web has emerged as the dominant source for market response in the United States In Europe and South America, researchers typically collect market response data in face-to-face interviews in respondent homes.

According to Bases, the number of completed questionnaires per mall location per day fell from thirty in the 1970s to 5 in the 1990s. Bases found that 80 percent of all shoppers avoided recruitment and a third who qualified refused to participate. Time-constrained consumers were willing to participate in the research, but at their own convenience. Bases, FYI, and Synovate have now turned to the Internet for concept exposure and in-home usage evaluation of new and restaged products.

Bases states that it spent more than $1 million to develop and test the e-Panel concept. To validate the e-Panel, it conducted more than a hundred parallel tests over three years. Bases reports that the important measures from the mall tests and the e-Panel were highly correlated. Further, there was a high test/retest correlation. A comparison of the respondents to mall tests, Internet tests, and the e-Panel indicates the important demographics such as household size, age, employment, race, gender, and education are similar. Bases plans to maintain a panel of 90,000 participants.[3]

According to the company, using the e-Panel means savings of approximately 20 percent per study compared to traditional recruitment. Bases uses the Internet for both concept exposure and post-usage evaluation of a product that is delivered directly to the respondent's home. Bases estimates that approximately 80 percent of its studies are conducted through its e-Panel. The remaining employ mall intercept and occasionally mail or mail panels for trial exposure. Bases employs phone surveys for the results of in-home use evaluation with mall intercept samples. When Bases conducts a direct-to-consumer pharmaceutical study, there is often a component of research that includes doctor response to the campaign.

Research International uses in-home face-to-face interviews for concept exposure for most of its research in Europe. It typically gathers market response information for a follow-up from the in-home phase through phone interviews. It does a small proportion of concept exposure through mall intercept and the Internet.

NFO FYI has conducted tests with online samples. In more than 50 studies that were tested both online and through mall-intercept, NFO FYI found significant differences between the responses on important questions such as purchase interest. After much analysis, the research team developed calibrations that generated a high level of accuracy for market response data collected using the Internet. NFO FYI has now conducted hundreds of projects using the Internet and the number is rapidly increasing.

NFO FYI administers concept and concept product tests online with the test product delivered to the consumer's home. It administers a majority of concept exposures through an Internet panel and conducts the remainder of the concept exposures through mall intercept, mail, and phone samples. The in-home-use evaluations of new products that are initially exposed on the Internet are conducted online. When NFO FYI has recruited respondents in malls, it employs phone interviews to examine their evaluations of a new product after in-home use. NFO FYI includes a doctor component in many of the direct-to-consumer pharmaceutical studies.

Synovate uses its online consumer panel of over 1 million names in the United States for concept exposure and in-home-use evaluation in addition to its ION system in malls. ION is a multimedia technology that offers full motion video, advanced graphics, stereo sound, and a touch screen for self-administered surveys. Synovate also uses mall intercept for concept exposure combined with phone interviews for the callback stage.

Ipsos-Vantis uses online concept exposure when the purchase environment of the product allows. However, since many of the concepts are durables or services that do not lend themselves to the online environment, the firm generates most of its concept exposures through mall intercepts and recruitment to a central location. Many of the durable products have replacement parts such as filters that require a repurchase forecast. In such cases, Ipsos-Vantis may contact respondents by phone or in person to generate a repurchase interest forecast. When conducting research for a new medical product, Ipsos-Vantis usually includes the likelihood that a doctor would recommend the product to patients.

Copernicus, like its competitors, has moved rapidly toward undertaking STM studies over the Internet with consumers, business-to-business decision-makers, and physicians. When client and consultant believe that an Internet simulation is insufficient (e.g., when the focus of the experiment is on packaging or price), Copernicus employs a traditional methodology of recruiting respondents to a central location. Here they are exposed to the concept or advertising. The central location provides the ability to expose consumers to a half-hour television show with an advertisement for the new product and clutter ads embedded in the program. They are then brought into a simulated store environment where they can purchase (or not) the available products, priced similarly to actual market conditions, with follow-up interviews one to two weeks later to gauge reaction to the new product.

M/A/R/C Research is a pioneer in the use of Web-based research. In 1995 M/A/R/C partnered with America Online to develop Internet interviewing methodologies for consumer and business-to-business projects. Since 1995 M/A/R/C Research has conducted over a million online surveys, according to company statements. M/A/R/C has introduced a new interviewing methodology, Web Intelligent Technology, that allows the firm to conduct research using a combination of sample sources—Web, central recruitment, mall intercept, and phone. To move the Web-based interviews to completion, M/A/R/C uses a proprietary technique, NeuroKnowledge, that combines principles from neuroscience and cognitive psychology to prevent respondent boredom.

TYPICAL SAMPLE SIZES

The typical sample used in an STM evaluation varies widely based on the study type. Concept-only forecasts and consumer package goods typically require smaller sample sizes than services and durable goods with low penetration rates. The typical concept-only sample for a consumer package good forecast ranges from 150 to 300 to test one concept.

Very often the marketer examines more than one concept, price, positioning, or advertising. Each change in a concept requires an additional cell. For example, a client may be testing a new wine and is not sure what label design generates the strongest trial interest. It must test different labels in individual cells; a study evaluating interest in a new wine with two different labels will require two cells, each requiring at least 150 respondents.

Sample size increases when the research conducts an in-home evaluation of the product or service. Most of the models require 150 to 200 consumers be recontacted to forecast repurchase interest and purchase units. Respondents typically drop out of the research at each stage. Therefore, if the researchers expect that 70 percent of consumers will have a positive purchase interest and 80 percent of those will be recontacted, a concept exposure sample size will range from 300 to 400 respondents for a concept test with an in-home use phase.

The sample size grows larger when the research requires multiple in-home-use tests. These are typical with niche products that may experience wear-in or wear-out among consumers. If the product experiences significant wear-out after multiple uses, the forecast will be too high if the marketer applies only one in-home-use phase because the anticipated purchase units are too high. However, multiple in-home-use phases will generate a more realistic forecast for anticipated purchase units. Since respondents typically drop out during each phase of research, multiple use phases require a larger initial sample size.

NFO FYI indicates that its typical sample size for consumer package goods evaluations is 150 for a concept-only evaluation and it requires 150 placements for concept tests with an in-home-use phase.

Research International requires a minimum of 200 respondents for a single consumer package goods concept test. The in-home-use phase requires 200 product placements.

Ipsos-Vantis sample sizes vary greatly, ranging from 300 to 1,000 respondents. The large range is a result of custom research in very different categories from financial services to medical products and consumer durable goods.

Synovate requires a sample of 250 to 300 respondents for single concept forecasts. The company needs a sample of 200 completed placements for in-home product evaluations.

Copernicus typically studies a concept or an ad with in-home placement. A typical sample for a one-cell study is 400 to 500 respondents.

M/A/R/C Research indicates that a concept test requires a sample of 225 while a concept product test requires a sample of 300.

PRODUCT AND CONCEPT EXPOSURE—TRIAL AND REPURCHASE

Simulated test marketing models generate forecasts at various concept and product stages. In the very early stages of product development, marketers often expose consumers only to the concept or to a group of concepts in a concept screen. At this early stage of product development, the product is not available for in-home use. Thus, the accuracy of such forecasts is typically lower than, say, the accuracy of repurchase interest and purchase frequency forecasts based on in-home product use.

When the product is available for in-home use and the packaging is not an important part of the purchase decision, the marketer may generate a forecast through concept exposure with an in-home-use phase or phases. With concept exposure, the marketer evaluates purchase interest based on consumer attitudes. When the product is high tech and has complex features that are truly innovative, the exposure is often Web-based. When the packaging is important to the product image, such as an alcoholic beverage, researchers expose consumers to it via the shelf set.

When the advertising is at a final stage, marketers can use an STM. In this case, they expose consumers to the product in a simulated store environment, and they base purchase interest on actual consumer behavior; people buy the product with their own money. When a product is in a test market, marketers can use the real-world trial, repurchase rate, and purchase frequency at two, three, and six months to forecast Year 1 sales.

In the simulated environment, most forecasting systems use a concept that includes a price. Some systems expose consumers to the new product in the presence of a competitive set to simulate the real-world environment.

Bases indicates that approximately 25 percent of its studies have an in-home placement component. Purchase interest is based on a five-point attitude scale. Typically, Bases exposes the concept with a price but without a competitive set. When in-home use is a component of the research, Bases generates a repurchase forecast through a model that uses an attitudinal scale. When it does not test a product in the home, it uses database norms to forecast repurchase interest.

Research International specializes in concept tests with in-home placement since 90 percent of its studies using the MicroTest model include in-home placement. Research International generates a purchase interest forecast at the concept phase based on a purchase intention question. The firm initially exposes concepts without prices. It asks about purchase interest after consumers have been informed of the price together with a priced competitive set. Since most of Research International's new product forecasts use in-home placement, it employs a model that uses an attitudinal scale to forecast repurchase interest. When in-home use is not feasible, the firm employs database norms to estimate repurchase interest.

While Bases focuses on concept-only exposures and Research International focuses on concept tests with in-home placement, NFO FYI has a mix of both. Approximately 40 percent of its studies include in-home product placement. The firm evaluates purchase interest at the concept stage through a model based on a rating scale. The concepts NFO FYI tests always include prices. It employs a competitive set, however, only as required. NFO FYI employs a model using an attitudinal scale to forecast repurchase interest with in-home use. In the absence of in-home use, it uses a database and norms to forecast repurchase interest.

Synovate's MarkeTest model has been used primarily at the early stages of product development, testing concepts. Synovate is now repositioning itself to increase its focus on forecasts that include product placement. The firm determines purchase interest through a weighted five-point scale. The concepts Synovate tests always include prices; however, they do not include a priced competitive set. The monadic evaluation relies on the consumer mindset. Synovate believes that a competitive set creates an artificial environment of competitive awareness and imagery. Synovate employs an attitudinal model to forecast repurchase interest for the products that have an in-home-use phase. In the absence of in-home use, the firm employs category norms to estimate repurchase probability.

Since Ipsos-Vantis's focus has been nonpackage consumer goods, its research has been limited to the concept stage. Recently, however, Ipsos-Vantis has placed products in homes to evaluate reordering of parts—such as reusable cartridges. The firm exposes consumers to concepts that include prices and to other products on the market. It often uses a shelf set for the concept exposure.

Approximately 25 percent of the forecasts generated by the Discovery system of Copernicus are concept only, while another quarter are concept with product placement, and the remaining are complete simulations where respondents are exposed to rough advertising rather than a simple concept. In every Copernicus study, a competitive set is introduced, including price. According to Copernicus, prices and a competitive set are key components to a true simulation of the real world purchasing environment. When an in-home-use phase is included in the research design, Copernicus forecasts repurchase probability through a multidimensional attitudinal model. When forecasting the sales of very different or niche products, typically food products, second and third in-home-use periods are used to examine the "wear-in" and "wear-out" phenomena.

Approximately 60 percent of the forecasts generated by M/A/R/C Research using the Assessor system are concept exposures with product placement. The firm generates a purchase interest forecast using logic, through Assessor Gates questions. It uses a five-point purchase interest question with multiple measures, including likelihood to use, importance of benefits, perceived difference or uniqueness, and willingness to pay. M/A/R/C also observes preference based on the respondent's own competitive set. For high tech products, it employs diffusion modeling to generate longer-term forecasts. M/A/R/C classifies respondents as "innovators" or "imitators" based on response to stimuli and uses an algorithm to forecast adoption of the new product.

TYPES OF FORECASTS AND NUMBER OF MARKETING PLANS

All of the simulated test marketing systems generate Year 1 unit sales forecasts for the new product, service, or repositioned product. Additional forecasts include Year 1 awareness, share, and incidence. To provide additional guidance, some systems provide monthly, four-week, or quarterly forecasts for Year 1. Many of the systems also provide Year 2 or sustaining forecasts.

To generate a volumetric forecast, the client supplies the research company with a detailed marketing plan. Typically, clients provide three marketing plans to generate alternative forecasts for the launch year. The plans typically vary in weight, or overall spending. In some cases, the plans allocate the same number of dollars differently by promotional vehicle. For example, the client may want to test the impact of couponing versus prime-time media on Year 1 sales. In other cases, the client may want to test various media schedules—short, intense advertising bursts versus sustained, for example.

The Bases system forecasts Year 1 sales and four-week sales for the launch year for all concepts tested. The firm generates trial, repeat, and depth of repeat forecasts for each concept tested. When the research does not include an in-home-use phase, Bases uses norms to forecast repurchase interest. Bases generates an overall Year 2 forecast for the concept, and the firm typically evaluates three marketing plans for each concept.

Research International's MicroTest forecasts Year 1 and Year 2 sales, share, and incidence. It generates quarterly sales forecasts for the launch year. In addition to a forecast of trial, Research International provides a first repeat forecast. Clients supply three marketing plans for the launch year forecast.

NFO FYI provides trial, repeat, and Year 1 sales forecasts. It provides incidence for the concept tested for the launch year when requested, and it provides a Year 2 volume forecast. However, the Year 2 forecast is limited by the accuracy of the Year 2 budget plan the marketing manager makes available. While NFO FYI will evaluate one to eight marketing plans, the average number is two.

Ipsos-Vantis specializes in durable goods, high tech products, services, and alcoholic beverage forecasts, where the purchase cycle can be very long. Thus,

Ipsos-Vantis has no typical forecast; it customizes each for the category. In some cases, it generates both Year 1 and Year 2 forecasts. For some durable products the forecast time frame may be longer. Clients typically supply two to four marketing plans for the research.

Since the focus of Synovate's MarkeTest forecasting system has been early-stage concept testing, Year 1 trial forecasts have been the primary output. More recently, however, Synovate has provided forecasts of awareness, trial units, repeat units, retail dollars, and factory dollars for two or three client-supplied marketing plans for each forecast.

Copernicus's Discovery system forecasts consumer awareness, trial and repeat, total dollar and unit sales, market share, and profitability for every month following launch for one to three years. The model's sensitivity analysis feature enables clients to discover alternative marketing plans forecast to be more profitable than the original.

M/A/R/C Research generates Year 1 unit sales and share forecasts. It provides trial, first repeat, and second repeat forecasts and sustaining Year 2 unit sales. It typically evaluates three marketing plans for each concept tested.

ADDITIONAL DIAGNOSTICS THE MODELS CAN SUPPLY

These systems vary greatly in the additional diagnostics they provide. Some generate only sales forecasts for the new concept. Others, however, are part of a larger custom research system and provide guidance concerning the target market, product positioning, price sensitivity, cannibalization analysis, and marketing plan optimization.

The sales forecast is the focus of the research provided by Bases. However, Bases will provide a core target analysis and it addresses cannibalization in product concept tests using a chip allocation methodology. Bases Price Advisor offers multicell price testing.

Since Research International generates forecasts for concepts with product evaluation in the home, it is providing forecasts for products at the mid-to-late stage of development. Thus, it provides guidance concerning the target market, price sensitivity, positioning, and cannibalization.

NFO FYI is positioned as an accurate and economical forecasting system. Therefore, the forecast is the focus of the services it offers and not additional diagnostics.

Ipsos-Vantis approaches each forecast as a custom research study and offers many diagnostic services. Target market analysis, cannibalization, and positioning are typical diagnostics for a forecast. The firm will examine price sensitivity through monadic concept exposures with a choice model. Competitive response is occasionally examined through a price reaction analysis.

Synovate provides a profile of the target market for line extensions and restages. Cannibalization analysis is generated through a pre- and post-concept exposure chip allocation analysis.

Copernicus offers many diagnostics in addition to a volumetric forecast. It will do a complete analysis of the category behavior and demographics for the target market and insight into a financially optimal target. It employs two different proprietary models to identify the best positioning for the new concept, and it uses four convergent methodologies to evaluate cannibalization. The firm establishes price sensitivity through built-in trade-off analysis and price analysis with each exposure. It offers sensitivity analyses to investigate the impact of every marketing input variable on sales and profitability, and, optionally, a media optimization submodel to guide media planners. Finally, Copernicus provides marketing plan optimization, a unique approach to determine the optimal marketing plan for a new or restaged product or service.

M/A/R/C Research approaches each forecast as a custom consulting project. The firm provides a target market analysis and uses a choice model to evaluate price sensitivity and competitive response. Cannibalization analysis is a part of the forecast for a line extension.

VALIDATION RATES OF THE MODELS

Simulated test marketing is arguably the single most validated research tool in all of marketing. Typically, after Year 1 of a new product launch, the marketer compares the actual sales achieved in the market to the forecast generated by one of the models discussed here. The forecasts often must be updated with actual marketing data used for the launch, since often the actual plan differs from the one used at the STM stage.

All of the models discussed here have strong validation records. Most validations are based on the introduction of a new brand in an existing product category. For new brands in new product categories, limited evidence (there are not enough cases to draw firm conclusions) suggests that the confidence range may increase; plus or minus 10 percent may go to plus or minus 12 to 15 percent.

Bases publishes its validation history[4] and reports over 1,023 validations worldwide. North America accounts for 59 percent, Europe and the Middle

East accounting for 35 percent, and the remainder are in Asia and Latin America. According to the ACNielsen Bases website, the average Bases forecast is within 9 percent of actual sales. Bases indicates that 95 percent of its forecasts are plus or minus 25 percent of actual sales; 91 percent are plus or minus 20 percent of actual; 80 percent are plus or minus 15 percent of actual; 62 percent are plus or minus 10 percent of actual; and 37 percent are plus or minus 5 percent of actual sales.

Research International publishes its validation history in its publicity material. In addition, its clients publish the results of specific applications of MicroTest. Research International claims a validation history of between 350 and 400 new product launches. The average error by MicroTest forecasts is 9 percent. Research International reports that 85 percent of its forecasts are within 20 percent of actual sales and 60 percent are within 10 percent of actual.[5]

NFO FYI has a validation history for more than 60 consumer goods and services. The overall average error generated for consumer goods and services, including some direct-to-consumer campaigns, is approximately 11 percent, according to the company. The forecasts for concept tests with in-home placement are approximately plus or minus 15 percent of actual sales, while the forecasts for concepts without in-home placement are approximately plus or minus 20 percent.

Synovate reports a successful validation history for 150 new product launches with MarkeTest. Forecasts generated with concept only are plus or minus 20 percent of actual sales. Forecasts generated with in-home placement are plus or minus 17 percent of actual sales.

Ipsos-Vantis tracks actual sales of new products launched with the assistance of Market Simulator with its clients. Since there is limited data for the products that are evaluated through the use of Market Simulator, it uses shipments and through-sales to evaluate the model's accuracy. Ipsos-Vantis has 100 validations; in 80, actual sales were plus or minus 20 percent of forecast sales.

Discovery, as we have pointed out, is an elegant derivative of the Litmus model, which we discussed earlier. Combining the validation histories of both models, there are approximately 260 validation exercises. Validations are traditionally done by rerunning the model with actual marketing plans and comparing the results to real world performance. In 80 percent of the cases, concept tests followed by in-home use generate forecasts that are plus or minus 15 percent of actual sales. A true STM (which includes exposure to advertising followed by actual buying behavior) yields forecasts that are generally plus or minus 10 to 15 percent of actual sales in 90 percent of cases. In-market tests generate forecasts that are plus or minus 7 percent of actual sales.

M/A/R/C Research has generated most of its validation history for concept tests with an in-home-use phase. The Assessor system has been validated with 160 cases. According to the company, actual sales were within 10 percent of the forecast in 92 percent of the cases.

MANAGEMENT IMPLICATIONS

In discussing various STM models with the experts, it becomes clear that while the models have many similarities and differences, the depth of experience and marketing science background of the professionals who generate the forecasts are key to generating accurate forecasts for every system.

In a dynamic world, as categories change, globalization spreads, and the Internet's influence grows, these professionals learn from their forecasts and validations and they update their models. In addition to updating the models with market structural changes, they apply their experience when evaluating the inputs for a specific forecast.

Before doing a forecast, researchers must evaluate the accuracy of the marketing plan data clients provide. For example, many clients are over-optimistic in their projections for Year 1 ACV distribution or for the gross rating points generated by a particular budget. The experienced forecaster examines the proposed marketing plans and questions the ACV distribution or gross rating points to ensure the best possible forecast. Often, when questioned, the client submits revised and more realistic marketing plans.

This chapter has shown that there are many differences in the major simulated test marketing models available today. Although there is no independent audit of the claims made by competitors in this industry, the popularity of STM models is evidence that they do work and that any of the major systems will provide management with a reasonably accurate estimate of the sales expected for a new product or restaged product or service. Indeed, we regard simulated test marketing as the single most validated tool in all of marketing research.

NOTES

1. Kevin Clancy, Robert Shulman, and Marianne Wolf, *Simulated Test Marketing: Technolgy for Launching Successful New Products* (New York: Lexington Books, 1994).

2. Information provided by Todd Kaiser of Synovate based on a Web search and personal conversation with Steve Tipps of Copernicus.

3. Jim Miller and Sheila Lundy, "Test Marketing Plugs Into the Internet," *Consumer Insight Magazine*, Spring 2002, acnielsenbase.com/news/Test Marketing Plugs into the Internet.pdf

4. Company literature and http://www.bases.com/research/validation_record.html.

5. Company literature and http://www.research-int.com/pages/pages.asp?id=15& lang=0

5

Mathematical Modeling Marries STM: The Discovery and Litmus Models

Simulated test marketing technology, as we discussed in chapter 3, has evolved over time to reflect the gradual convergence of two different approaches to forecasting: mathematical modeling and laboratory experimentation. Mathematical modeling involves the use of statistical and mathematical equations to predict real-world sales performance from detailed marketing plan inputs. Laboratory experimentation involves the exposure of the new product concept to a cross section of prospective buyers to gauge their reactions to the idea and to the product itself under real-world usage conditions. The laboratory experiment stage has now evolved to incorporate the use of Web panels for concept exposure and evaluation after in-home use.

The first system to incorporate *both* laboratory experimentation and mathematical modeling was Litmus, initially introduced as a diagnostic tool by Yankelovich, Skelly & White in 1981, formally introduced as a stand-alone new product forecasting system by Clancy Shulman Associates in 1982 and successfully employed after 1986 by Yankelovich Clancy Shulman (and, later, Yankelovich Partners) until January 2001 when it was sold to Harris Interactive with other custom marketing-research tools. As we noted earlier, the developers of the Litmus system have now developed a more advanced system, Discovery.

During the past decade, a number of simulated test marketing systems have made great progress in incorporating both mathematical modeling and laboratory experimentation in their methodologies. Discovery represents a powerful example of modeling and laboratory approaches while Assessor, Bases, and NFO FYI have all taken strides to improve their methodologies, reflecting the best of the modeling and experimentation paths to new product forecasting.

In this chapter we will use the Discovery system to describe how a marketer may employ a simulated test marketing system to forecast a new product introduction's success or failure. The chapter outlines the kinds of forecasts the system generates for a new product, and the technical appendix at the end of the book sketches the mathematics used to create the forecasts.

As we pointed out in the last chapter, the specific types of forecasts that simulated test marketing research provide vary by system. All simulated test marketing systems provide volume forecasts. Like its predecessor Litmus, the Discovery system generates a variety of different forecasts on a monthly basis for up to 24 months following the introduction of a new or re-staged product or service. Both models forecast

1. total brand awareness for a new product or campaign awareness for a re-staged brand;
2. penetration (percent of consumers purchasing at least once);
3. repeat buyers;
4. unit sales;
5. market share in units and dollars;
6. profitability—if the marketer provides detailed information on the cost of the marketing program, manufacturing, packaging, and distribution; and
7. return-on-investment—profitability relative to investment.

THE INFRASTRUCTURE OF AN STM MODEL

To accurately forecast a new product's launch or an existing brand's restaging through simulated test market (STM) methodology, a simulated test marketing system must model the marketing environment that will exist at the time the product (or service) is launched or restaged. A smart system models the entire marketing mix (see figure 5.1), and the system requires three kinds of intelligence: market response information, product category data, and marketing plans (the next chapter covers these in more detail).

In direct-to-consumer (DTC) pharmaceutical campaigns, the marketing plan for the physician and the physician market response also must be modeled. (Chapter 10 covers the special considerations of DTC campaigns.)

A Model of the New Product Introduction Process

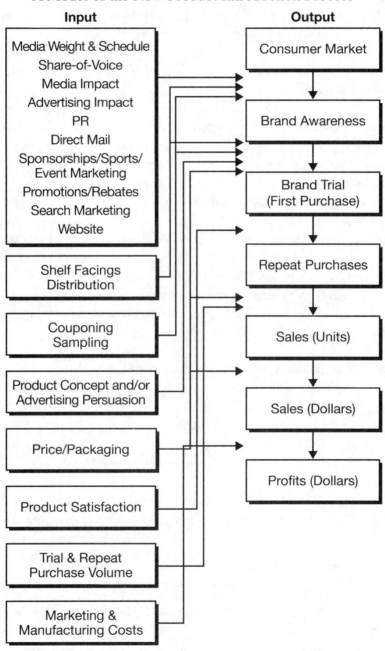

FIGURE 5.1.

Market response is the consumer or physician response to the test product; the laboratory experiment provides this information. The key consumer response components include trial probability, repurchase probability, usage rate, and preliminary estimates of the new product's purchase cycle. The physician response is the probability a physician will prescribe the product in response to a consumer request.

The company's marketing management provides the product category data and marketing plans as we discussed in the last chapter. These are necessary to establish the general framework for doing the forecast and the competitive environment that will exist during the launch or restaging.

The Discovery system characterizes the new product model by a Markov process with trial and purchase probabilities that change over time. Figure 5.2 shows the model's basic structure through the first trial state for consumers. The model allows a new or restaged product to begin with some initial awareness, initial trial, and even initial repeaters (at levels set by the user). The rectangles and circles show general state categories that the company can achieve over the product introduction period. They denote points in the process at which the consumer's behavior is subject to chance effects that can alter the consumer's awareness of the product.

MODEL DEVELOPMENT AND THE PURCHASE CYCLE

As with other new product sales forecasting models, Clancy and Blackburn's model was originally built around a time period that corresponded to the product's normal purchase cycle. Researchers had observed that the product's purchase cycle works quite well for package goods that people purchase frequently, when, for example, the consumer buys the item once a month or more often.

Such a purchase cycle did not work well, however, for the infrequently purchased new product, when, for example, the consumer buys the product only once or twice a year. To illustrate, consider a genuine situation: a new solid room air freshener whose real-world performance was wildly overstated by an STM.

Category data suggested that the expected purchase cycle would be every four months. The company built its marketing plan on a monthly basis, although consumers would buy the product on average only three times a year. The marketing plan provided, as customary, month-by-month gross rating

Model Structure Through The First Trial State

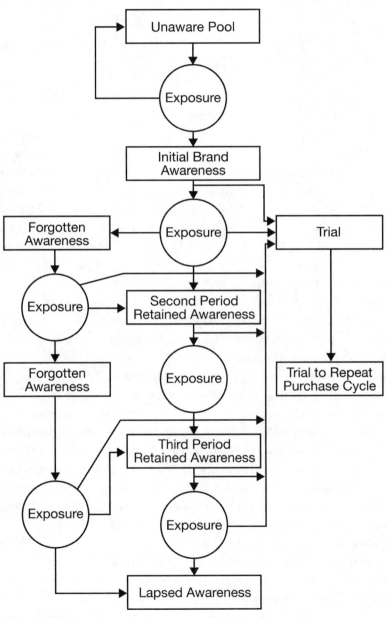

FIGURE 5.2.

points by media type, couponing, sampling, distribution figures, and all other marketing information.

There are two obvious "solutions" to this conflict between purchase cycle and marketing plan. Each solution leads to a different and incorrect conclusion concerning the product's performance. The first solution is to treat input and output data as if there are only three periods during the year—the every-four-months approach. In this construction, the company adds media and promotional figures into three periods of four months each while it averages distribution figures for each of the periods. Taking this approach, however, overstates performance. Awareness, trial, and sales forecasts far exceed actual real-world activity.

This approach generates a "hyperforecast" for two reasons. First, the same number of gross rating points produces different awareness levels depending on the exposure period's duration. For example, 1,000 gross rating points spread over four months yield considerably less awareness than when they are spread over four weeks. Yet the original Litmus model was not able to recognize this difference. Because the model overestimated awareness, it overestimated trial as a function of awareness.

Second, the short time—three four-month periods during the launch year—did not permit the decay function to play a role in determining sales. In other words, there was not enough time for consumers who tried the product to drop away from it. The model assumed that everyone who tried the product would continue to buy it, which never happens.

The second solution is a two-year approach: base the model on, in this case, six periods. Increasing the number of periods permitted the company to observe the anticipated decay in repeat purchases. Moreover, the company adjusted the awareness forgetting coefficient upward to compensate for the longer-than-usual time periods between "bursts" of gross rating points. In other words, since the period between advertising bursts was longer than usual, the advertiser expected more consumers than usual to forget about the product between the advertising exposures.

The result was that the model showed awareness down considerably by the end of the six periods. The model still overestimated trial—in contrast to awareness—because trial never declined. Sales decelerated rapidly because the model increased the proportion of consumers who did not repeat their purchases. The total repeat forecast was less than half the original plan's forecast.

The sales estimates generated by these two solutions were very different, and could not be reconciled with the need for a one-year forecast of a product that consumers buy on average three times a year. The model required another approach.

In working with marketing managers who used the STM system, Clancy and Blackburn encountered a number of these infrequently purchased new products and services. These were situations in which the managers needed both the marketing plan inputs and awareness and sales projection outputs on a month-by-month basis, but consumers do not buy the product every month. Thus, Clancy and Blackburn found a basic inconsistency between the input and output time period definitions and the model's internal time clock.

Clancy and Blackburn considered another alternative in which they applied monthly time periods in the model while reducing the trial and repeat probabilities. This solution also proved unsatisfactory because there was no consistent way to compensate for the lower trial and repeat rates that resulted.

Ultimately, they found a solution by making the time interval units equal to the time period defined by the marketing plan. In other words, if the marketing input is weekly, the model provides for transitions from one awareness and purchase state to another on a weekly basis. If the marketing input is monthly, the model provides for transitions from state to another on a monthly basis. The model then defines the purchase cycle as the number of time periods between purchases, which can, of course, be virtually anything.

To accommodate a purchase cycle that may be several months long, the system superimposes the purchase process onto the model's time increments (figure 5.3). For example, if the time between purchases is three periods, a consumer who makes a transition from awareness-to-trial in Period 2 will not make another transition until Period 5, when she has consumed the product and may make her first repeat purchase. If she does so, and becomes a regular purchaser, subsequent repeat opportunities would occur in Periods 8, 11, 14, and so on.

Although this change in the model complicates the Markov chain representation, it provides the flexibility necessary to predict accurately what will happen when a company introduces a product consumers buy infrequently. Clancy and his colleague Dr. Steve Tipps incorporated this flexibility in the purchase cycle into the updated Discovery system.

Opportunities to Try and Repeat as a Function of the Purchase Cycle

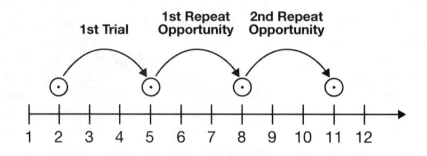

FIGURE 5.3.

CALCULATING AWARENESS PROBABILITIES

Over the years, researchers have found that the more determinants of aware-ness they include in the forecast, the smaller the error range in the awareness estimates (figure 5.4). Today's model employs many input variables to forecast awareness; among them mass media, distribution, couponing, sampling, di-rect marketing, Internet and outdoor advertising, a website, public relations, and marketing experiences (e.g., street theater).

We discuss the inputs for these factors in chapter 6, but it is important to note that in each purchase period, prospects who do not know of the product (the members of the unaware pool) have the potential to become aware of the new product through advertising, couponing, sampling, public relations, di-rect marketing, distribution, or some combination of all six. Advertising in-cludes mass-media-awareness-generation vehicles such as advertising on television, radio, print, and outdoor. Public relations campaigns include press releases, Web articles, radio and television talk shows, and event sponsorships because they are evaluated similarly, using gross and targeted rating points. As a result, a certain fraction of these prospects moves into an awareness state—awareness prior to trial. They know the product exists.

We assume exposure to the product by advertising or through couponing, sampling, or distribution to be independent effects. In early versions, the

To Hit the Bullseye (i.e., an accurate forecast)
Requires a Sophisticated Model

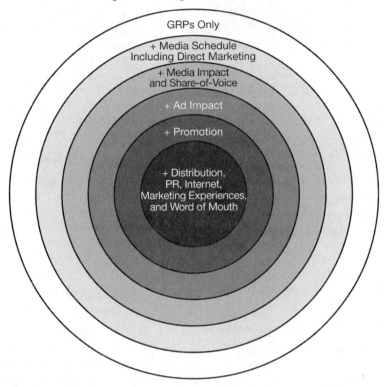

GRPs Only

+ Media Schedule
Including Direct Marketing

+ Media Impact
and Share-of-Voice

+ Ad Impact

+ Promotion

+ Distribution,
PR, Internet,
Marketing Experiences,
and Word of Mouth

FIGURE 5.4.

model used a simple exponential relationship between advertising gross rating points and brand awareness patterned after the function used in the News system.

Case histories show this simple model's shortcomings. A leading manufacturer of plastic trash bags employed the system to forecast a new bag's performance, one supported by a $15-million advertising effort. The marketer allocated advertising dollars to daytime television (approximately 40 percent), prime-time television (35 percent), and print (25 percent). Following the forecast, the marketing manager wanted to know the proper mix of dollars by media and requested a sensitivity analysis, one that would show the effects of gross rating points, by media, on sales and profits.

At about the same time, a major tobacco company's manager made the same request. The company's advertising budget was much larger, $50 million, and the media choice was unusual, and included outdoor, news magazines, shelter magazines, and newspapers. In both cases the clients wanted to know what effect different spending levels in different media would have on consumer brand awareness and, ultimately, on product sales.

We used the system to generate a number of simulations. We examined the impact of adding variables that account for the media schedule, the media impact, the share of voice, and the advertising impact. We found that adding the media schedule—versus using gross rating points only—reduced the forecasting error by 29 percent (figure 5.4). When we included the media schedule, media impact, and share of voice, we reduced the error by 55 percent. And when the forecast included the media schedule, media impact, share of voice, and advertising impact, the forecasting error dropped from 28 percent to 9 percent—a 68 percent improvement.

Because including the media schedule, media impact, share of voice, and advertising impact significantly improved the system's awareness forecasting power, we revised the advertising awareness submodel to include them. This change increased forecast accuracy, and it allowed marketing management to test the media mix's effectiveness. The trash bag manufacturer, for example, learned that dollars the company spent on daytime television were more effective than the marketing dollars it spent elsewhere. The cigarette company discovered that outdoor advertising did little to advance brand awareness or, as a consequence, sales.

MODELING COUPONING AND SAMPLING AWARENESS

Since many new product launches involve extensive promotions that include coupons and samples, systems that have inadequate models of these elements of the process are seriously handicapped. With heavy promotional activity, a danger exists that the model will inflate the predicted aggregate awareness. This can have the counterintuitive effect of underestimating the predicted trial rate in subsequent periods. To see how promotional activity can distort the process, consider the following.

Two decades ago, a major health and beauty aids marketer used the system to forecast and diagnose a new toothpaste's sales. Although the system indicated initially that the launch would be successful, the marketing manager asked for an evaluation of 18 different marketing plans. Many of these employed heavy promotional activity—sampling and couponing. Other plans employed low promotional levels. Moreover, the client requested a sensitivity analysis of the projected effects of each marketing input on sales. Since the sensitivity analyses were easier to produce than the 18 forecasts, we provided the sensitivity analyses first.

These analyses and simulations revealed discrepancies. The sensitivity analysis of some marketing plans, for example, showed that sales were very responsive to gross-rating-point changes. The plan simulation results suggested precisely the opposite: on average, plans with high advertising levels failed to produce sales significantly higher than plans with lower advertising levels.

These discrepancies, of course, did not please the marketing manager who requested an analysis of model failure. We traced the problem to the promotion-to-awareness function built into the original model and into several other simulated test marketing models. These models treated coupon and sample recipients as consumers who are "Brand Aware."

Given "normal" promotional activity levels, the harmful effects of such treatment are minor. Given massive promotional activity, however, especially promotion that is "front loaded" (as was the case for the new toothpaste), the effects can be calamitous. As more and more consumers become aware of the product due to promotion, the proportion remaining to become aware due to the advertising becomes smaller and smaller. Promotional awareness stops only at 100 percent or, in the case of the original LITMUS and NEWS, at a maximum figure, which, as set by the model's designers, was less than 100 percent.

In the real world, of course, not every prospect who receives a sample or a coupon becomes "Brand Aware." A company distributes samples that many prospects never receive; many prospects ignore or discard the samples they do receive; and some prospects notice the sample but do not use it for some reason.

This is even more common for coupons. When the original Litmus assumed that everyone who receives a sample or a coupon is aware of the product, it and other models exaggerated awareness and mistakenly reduced the pool of unaware consumers. As a consequence, the model erroneously reduced new awareness and trial in future periods, which attenuates the likely sales forecast and, simultaneously, the model's predictive accuracy. In this case, we learned that instances occur when advertising is more efficient than promotion. When advertising is more efficient and the marketer applies strong promotional pressure early, models that assume every coupon and sample recipient is aware of the product will suppress advertising's "true" effects.

To deal with this situation, we added a stage to the promotion process that provides a closer approximation to reality. First, the Discovery model calculates a sample's reach by time period and inputs it to obtain the fraction of the market the company has scheduled to receive the sample. Second, the model estimates the probability of sample awareness given a sample receipt, and it uses this figure to compute the awareness fraction. The model computes a trial estimate from the sample awareness-to-trial probability. Adding this stage to the calculations improved the consumer awareness estimates and ultimately sales and market share forecasts. We formulated a similar process to deal with coupon promotions.

During the late 1980s, promotion budgets became a larger and larger portion of marketing budgets. As corporations spent more and more on promotion, they used multiple coupon events throughout the year and during the same period. Although the system improvement corrected for the hyped awareness, it did not account for the interaction effects of different coupon events. In many cases, multiple free-standing inserts, run-of-paper ads, cross ruffs, and samples will seem to yield a reach of over 200 percent.

Since it is possible to reach only 100 percent of the market, we modified the system again to account for the interactions. First, we put the reach for each coupon event into the system separately and matched it with the appropriate couponing awareness-to-trial figure. Second, we put a maximum coupon reach constraint into the model. The model accordingly adjusts the reach of each event in each time period. These improvements have enhanced the system's capability to handle heavy promotions with multiple events and to provide keener diagnostic capabilities at any promotional activity level.

MODELING DISTRIBUTION AWARENESS

A major durable goods marketer used the system to diagnose sales for a new product. Although initial indications were positive, the marketing manager believed that the awareness forecast was lower than forecasts observed for similar new product introductions and spending plans. After we compared awareness levels achieved by other plans and reviewed all other marketing parameters, we realized that awareness generated through distribution was an important factor missing from the awareness equation for a product in this category. In this category, shelf (or sales floor) presence is a more important factor in generating awareness than it is for, say, consumer package goods.

The original Litmus generated accurate forecasts without distribution awareness for low-involvement products with high advertising expenditures, such as cold cereals or frozen entrees. In product categories that have traditionally lower advertising levels and higher involvement categories, where a motivated consumer actually searches the aisles to find what she is looking for (e.g., a Black & Decker power drill or a Sony DVD player), distribution awareness becomes more significant. The system therefore evolved once again to include awareness due to distribution. The probability of awareness due to distribution is a linear function of the all commodity volume (ACV) distribution during each time period. The parameters of the equation vary based on the level of involvement of buyers in the category.

TRACKING 16 AWARENESS STATES

To keep the following discussion relatively simple, consider that in a product introduction's first month there are 16 awareness states (we're ignoring many of the factors previously discussed, such as public relations and direct marketing). These result from the possible combinations of advertising, promotion, the Web/viral generation, and distribution—advertising alone, advertising plus promotion, advertising plus the Web, and so on (figure 5.5). By Month 2, the number of possible awareness states has increased to 256. By Month 12, the number of possible awareness states has increased to 4,096 (16 × 16 × 16), all which the Discovery system considers (figure 5.6).

Once the product achieves consumer awareness, the system assumes a person has as many as three time periods to try the product; that is, to move from an awareness state to a new-trier state. The probability of purchase diminishes over this time interval, but the probability also depends on the number and type of exposures. For example, a consumer may see the advertising in Period 1, see no advertising in Period 2, but clip a coupon and see an in-store promotion in Period 3. The model then bases the trial probability in Period 3 on the consumer's entire exposure history.

The probability of trial in any given time period, therefore, depends on the consumer's awareness states in the three most recent time periods. We

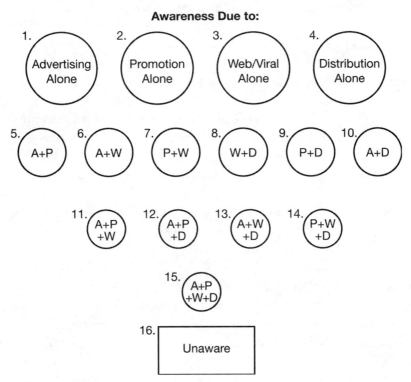

FIGURE 5.5.

describe the trial probabilities for prospects newly aware first, followed by the two-period-aware consumers, and finally consumers who first became aware of the product the third period. The current Discovery system, incidentally, employs a much larger number of states of nature to capture the richness and complexity of the awareness-to-trial process than its precursors.

If the prospect is aware of the product because of the advertising and having received a sample, the model assumes trial to occur as a result of one of these two effects. Although some might hypothesize an exceptionally positive interaction between the two effects, no empirical evidence supports this hypothesis. Experience with the Discovery simulated test marketing model and with consumer test marketing suggests that the interactive effect is negligible.

Escalating Number of Awareness States by Month 2

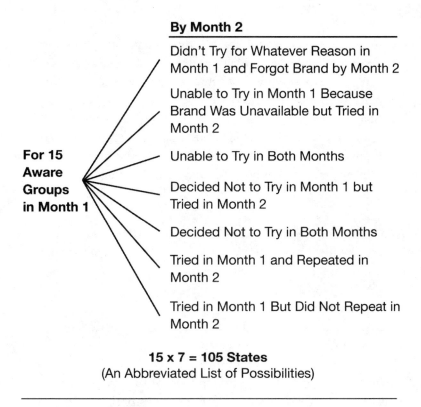

By Month 2

Didn't Try for Whatever Reason in Month 1 and Forgot Brand by Month 2

Unable to Try in Month 1 Because Brand Was Unavailable but Tried in Month 2

Unable to Try in Both Months

Decided Not to Try in Month 1 but Tried in Month 2

Decided Not to Try in Both Months

Tried in Month 1 and Repeated in Month 2

Tried in Month 1 But Did Not Repeat in Month 2

For 15 Aware Groups in Month 1

15 x 7 = 105 States
(An Abbreviated List of Possibilities)

FIGURE 5.6.

Two additional factors complicate computing trial probabilities for prospects who have maintained awareness for two purchase periods. Since these prospects have failed to try the product during one purchase period, their probability of trial should be less than that of newly aware prospects.

In addition, the marketer has exposed these prospects to new advertising or a promotion in the current period and this will alter the degree of their awareness and, as a result, trial probability. To account for this latter factor, the system denotes the awareness state by two components (i, j) where

i = one of the 16 possible awareness states in time period t, including unaware (these are the states indicated in figure 5.5), and

j = the awareness state in time period $t-1$.

For example, (1, 6) is the initial awareness due to advertising (State 1) in time period t, and initial awareness due to advertising and sampling (State 6) in time period t-1.

State 16 indicates no new awareness in the current time period. So (16, 1) indicates a consumer who was initially aware solely through advertising. Since there was no new exposure, the consumer simply retained the awareness in period t, the current time period.

Since State 17 indicates forgotten awareness, (2, 17) denotes a consumer who became aware of the product in period t-2, forgot about the product, and became aware of the product through couponing in the current time period. The technical appendix shows how the model employs these factors in its calculations.

UPDATING AWARENESS AND NEW TRIER FRACTIONS

Consumers who first become aware of the product in the first time period can be in one of three states in the next period:

1. they can be a new trier;
2. they have retained awareness, but did not try in first period; or
3. they have forgotten about the product.

The effect of imperfect distribution in the first time period is to diminish the probability of trial by a factor denoting the probability the product is available to a prospective purchaser. Of the prospects who do not buy the product (the nontriers), a fraction will retain awareness and the remainder will not.

A prospect who forgets about the product can still become a trier, given that renewed exposure regenerates awareness within two periods of initial exposure. Otherwise, the model assumes that the prospect will not try the product. In the event of regenerated awareness, the probability of trial will be lower than the probability that a prospect who is newly aware of the product will try it. Consumers who fail to retain awareness can achieve new awareness states.

Consumers who have been aware of the product for the past three periods become people who try the product during the period or who have a negligible probability of trial. These latter consumers ("lapsed people"), who are aware of the product but do not try it, remain in this state for the study's duration.

THE TRIAL-TO-REPEAT PURCHASE PROCESS

Once a consumer has tried the product, then in each succeeding purchase period there is an opportunity to make a repeat purchase. The probability of a repeat purchase increases with the number of prior purchases and decreases whenever a consumer fails to purchase during a period.

Figure 5.7 shows the repeat purchase process schematically. The nodes represent repeat purchase process states and the arrows denote the probability of moving from one state to another between purchase cycles. Primes indicate the number of purchase periods in which a consumer has failed to make a purchase since trying the product.

1 denotes a new trier, one who first tried the product in the preceding time period.

1' denotes a new trier who failed to purchase last period.

1" denotes a new trier who has failed to purchase in the preceding two periods.

2 denotes a consumer who made a second purchase in the preceding purchase cycle.

2' denotes a consumer who has made two purchases, but has failed to purchase in one purchase cycle.

A consumer who fails to repurchase during a period is less probable to repurchase in the next time period than a consumer who does repurchase. The

Markov Model of the Repeat Purchase Process

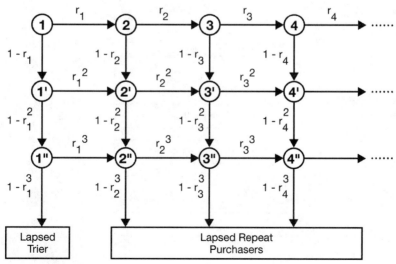

FIGURE 5.7.

first failure reduces the probability of repeat purchase and the second missed purchase opportunity reduces it by another factor. After three purchase periods without repurchase, a consumer's repurchase probability drops to zero; these consumers move into the lapsed purchaser state.

Figure 5.8 shows a simplified summary of the process used to generate sales and share. This is basically the back-of-the-envelope approach that we talked about in chapter 3 and will again discuss in chapter 12.

Simplified Overview of a Sophisticated STM Model

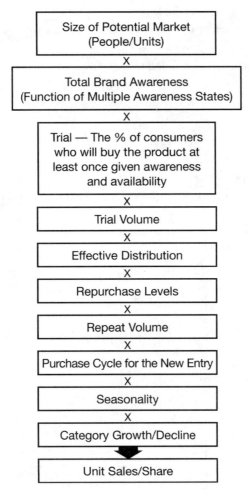

FIGURE 5.8.

APPLICATIONS OF AWARENESS, PENETRATION, AND SHARE FORECASTS

Marketing managers use the Year 1 awareness, penetration, share, and volume forecasts in their decisions whether to continue in the development and launch of the new or restaged product. Management uses the month-by-month forecasts to aid in inventory planning. Moreover, they use the month-by-month forecasts diagnostically to decide how to schedule marketing plan expenditures.

The awareness forecast is the key to the volumetric forecast. The company must make prospects aware of a new product before they will buy it. After they become aware of the product, consumers will buy it if they have decided they want it and if they can find it.

Marketing management can use the awareness forecast from STM research to evaluate a marketing plan's effectiveness. Marketing managers who test a number of marketing plans usually compare the awareness forecasts generated by the different plans. They often use the awareness forecast diagnostically by comparing it with other marketing factors such as seasonality and distribution.

Figure 5.9 is an example of the month-by-month forecasts the model generated. The forecast reveals that awareness peaks in Month 3 (December in this example) and continues to fall thereafter. If this forecast is for a product with high seasonality, and Month 3 is the month every year with the greatest sales, then the marketing plan may be appropriate. If the product's seasonal sales are relatively flat, however, or if it is a seasonal product but the peak month falls later during the launch year, management should examine a marketing schedule that is more consistent with the product's seasonal performance.

It is also useful to compare the awareness build with the ACV distribution build—the percentage of the category's total volume reflected in stores that carry the new brand. In other words, if the stores that carry the new product account for only 5 percent of total category volume, the new product could not obtain more than a 5 percent share of market even if it entirely replaced all other brands. If a product attains peak awareness early in the launch year, but the distribution build is slow, the product may lose those prospects who would try the product but do not because it is not available on the shelf when they are aware of it.

The month-by-month penetration forecast generates a cumulative penetration rate and a net (incremental) penetration rate based on the sample

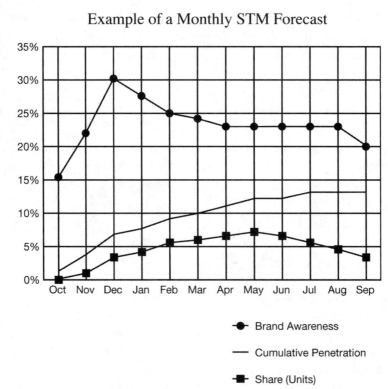

Example of a Monthly STM Forecast

- ●— Brand Awareness
- —— Cumulative Penetration
- ■— Share (Units)

FIGURE 5.9.

represented by the study. The cumulative penetration rate is the projected cumulative percentage of potential purchasers who have bought the product in each month. The net penetration rate represents the projected incremental percentage of potential purchasers who have bought the product in each month.

If the sample used to generate the forecast illustrated in figure 5.9 is representative (in this example, all households are potential purchasers), the 13 percent year-end penetration indicates a forecast that 13 percent of all households will buy this product at least once during the introductory year.

If the sample is a user-based sample that represents, say, 75 percent of total households (if a potential purchaser must own a microwave oven to use the product, for example, oven ownership limits the market), then the figure indicates that 13 percent of this smaller market will buy the product, or a 9.75 percent penetration among total households.

The marketing manager who analyzes the month-by-month penetration forecast can diagnose the link between awareness creation and the generation of people who try the product. The figure 5.9 forecast indicates that the product's net penetration increases with awareness during the first three months. After Month 3, however, awareness falls and net penetration declines with it.

By Month 4, the product has achieved 55 percent of its Year 1 penetration and 20 percent of its sales. Such a rapid build in penetration combined with a subsequent decline in net penetration and awareness levels may signal a need to test marketing plans with different media and promotion flights and schedules. Since the awareness and penetration build is rapid in the first three months, followed by a decline, testing plans with less activity in the beginning (are less front-loaded) may yield an increase in projected sales and penetration.

The model generates a volume forecast in the units most useful for the client: packages, standard sizes, or cases. The number of units sold each month reflects both trial and repeat units.

The forecast the system generates for a line of items is the total line volume. The model further provides the distribution of items within the line based on consumer preferences at the trial and repeat stages. The model derives the monthly share figure by dividing the sales volume projected for the product by the total category sales each month.

The share and volume forecasts interest marketing managers because they most often base the decision to continue development toward launch on a volume or market share goal. The test product's profitability is often a function of the market share it obtains.

The monthly sales build is key in achieving distribution. If the new product does not move off the shelf as quickly as retailers have come to expect in the category, they may not restock and the new product thereby loses distribution. Marketing managers are familiar with their product category's requirements, and they compare the annual and monthly forecast figures with these retailer requirements for sales movement.

Marketers use the awareness and penetration forecasts, plus the month-by-month share and volume forecasts, to adjust the marketing plan. For example, in figure 5.9 monthly total sales and share peak in Month 8 (May) and decline thereafter. It appears that the repeat generated by the consumers who try the product early is not enough to maintain the market share.

The share drop may result from the reduction in the awareness and net penetration, or the product's performance, or both. If the estimated repeat sales figure is strong and other post-usage diagnostics are positive, it is likely that the monthly share decline is a result of the drop in awareness and net penetration.

This example shows that the forecasts generated by STM research are helpful not only in making the decision whether to launch a new product or not, but in evaluating the effectiveness of the marketing plan used to launch it.

MANAGEMENT IMPLICATIONS

The purpose of this chapter was to describe how the evolving marriage between mathematical modeling and laboratory experimentation has provided marketing management today with the capability to accurately forecast the performance of marketing programs for new and restaged products and services long before an expensive real-world introduction.

In chapter 3 we provide details concerning the genesis of one contemporary model that combines the mathematical elegance and construct validity of BBDO's News model and its parent, Demon, with the pioneering laboratory simulation work of Florence Skelly and her colleagues at the Yankelovich organization. That model, called Litmus, went through numerous iterations over time eventually metamorphosing into Discovery. Once joined, the two partners grew significantly in sophistication and complexity to become an "ideal type" for simulated test marketing in the new century.

This chapter showed the key parameters underlying a sophisticated STM system and how each can be modeled today. The chapter also described procedures for modeling awareness, the effects of promotion and sampling, and the purchase cycle.

Finally, we presented examples of the types of forecast a smart system can generate and how this forecasting capability can be employed by marketing mangers to build better plans. In addition, this chapter explained how marketing management can apply the forecasts to improve the marketing plans of the new or restaged products.

6

Inputs for a Simulated Test Marketing Model

The last chapter described in detail a sophisticated test marketing model used to generate a volume forecast. Three types of information fuel every new product forecasting model, including Discovery: product category data, marketing plans, and research-based estimates of market response. Marketing management provides the category data and the marketing plan for the introductory year of the new product's life. The simulated test market consulting firm designs and implements the study to measure market response.

Product category data describes the size and nature of the category in which the new brand will compete. The new product's marketing plans indicate in detail how the company proposes to generate awareness and trial for the new product. Advertising, public relations, promotion, distribution, and other issues need to be covered. And finally, by "market response" we mean consumer reaction to the new product at the trial and repurchase stage; simulated test marketing research provides this information. This chapter describes the inputs consultants use to do a simulated test market and make a valid forecast.

THE CATEGORY DATA REQUIRED
The marketing manager sets the stage for the simulation with secondary data pertaining to the new product's category. The category data that provides the background for a volume forecast includes

1. the potential market's size in millions of buyers;
2. the market's size in dollar sales and in millions of units or cases;
3. the purchase cycle for the product category (i.e., how often the product is purchased per year on average);
4. the average standardized price of the product sold at retail (e.g., price per ounce);
5. a market seasonality index by month;
6. a category sales trend index by month;
7. total advertising spending in the product category;
8. a list of brands in the category that in total account for 80 percent or more of category sales in dollars and units, and the market shares for each;
9. the nature and magnitude of promotional activity by month;
10. insights into likely competitive response to a new product; and
11. new developments taking place in the category (e.g., other introductions, packaging changes, pricing changes, and the like).

If the product is truly new and innovative and no category currently exists, the category data must be inferred from analogous categories.

A critical part of the forecast is the response of buyers to the new product. This requires research among a specific group of consumers. The sample may represent all households or it may be a subset, such as buyers in a given product category. When the sample is a subset of total households, the potential market's size is that group's incidence in the general population.

If, for example, only purchasers of wine are potential consumers, the group of consumers who are wine purchasers—approximately 21 percent of adults who are of drinking age—defines the market's limit. If the sample includes only wine purchasers, and if 20 percent say they would buy the product, the total sales potential can be no more than 20 percent of approximately 21 percent of all adults.

The marketing manager provides this incidence figure. Since a model generates its volume forecast based on the size of the buyer group, the incidence figure directly affects the volume forecast. It is the forecast's cornerstone. If the marketing manager gives an incorrect incidence figure, the resulting volume forecast may be wrong by the percentage that the incidence figure was incorrect.

In one famous case, which resulted in a lawsuit, a client overstated the incidence of product category users by 100 percent. The research firm, basing its forecast on that estimate, overstated the sales potential for the new product. The unhappy client facing the prospects of another major new product failure, turned on the research firm and blamed the model for the problem when the model, in fact, produced an accurate forecast when adjusted by the—later to be discovered—correct category incidence numbers.

Take as an example a company launching a new value-added vegetable product, a genetically altered fresh tomato, one that looks red and ripe and tastes delicious throughout the year. The marketing manager assumes that the potential buyers will be consumers who have bought fresh tomatoes during the past year. To determine the market response from such a sample, the forecast depends on the number of fresh tomato buyers. The marketing manager has several data sources: one of them indicates that 50 million American households purchased fresh tomatoes during the past year; another source of share information, suggests that 40 million households have purchased fresh tomatoes during the past year.

Assume that the research forecasts a 10 percent Year 1 penetration of American households. Such a forecast means that when the model uses a base of 50 million households, 5 million will try the product during the launch year. If the model uses a base of 40 million households, however, the forecast will be for 4 million purchasers of the new tomatoes during Year 1—a significant difference. The potential buyer base reduction produces a 20 percent reduction in the number of purchasers forecast during the launch year. For the eventual forecast to be accurate, category data must be accurate.

To generate market share forecasts, the model uses the market's size in millions of cases (or some other standard measure) provided by the marketing manager. In addition, the model uses the category buyer data to generate an average category purchase rate. It compares this purchase rate with the purchase cycle provided by the marketing manager. When the model uses seasonality factors, it increases or decreases the buying population's size on a month-by-month basis to account for this real-world change.

As in the case with seasonality, the system adjusts for total category growth or decline. This issue is particularly problematic when the marketer cannot know the market's size—in cases or dollars—at the time of the research because the category does not exist. In this situation, models such as Bases or Discovery will base their forecast on the number of prospective households that might be the target for the new category; market share models such as

Assessor or Designor might be forced to punt—that is, turn down the assignment.

The model adjusts the buying population's size to account for an increasing or decreasing number of people in the target universe who are likely to try the product.

The system needs additional category data when the objective is to generate a forecast for a restaged (repositioned, relaunched) product versus a new item. The Discovery system and other sophisticated simulated test marketing models such as Designor recognize the brand's history by incorporating the brand's "going-in" sales share as well as the brand's annual growth or "erosion rate." A smart model obtains the latter information by a trend or regression analysis of brand sales over the past five years. The restaged brand must strive to surpass whatever sales level this analysis projects.

THE MARKETING PLAN'S ROLE IN THE SYSTEM

The marketing plan is a key component in successfully launching a new or re-staged product. The marketing plan's elements describe how the product will obtain awareness and distribution and encourage trial. The simulated test marketing research model therefore simulates the marketing environment through a month-by-month procedure that details advertising, couponing, sampling, and distribution (shelf presence). Consider each of these:

Advertising

To generate an awareness forecast, each of the systems use some common inputs. However, the more sophisticated models incorporate at least ten components of the marketing plan for advertising and public relations, including

1. total gross rating points (GRPs) or target group rating points;
2. GRPs allocated by media type (e.g., prime-time network television, newspapers, drive-time radio, outdoor, Internet);
3. GRPs allocated by media type by month (i.e., the media schedule);
4. share of voice for each competitor;
5. attention-getting power of the advertising compared to norms;
6. attention-getting power of each media vehicle compared to norms;
7. brand awareness before the marketing program is launched;

8. maximum likely brand awareness;
9. the probability that a buyer will remember the brand in the absence of subsequent advertising exposures; and
10. assumptions about interactions between awareness due to advertising and awareness due to other marketing mix drivers.

Simulated test marketing researchers can conduct surveys among media experts to obtain a consensus estimate of the attention-getting power of various media vehicles ($ß_i$ in the technical appendix, page 310). The results of such work show that attention-getting power varies by medium. For example, studies indicate that a commercial shown on prime-time network television has 30 percent more attention-getting power than the same commercial shown on daytime network television. The GRPs for vehicles (GRP_i in the technical appendix) that differ in attention-getting power are put into the model separately so the model can account for the differences. Figure 6.1 is an illustration of the template the Discovery system employs, which takes marketing inputs into account on a monthly basis.

Bases, NFO FYI, and Synovate's MarkeTest use marketing inputs on a four-week basis. Thus, 13 periods of data are required for the marketing plan for these systems. Research International's MicroTest uses quarterly data to forecast awareness. Vantis is flexible in the use of marketing plan inputs. It uses monthly inputs if they are available from the client. Assessor uses monthly marketing inputs.

Most new product introductions employ a combination of television and print advertising. Companies also frequently schedule radio, Internet, and outdoor advertising. Television advertising includes network, spot, and cable vehicles. These television vehicles are further divided into day parts: early morning, day, early fringe, prime, and late fringe. Before a company even considers program content, the combination of vehicle and day part offers 15 media placement options for television alone.

Studies have shown that commercial length (30 seconds versus 5, 10, 15, or 60 seconds) also affects its attention-getting power. When a company employs different length commercials, a smart model differentiates each spot's GRPs by length and by each day part to forecast consumer awareness.

Likewise, print vehicles differ in their attention-getting power. Typically, magazine advertisements show greater attention-getting power than do newspaper

Selected Marketing Plan Inputs

Media Schedule
Note: -- GRPs must be against all product category users or the market target
        -- Enter any additional media on separate lines
        ❑ Enter 30 sec., 20 sec., 15 sec. ads separately
        ❑ Enter interned web sites, banner ads, pop-ups, etc. separately

↓ Start of Advertising **Allocation by Month**

	1	2	3	4	5	6	7	8	9	10	11	12	Total
	GRPs	GRPs	GRPs	GRPs	GRPs	GRPs	GRPs	GRPs	GRPs	GRPs	GRPs	GRPs	GRPs
A. Total													
B. Network TV													
i. Prime													
ii. Day													
iii. Early Fringe													
iv. Late Fringe													
v. Early Morning													
C. Spot TV*													
i. Prime													
ii. Day													
iii. Early Fringe													
iv. Late Fringe													
v. Early Morning													
D. Cable TV													
i. Prime													
ii. Day													
iii. Early Fringe													
iv. Late Fringe													
v. Early Morning													
E. Magazines													
F. Newspaper													
G. Radio													
H. Internet													
Web site													
Banner													
Pop-ups													
Other													
I. Outdoor													
J. Public Relations*													
K. Word-of-Mouth, especially among influentials*													

*Estimated in terms of GRP or TRP equivalents, based on historical norms.

*Spot GRPs should be equivalent to national — not merely GRPs in designated spot markets, but expressed on a national basis.

FIGURE 6.1.

ads. Moreover, full-page four-color ads typically obtain more consumer attention than do half-page color ads in the same publication. A good model considers such differences and adjusts accordingly.

Discovery, Research International's MicroTest, and Synovate's MarkeTest, apply a share-of-voice factor (sov in the technical appendix) to account for the advertising spending variation between categories. For example, in the plastic wrap category, a $20 million advertising expenditure during Year 1 will yield a large share of voice because the companies in the category spend relatively little on advertising and therefore the category generates less clutter.

In the laundry detergent category, however, a $20 million Year 1 expenditure obtains a relatively small share of voice since laundry detergent advertisers spend so much. The plastic wrap $20 million will generate greater awareness than the same $20 million in the more highly advertised laundry detergent category because it is easier to be heard in the category with lower spending. The systems model a share-of-voice parameter to account for such differences, the way the same expenditure levels generate differential awareness in different product categories. The Bases system does not model share of voice; however, when the client expects a competitive response to the new or restaged product, Bases incorporates the competitive response into the forecast.

The advertising's attention-getting power by media type (a function of g in the technical appendix) used in Discovery reflects the related recall score generated through copy testing using ARS, ASI, MSW Research, or similar advertising testing service. The model expects an advertisement that scored below average on a copy test to generate less awareness than one that scores at the norm. Conversely, a smart model expects an advertisement that scores well above the norm to generate higher awareness levels. Simulated test marketing systems apply the copy test recall score to the norm in the category to reflect the advertisement's awareness-generating power.

Over time, the better simulated test marketing systems have developed historical data bases to estimate initial brand awareness, maximum likely brand awareness, and the probability that a prospect will remember the brand in absence of additional advertising exposure.

Couponing

Chapter 5 discussed why it is important to enter the planned coupon event for each month. Discovery, Research International's MicroTest, NFO FYI,

Vantis, and Assessor model the coupon plan for a product launch. Often, a company will plan multiple free-standing inserts and run-of-press ads for the new or restaged product during the launch year. We enter each event separately to allow a model to account for interaction effects between events. Figure 6.2 illustrates the coupon plan information form the Discovery system employs.

The marketing manager supplies the reach and anticipated redemption rate for each event for every month, and we input these figures to the model. Reach is the percentage of potential prospects who will receive a given coupon. For example, if the marketing manager expects that 10 million of the 30 million dog food purchasers will receive a new dog supplement coupon, the reach is 33 percent.

The marketing manager also furnishes the anticipated redemption rate (adjusted for misredemptions). The redemption rate is the percentage of coupons consumers actually redeemed for the product. If consumers redeem 250,000 of the 10 million coupons distributed for the new dog supplement, the redemption rate is 2.5 percent. We compare such projected redemption rates to historical experience to confirm that the marketer is using a realistic rate.

Couponing Input Form

	1	2	3	4	5	6	7	8	9	10	11	12

Coupon Events: (Indicate if Purchase is Required Before Coupon Can be Redeemed - i.e., On-pack Coupon, Bounce Back)

i. Type

ii. Value

iii. Projected Reach (Millions)

iv. % Reach

v. Projected Redemption Rate (Net of Misredemptions)

FIGURE 6.2.

Sampling

Direct mail sampling, on-door sampling, trial size samples with coupons, free in-store sampling, and taste sampling are marketing tools that companies often use in new product introductions. Discovery, Research International's MicroTest, NFO FYI, Vantis, and Assessor indicate that they model the sampling plan for a product launch. When marketers do employ such events, we add the trial due to sampling and the corresponding reach to the system for each month (or time period the model uses) of the launch year. Figure 6.3 illustrates the sampling plan information form that the Discovery system uses.

The sample reach is the percentage of the potential buyers who receive the sample. If 300,000 of the 30 million dog food purchasers receive a new dog biscuit sample through the mail, the reach is 1 percent. The sample conversion rate is the awareness-to-trial *due to sampling*. When sampling is a small part of the marketing plan, the marketing manager estimates this figure based on his or her experience in the category. All of the major simulated test markets employ marketing research methods to estimate the conversion rate when sampling accounts for a large portion of the marketing budget.

Distribution

The trial information generated by "laboratory" research reflects "ideal" marketing conditions: 100 percent awareness and 100 percent distribution. As we discuss later, one role of distribution for any new product is to generate

Sampling Input Form

	1	2	3	4	5	6	7	8	9	10	11	12
Sampling:	(Indicate if Sample is Purchased or Given Away)											
i. Type	—	—	—	—	—	—	—	—	—	—	—	—
ii. Number	—	—	—	—	—	—	—	—	—	—	—	—
iii. Projected Reach (Millions)	—	—	—	—	—	—	—	—	—	—	—	—
iv. Anticipated Rate of Conversion	—	—	—	—	—	—	—	—	—	—	—	—

FIGURE 6.3.

awareness. Even in the absence of advertising, couponing, and sampling, some consumers will become aware of the new entry due to distribution alone. The higher the distribution level, the greater the distribution-induced awareness level.

The most important function of month-by-month distribution in a test market simulation model, however, is to temper ideal trial to create a "real-world" shopping environment. All models employ all commodity volume (ACV) distribution information to reflect the probability that consumers will be able to find the new or restaged product if they want it. In most new product simulation models, distribution has a powerful, almost linear impact on the volume forecast. The wider and deeper the distribution, the greater the sales. If marketing management gives the model an ACV distribution figure 10 percent higher than the amount the product actually achieves during each month of the launch year, the model's forecast will be approximately 10 percent too high.

Take, as an example, a new salad dressing. Historical data indicated that the corporation had achieved an 80 percent average Year 1 ACV distribution for the last three new salad dressings it had introduced. Since the corporation planned to spend more on advertising and promotion for the *new* dressing than it had budgeted for the last three introductions, the marketing manager believed that she would achieve even higher levels of distribution. The number she decided to use was an 85 percent average Year 1 distribution. This became the basis for a first year forecast and the new brand was launched.

At the end of Year 1, however, faced with lower sales than expected, an autopsy revealed that the dressing achieved only a 77 percent average ACV distribution, 10 percent less than the level anticipated. This meant that, contrary to the forecast's assumption, 10 percent fewer potential consumers who would try the salad dressing were able to find it in stores. Since all other factors remained constant, the product's actual sales at the end of Year 1 were in fact approximately 10 percent lower than the sales forecast.

Distribution Search

One of Blackburn and Clancy's discoveries in developing and implementing the Litmus model, and incorporated into the Discovery system, was that the typically assumed linear relationship between distribution and sales is a myth in many cases. Under some conditions, a low level of distribution can "work" as well as a very high level of distribution for a different product. The key to understanding the true effect of distribution is to know how involved consumers are in the product category, in the new product in particular, and how many stores they will shop to find it. The more stores they will shop in, the less important the absolute level of distribution will be.

The Discovery system addresses this issue with a distribution search feature for those product categories in which consumers shop in more than one store to buy the item. Typically, such categories contain many high-involvement consumers who will shop in multiple stores until they find what they want. Consider a new cosmetic guaranteed to remove wrinkles overnight, an R&D breakthrough supported by $100 million in advertising and minimum distribution. This product would be a success even if it meant that people had to shop 10 stores to find it.

The laboratory research study includes measures of consumer involvement in the product category and self-reports of the number of stores they would visit to find the new product. This enables us to estimate the percentage of consumers who will shop in only one, in two, three, or even more stores to find the new product. Model input, as a consequence, calls for "effective distribution" as opposed to simple ACV distribution.

To illustrate: if every consumer would shop in two stores to find the new entry and if the stores were independent of each other, then a 50 percent ACV distribution level would represent an effective distribution of 75 percent.

Marketing Program Costs

Marketing program cost data that marketing management supplies for profitability analysis includes

1. average cost per thousand GRPs by medium;
2. average cost per coupon by promotion type;
3. average cost per sample by promotion type; and
4. the cost of distribution.

The analysis can also include manufacturing costs, research, and other costs.

Depending on the marketing manager's needs, the profitability analysis can range from the gross margin level to an operating profit level. Not only will this information improve the value of a volume forecast, but it can also be used in a sensitivity analysis to determine the relative efficiency of each of the marketing mix components.

SIMULATED MARKET RESPONSE

Market response measures consumer reaction to the new or restaged product after advertising, couponing, sampling, or all three makes them aware of it. The three market-response components essential to forecasting a new product's sales are the item's 1) trial, 2) repeat, and 3) purchase cycle. We measure these components of market response through survey research and electronically through the use of scanner data in test markets, regional introductions, and national introductions. The simulated test market research's interview process generates consumer response to a new or restaged product in a simulated test market. We will first describe the interview process that collects the market-response information, then describe how a system forecasts each of the measures.

Simulated test marketing systems use different methodologies depending on the test product's development stage. One methodology is employed when the test product is not available for the consumers to use at home and the marketer is limited to a product concept description, a shelf set, or a finished advertisement that can be displayed during an Internet product exposure. Most systems use this approach.

An alternative methodology is employed when the marketer has competitors, advertising for the new product, and sufficient quantity of the packaged new product to display and "sell" it in the simulated store. We call the first approach a concept test market (CTM) while the second is a simulated test market (STM). The STM is currently used for a very small proportion of product tests due to the high costs of executing such an experiment.

The interview process for a Discovery system CTM and a simulated test market occurs in three stages. For the details of process flow, see figures 6.4 and 6.5. For both methodologies, the research often begins by screening thousands of prospective respondents on the Web or by phone using random selection processes in several geographically dispersed locations. The locations are selected so that they reflect national product category and brand usage patterns.

Concept Test Market Data Collection Process

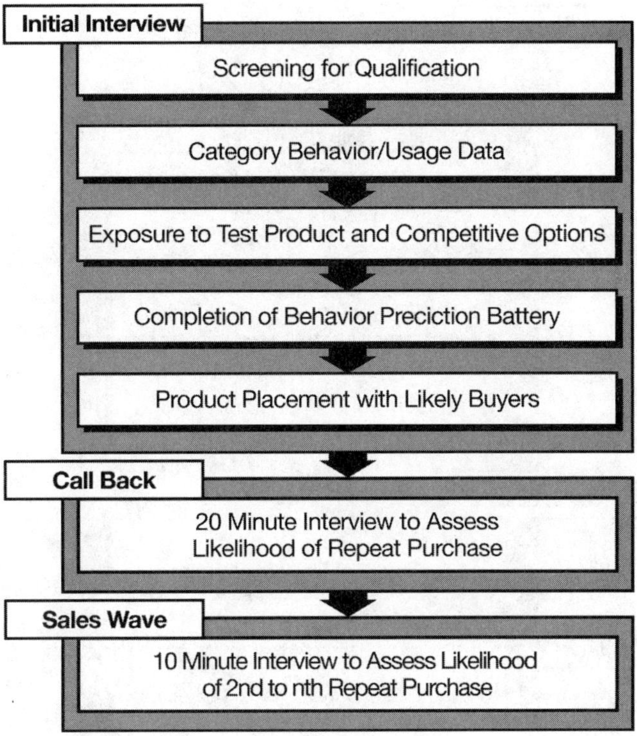

Initial Interview

Screening for Qualification

Category Behavior/Usage Data

Exposure to Test Product and Competitive Options

Completion of Behavior Preciction Battery

Product Placement with Likely Buyers

Call Back

20 Minute Interview to Assess
Likelihood of Repeat Purchase

Sales Wave

10 Minute Interview to Assess Likelihood
of 2nd to nth Repeat Purchase

FIGURE 6.4.

THE CONCEPT TEST MARKET PURCHASE SIMULATION

The basic data collection vehicle for a CTM study is a one-on-one interview. We either recruit using a telephone interview or recruit qualified consumers using mall-intercepts to find respondents for interviews at a research facility or we use an e-based panel for a web-based interview. The sample definition determines consumer qualifications. For example, if a client is testing a cat food, the sample definition will probably include cat ownership and a three-month cat food purchase history. Furthermore, consumers must satisfy the appropriate demographic profile and security, which means they do not work for a competitive company or for a market research company.

Simulated Test Market Data Collection Process

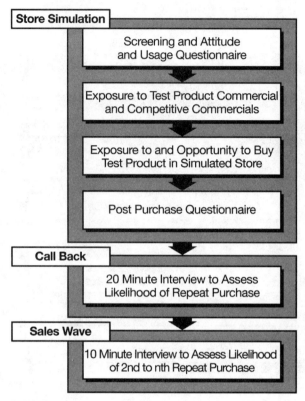

FIGURE 6.5.

The initial one-on-one interview is approximately 40 minutes long. This interview screens the consumers again to confirm their qualifications and it obtains background information concerning consumer attitudes and practices in the category.

For example, the interviewers establish for each respondent the number of units the consumer has bought in the test product's category in the past x weeks or months (depending on the category's purchase cycle) and each brand's share. This background information identifies heavy, medium, and light purchasers. It also identifies current brand buying among purchasers and nonpurchasers of the new (test) product. Further, it forces the respondents to think about their purchase decisions in the category and prepares them for the concept exposure.

In the Discovery system, respondents also rate a short list of category attributes and benefits in terms of desirability for the positioning research that we discuss in chapter 7.

Once the interviewer collects this background information, he or she exposes the respondent to the concept in a competitive context. We always show the concept with a price and accompany it with a competitive array of the key entrants priced appropriately for the market. Copernicus uses this approach because it mirrors the real world. As discussed in chapter 4, concept exposure varies between the systems. For example, typically, Bases exposes the concept with a price but without a competitive set.

Following exposure to the test concept, respondents evaluate it on one or another purchase probability scales. For a Discovery forecast, Copernicus employs a behavior prediction battery. Figure 6.6 shows one of the model's components.

We use a concept board and a competitive board as stimuli. The test product is positioned near the middle of the competitive board, with category leaders all priced according to the market. The presence of a competitive set is key to simulating the real-world purchasing environment. (It should be remembered that in some other systems no competitive stimuli are shown.)

After we have exposed respondents to the concept, they rate the critical attributes of the test product and its key competitors. Further, the interviewer establishes an anticipated purchase cycle for the test product, and collects attitudinal, behavioral, and demographic information that can be used to profile people who are likely to try the product and those who probably will not try it.

One Component of the Behavior Prediction Battery

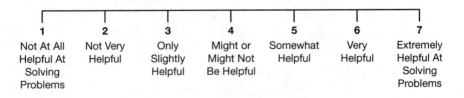

How helpful do you think this new (test product) would be in terms of solving any problems you may currently experience with regard to the brand you currently use?

1	2	3	4	5	6	7
Not At All Helpful At Solving Problems	Not Very Helpful	Only Slightly Helpful	Might or Might Not Be Helpful	Somewhat Helpful	Very Helpful	Extremely Helpful At Solving Problems

FIGURE 6.6.

We then place the product with respondents who express a purchase likelihood of 70 percent or more. If the test product is a line of items that vary by size, flavor, or form, we give respondents the one or two varieties they say they would buy first. When a client wants to build the user base for diagnostic purposes, we give additional products to people who rejected the concept.

After a reasonable time period (an interval that matches the product usage pattern), we contact respondents who have the product to gauge their reaction and likely repeat purchase. Most firms measure repeat purchase with one or more simple four- or five-point purchase probability scales.

A TRUE STM STORE SIMULATION

The initial interview for a "true" STM incorporates a self-administered questionnaire. Interviewers recruit qualified consumers by telephone; groups of 20 to 25 meet at a central facility. As in the CTM, the sample definition describes the consumer qualifications, and the interviewers screen prospective buyers to satisfy the appropriate demographic profile and security requirements (no competitors, ad agency, or research company employees).

When consumers arrive at the central location, they complete another screening questionnaire. Although the interviewers questioned the respondents during the initial telephone call, we administer the additional screen as a check on the respondents' qualifications. To ensure the sample's quality, the field personnel verify qualifications before the interview process continues.

After confirming respondent qualifications, the interviewer administers a background questionnaire. Similar to a CTM study, this form collects background information concerning the prospect's attitudes and practices in the product category, including category purchasing volume, brand purchasing behavior, and attribute desirability.

Following the background questionnaire, the interviewers expose respondents to the test product through an advertisement in a competitive environment, typically a 30-second commercial inserted into a half-hour television program. For product categories that rely heavily on print or radio advertising, the research uses those vehicles. Although most product categories use more than one medium, the STM research generates awareness of the new product (or restaged brand) by way of the category's primary advertising vehicle.

When the study uses a television commercial, respondents watch a 24-minute television program, usually a highly rated situation comedy in a theater-like setting. Four normal commercial breaks appear within the program. The third commercial break includes the test ad with "clutter" ads from unrelated categories, reproducing as closely as possible the real-world situation. The three other commercial breaks contain spots for the most heavily advertised competitors and clutter ads. The test commercial may be finished or animatic. If the study must use an animatic spot, at least one of the competitive or clutter ads is also an animatic.

For test products that rely heavily on print advertising, the research takes the portfolio approach. This is a collection of eight to ten print ads, with the test ad three-quarters into the portfolio. We do not require the ads to be "tipped in" to a magazine. Typically, however, the ads are in finished form. When a product category relies heavily on radio for its advertising, respondents listen to a radio program with a commercial break with the test product ad three-quarters into the break.

The interviewers give respondents an additional questionnaire after they see the television or print advertisements or listen to the radio spot. This questionnaire generates diagnostic information concerning advertising recall and communications: what did the test advertising communicate and how persuasive was the message?

After completing this questionnaire, respondents go into the simulated store. What happens next varies somewhat depending upon the STM service. Discovery appears to be the only system that continues to conduct an STM as described here. Respondents are brought into the store in groups of four or five where interviewers give them an order form. To simulate the local market, the competitive brands on the shelf represent approximately 80 percent of category volume, each priced appropriately for the local market. The prices on the shelves reflect the products' average, everyday retail price, not a discount or promotion price.

The test brand is always positioned near the center of the eye-level shelf, which is typically the second from the top of four shelves. Test and competitive brands are usually given one shelf facing, with dominant market brands receiving two or three facings as a maximum. And they usually stock products three deep within the test category.

To establish ambiance, we include surrounding products not in the test category. Respondents, however, may not buy them. These products consist of those items that typically appear near the test category. For example, if the test category is shampoo, conditioners and styling gels surround it.

To insure awareness of the test product, the Discovery interviewer leads respondents to the simulated store's test category section and informs them that they may buy any of the products with their own money. The interviewers further advise them to behave as they would in a real store. Often respondents pick up the merchandise to examine it and read the labels. Some respondents smell the products.

We stimulate purchasing in the simulated environment through a discount that applies to all test category products—typically 30 percent. Although the shelf prices are average, everyday retail, the order form lists both the retail price and the discounted price for each test category product. When the respondents complete their shopping, they either answer a postpurchase questionnaire or take part in a focus group discussion.

Copernicus uses focus group discussions following the visit to the laboratory store for diagnostic purposes. Though focus groups are not essential to the research, they sometimes produce interesting qualitative insights. Nine respondents who represent a mix of key segments make up each focus group(s): three people who bought the test product, three people who bought a competitive product, and three people who did not buy either.

The respondents who answer the postpurchase questionnaire rate the critical attributes of the test product and key competitors. We collect the brand share of requirements from the respondents with one significant difference: the test brand is included in the brand list. Further, this questionnaire produces an anticipated purchase cycle for the test product. Finally, the study collects demographic and psychographic information that we can use to profile purchasers and nonpurchasers.

After respondents complete their focus group discussion or postpurchase questionnaire, they return home with the products they bought. People are encouraged to use the products in their normal way.

THE CALL BACK INTERVIEW

All simulated test marketing services recontact consumers who "purchased" or who received the test product as a result of their initial interview. Indeed, the methodology is similar for the callback phase of a CTM study and an STM study. Category purchase cycle determines the callback timing to ensure that consumers have time to use the product. For example, a new cigarette callback will be three to five days after the initial interview. A new laundry detergent callback will be three to four weeks after the initial interview. On average, consumers will have used at least one-half of the test product when the interviewers call back.

The interviewers attempt callbacks for every person who bought the test product (an STM study) and for every person who received the test product (a CTM study). We expect an 80 percent re-contact rate. The callback interview is typically a 20-minute telephone conversation or Web-based survey where repeat purchase, purchase cycle, and diagnostic information about the test product are obtained.

The callback interview also elicits information concerning the amount of the product used, family/household member usage, occasions for use, and open-ended likes/dislikes. After the usage questions, the respondent typically answers repurchase intent on a five-point purchase intent scale. Based on these repurchase figures, the model estimates purchase volume.

Some of the systems, such as those provided by Copernicus, Vantis, and Research International, provide positioning guidance for an individual concept. In the positioning methodology used by Copernicus, respondents rate the same list of category attributes and benefits at the background stage during the initial interview and after the concept exposure stage. The survey thus gathers information about the product's performance versus the consumer's expectations.

At the conclusion of the callback interview, Copernicus researchers alone offer the product to the respondent at the regular retail price and ask if she would be interested in buying it again. If the study design incorporates an extended-use phase, the interviewer takes orders and the marketer delivers product.

THE SALES WAVE INTERVIEW

To differentiate between the initial callback and further interviews, researchers often use the term "sales wave" to identify those additional interviewing events. Similar to the initial callback, interviewers conduct the sales wave interview using the same methodology for a CTM study and an STM study. The sales wave timing is identical to the callback period; it matches the product purchase cycle. The sales wave is a 10-minute telephone or Web-based interview with few diagnostic questions. The key data that the sales wave interviews produce are purchase quantity and second repeat purchase probability. The same purchase quantity and repeat purchase questions are asked during the callback interview.

We conduct sales waves to assess long-term loyalty and purchase volume; sales wave interviews are necessary to determine changes in these market response variables over time. We use sales waves to assess potential "wear-out," declining interest in or usage of the product (or both), and to ascertain "wear-in," the consumer's increased commitment to the brand in terms of loyalty or purchase volume. Research has shown that sales waves are required in all tests involving food, breakthrough products, and unique products that may have a different usage pattern from the category at large. We employ multiple sales waves for products that indicate uncertain consumer loyalty and usage over time.

Again, as at the end of the initial callback, the Discovery system interviewers offer the product at the regular retail price. If the study incorporates an additional extended-use phase, the interviewers take orders and, again, the marketer delivers the product.

Although STM studies in the 1970s and 1980s routinely included sales waves, they have fallen into disuse in recent years for reasons having to do with saving time and money. This is a mistake.

It is a mistake because in some categories, particularly food products (e.g., cold cereals, energy drinks, a salad with chicken and ranch dressing, etc.) it takes several buying and eating experiences to gauge customer reaction to the product.

Recently we were informed by the chief marketing officer (CMO) of a major burger chain that STMs did not work in that category. The reason, he said, was that they overstated long-term sales of new entries. When asked whether he had employed sales wave research as part of their STM experience, the answer was no, he had not used it and wanted an explanation. When told that the purpose of the sales wave was to measure wear-out, he reluctantly admitted that perhaps with that addition, his STMs might have forecast more accurately.

MEASURING TRIAL IN A LABORATORY SIMULATION

The two methodologies we have just described—the CTM and the STM—measure buying behavior in a laboratory environment. All firms conducting simulated test marketing research employ proprietary adjustments to convert what people say they will do (in the case of the CTM) or actually do with their own money or full-face coupons (in the case of an STM) into estimates of real world trial. The technical name for this is the "awareness-to-trial conversion." That is, the proportion of people who will buy the product at least once under conditions of 100 percent awareness and 100 percent distribution.

Bases, Vantis, and MarkeTest, for example, have weights for their five-point purchase probability scale. According to company literature and interviews, weights that are used to make the conversion from the self-report into actual behavior vary by product category.

Copernicus employs a Behavior Prediction Battery at the concept stage we briefly touched on in the previous section. The Behavior Prediction model includes the following dozen measures that cover affective as well as cognitive reactions to the test product:

1. Visceral reaction (first impression): "What is your first impression of the idea for this product?"
2. Uniqueness: "How would you rate this product in terms of its uniqueness—that is, its similarity to or difference from other items on the market?"
3. Superiority: "How does this product compare to other products that currently exist?"
4. Problem solving: "How helpful do you think this product would be in solving any problems you may currently experience with regard to these types of products?"
5. Personal relevance: "Based on what you have just seen and read about this product, what types of people do you think would like this new product?"
6. Use occasions: "Can you think of specific use occasions you might have for this product?"
7. Value for the money: "What do you think of the value of this product in terms of value for the money?"
8. Absolute price: "What is your opinion of the price of this product?"
9. Likes/dislikes: "Which of the following best describes the degree to which you like or dislike anything about this product?"
10. Clarity: "Which of the following describes the degree to which you find anything about this product confusing?"

11. Credibility: "Is there anything about this product that you find hard to believe?"
12. Overall rating: "*Overall* how would you rate this product?"

We measure each factor on a seven-point scale that couples each point with a verbal description.

Finally, we ask consumers to rate the concept for purchase probability using an 11-point scale, created decades ago by Dr. Thomas Juster, then of the U.S. Department of Commerce. The scale couples word meanings with probability estimates to enhance serious thinking on the respondents' part. We have discovered through extensive experimentation that it predicts real-world behavior more effectively than the alternatives, especially for mixed- and high-involvement decisions. Figure 6.7 illustrates this scale.

Like all self-reported measures of consumer buying, this 11-point scale overstates the actual purchasing that takes place. Much of this overstatement comes about because the research environment assumes 100 percent awareness and distribution, something a company never realizes in the real world.

A Validated Purchase Probability Scale

10.	Certain Will Purchase	99 Chances in 100
9.	Almost Certain Will Purchase	90 Chances in 100
8.	Very Probably Will Purchase	80 Chances in 100
7.	Probably Will Purchase	70 Chances in 100
6.	Good Possibility Will Purchase	60 Chances in 100
5.	Fairly Good Possibility Will Purchase	50 Chances in 100
4.	Fair Possibility Will Purchase	40 Chances in 100
3.	Some Possibility Will Purchase	30 Chances in 100
2.	Slight Possibility Will Purchase	20 Chances in 100
1.	Very Slight Possibility Will Purchase	10 Chances in 100
0.	No Chance Will Purchase	0 Chances in 100

FIGURE 6.7.

Not all prospective consumers will be aware of the product and not all of those aware of it are able to buy it.

Even if we take the 100 percent awareness and distribution fallacy into account, people are more likely to say they will buy than in fact do buy. This is true in all product categories we have investigated. We have closely examined the relationship between people's reports on the 11-point scale and awareness-to-trial among people who were aware of the product and for whom product was available to be purchased for numerous consumer package goods.

We have also looked at this relationship in durable goods and financial service cases, including a hand-held microcomputer; a credit card; a flat-screen television; long-lasting light bulbs; new car dealer visits; overnight messenger services; trash bags; premium paper checks; personal computer printers; laptop computers; and medical equipment sold to hospitals. We also use this scale to forecast the likelihood that a doctor would prescribe a new pharmaceutical and the likelihood that a consumer would ask a physician to prescribe a new pharmaceutical (see chapter 10).

The higher the level of self-reported behavior probability, the greater the ratio of reported purchases to probability. Copernicus's experience indicates that usually no more than 80 percent of the people who assert they will buy, do buy. This figure declines monotonically but not linearly as self-reported purchase probability declines, but the ratio is not constant. We therefore apply different weights to account for respondent overstatements. Depending on the product category and the situation, virtually none of the people at the low end of the scale—from "Some possibility will purchase" on down—will buy the product or service. Figure 6.8 illustrates this relationship between actual behavior and self-reported probability of behavior.

Conventional wisdom says that purchase involvement is a function of the product or service; the more expensive, complex, or unfamiliar, the more time and deliberation the consumer gives the purchase. An automobile, by this view, is a high-involvement decision product; toothpaste is low. In fact, purchase involvement is not a function of the product, but of the consumer. Some toothpaste purchasers who score high in compulsive neuroses will spend more time in front of a supermarket display deciding between brands, sizes, and packages than some car buyers do in choosing a new car. We once found that the product that provoked the highest consumer involvement was bathroom wallpaper—not an expensive, complex, or unfamiliar product.

The Relationship Between Self-Reported and Actual Behavior

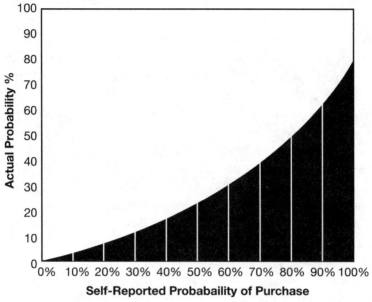

FIGURE 6.8.

Over time, Copernicus developed three sets of weights to adjust the scale for low-, moderate-, and high-involvement purchases. Low-involvement purchases reflect the greatest overstatement; they are typically priced under $10. Consumers spend the least time considering their purchase. They are low-risk, routine, or impulse purchases. Further, the product alternatives offer minimal differences.

Moderate-involvement purchases, which show moderate overstatement, are often priced between $10 and $99. The consumer spends a modest amount of time processing information during purchase consideration. Moderate-involvement purchases include such things as inexpensive services or durables and over-the-counter drugs.

High-involvement purchases, which experience the least overstatement, are usually priced over $99, involve a high level of personal or physical risk (e.g., a permanent hair color), or both. The consumer spends the most time learning about the product category, evaluating the different brands, and forming his or her attitude about the item during the purchasing process. The consumer sees these products more closely tied to one's identity and to peer group influence than are moderate- or low-involvement purchases. Greater differences exist among product alternatives. High-involvement purchases include more expensive consumer services and durables.

Adjusted scores on the 11-point purchase probability scale are then combined with the 12 affective and cognitive measures described earlier into a 13-factor individual-level equation that forecasts trial, given awareness, and distribution. Figure 6.9 shows the components of the model.

The model adjusts for responses that are inconsistent, such as the respondent who claims a 90 percent purchase probability but indicates that the product is not appropriate, will not be helpful, and will not have many uses.

Combining the 11-point purchase probability scale with the affective and cognitive dimensions reduces the discrepancies between the prediction and real-world performance. The full behavior prediction battery helps generate a forecast and so much more. It helps explain the forecast and provide insights into how it might be improved.

A Behavior Prediction Battery

Affective Measures	Cognitive Measures	Behavioral Measure
• First Impression	• Price	• 11-Point Purchase Probability Scale
• For People Like Me	• Value	
• For Occasions I Experience	• Clarity	
• Likeability	• Believability	
• Overall Impression	• Uniqueness	
• Helpful at Solving Problems	• Superiority	

[b1 (Factor 1) + b2 (Factor 2) + b3 (Factor 3) ... + b13 (11 Point Scale)] = Forcasted Behavior

FIGURE 6.9.

The conversion of laboratory behavior into estimates of real-world trial is a different process than a full STM (as opposed to a CTM we have just been discussing).

In contrast, at the simulated test marketing stage we rely exclusively on the proportion of people who buy the test brand. This percentage—adjusted by norms collected over a 12-year period—enables us to estimate what people will do in the real world based on what they do in the laboratory setting.

MEASURING TRIAL DUE TO SAMPLING

If sampling takes a large proportion of the marketing budget, the research tests its impact on trial. The Discovery system has tested plans that incorporate direct mail, trial size with coupons, free in-store sampling, and taste sampling. Since the system exposes all respondents to advertising or to a concept board, when the research includes sampling, the trial factor measured is the awareness-to-trial due to both advertising and sampling.

When a marketer uses direct-mail sampling, we send samples to a list of potentially qualified consumers. Since the recruitment success rate is approximately one respondent for three contacts, we must mail samples to at least three times as many prospects as the research requires. We then recruit consumers who have received the samples to take part in the research. To avoid bias, we do not tell these people that the sample they received in the mail is the test product. The percentage of respondents who buy the test product in the simulated store reflects the awareness-to-trial figure that we can attribute to direct-mail sampling and advertising.

We have tested trial size samples with "Act Now!" coupons in a simulated store by duplicating the promotion as it would be in the real world with a trial-size display. The percentage of consumers who buy in the simulated store denotes the awareness-to-trial figure that we can attribute to advertising and sampling with an Act Now! coupon.

We test free in-store sampling by handing samples to respondents as they enter the simulated store. The percentage who buy in the simulated store signifies the awareness-to-trial figure attributable to advertising and sampling.

We conduct food product taste sampling in both simulated and concept test market methodologies. We offer taste samples in the simulated store (an STM study) or during the initial interview (a CTM). The percentage of respondents who buy the product in the simulated store indicates the awareness-to-trial figure attributable to advertising and sampling. We use the Behavior Prediction Model to forecast the awareness-to-trial figure attributable to advertising and sampling in a CTM study.

MEASURING REPEAT PURCHASE PROBABILITY

Most simulated test marketing services obtain the first repeat purchase probability estimate through the initial callback interview after the respondent has had the opportunity to use the test product. Each system produces a purchase figure that is an "ever" repeat probability. That is, it forecasts the probability that a person who tries the test product will ever buy it again.

The first repeat purchase probability is a function of a four- or a five-point scale question. Discovery system researchers forecast first repeat purchase probability in a competitive context. Interviewers ask a five-point repeat purchase intent question using the test product's retail price. The interviewer also reminds the respondent of the competitive products' retail prices.

Besides the first repeat purchase probability, the Discovery system also provides a Year 1 repeat figure. The Year 1 repeat is the percentage of people who try the product and who buy it one or more times during the launch year. This figure is less than or equal to the repeat figure forecast because it depends on the trial build, ACV distribution, and the purchase cycle. The Year 1 repeat figure will be less than the first repeat purchase probability figure because people who buy the product for the first time during Year 1's last purchase cycle will not have the opportunity to buy again during the launch year.

For example, assume the research indicates a food product that has a first repeat purchase probability forecast of 55 percent; it has a purchase cycle of one unit every four months; and it has a slow trial build. Such a combination of first repeat purchase probability, purchase cycle, and trial build may yield a Year 1 repeat of 20 percent. In this case, only 20 percent of the people who try the product have an opportunity to buy it again during the first year. However, 55 percent of all people who try it will eventually repurchase the product—assuming the manufacturer maintains distribution.

THE PURCHASE CYCLE

The product's purchase cycle reflects the number of occasions the new or restaged product's franchise will buy it during the course of, say, the first year.

The franchise is that consumer segment the research anticipates to be the product's loyal consumers. Thus, we estimate the purchase cycle based on the franchise's responses to the callback and sales-wave interview questions about the anticipated purchase volume and the anticipated share of requirements.

For product categories with a known distribution of heavy and light purchasers, sophisticated STM systems include the option of using a purchase interval distribution rather than using an average purchase cycle. For example, if the STM research indicates that the franchise for a new food product will buy four units a year on average, the model will use a purchase cycle of one unit every three months. If the marketing manager provides additional research, however, indicating that half of the franchise buys two units a year and half buys six units a year (averaging to four units a year), a system such as Discovery will use the full distribution of repeat purchases, rather than the average, to forecast.

SHARE OF REQUIREMENTS

Most STM systems today evaluate purchase volume of the test product based on its anticipated share of requirements. The interviewer determines the test product's share of requirements in two ways during the callback and sales wave interviews.

First, the number of category units the respondent plans to buy in the next x weeks or months (depending on the category's purchase cycle) and the number of test brand units the respondent will buy in the next x weeks or months (again, depending on the category's purchase cycle). This generates a share of requirements in a noncompetitive context.

Second, the survey generates figures that show in a competitive context for each respondent how much each brand—including the test brand—accounts for the consumer's product category requirements. The average of these two share-of-requirement figures generates the purchase volume figure for the test product.

MANAGEMENT IMPLICATIONS

This chapter has described the three different types of inputs that drive any STM volume forecast. The first input is intelligence about the product category itself; the second is detailed information on a month-by-month basis about the marketing plans designed to support the new brand; the third is market response to the new entry as measured by the simulated test market laboratory experiment or concept test market.

Although the specific requirements of different STM consulting services vary to some degree, the similarities between them are striking. Marketers familiar with one service generally find it easy to understand another. Researchers who have worked for one STM consulting firm have generally found it easy to make the transition to another.

Marketers and researchers need to remember an important caveat in simulated test marketing research every time they conduct an STM: the three types of input are critical in determining the outcome. Marketers who provide flawed category data or hastily organized marketing plans or run questionable laboratory experiments risk a bad forecast. Given the increasing importance placed on STM forecasts by new product marketers, the high visibility and the amount of money at risk in new product introductions, the potential problem here is very serious.

Perhaps the most common problem in simulated test marketing study is a marketing plan that promises too much. This is the undoing of many new products and careers. Managers overpromise what they can actually deliver and the automated forecasting routines of an STM model carry out the plans, which may bear little relationship to what will actually be deployed in the real world. The result can be a forecast significantly higher than anything the company ever achieves. When this happens, marketing managers sometimes blame the model; they should blame themselves.

7

Diagnostic Tools to Improve a Marketing Plan

Today, many marketers—certainly the sophisticated ones—employ simulated test marketing to forecast a new product's performance prior to a real-world introduction. With many companies using similar technology (at least in theory), however, a volume forecasting capability offers no particular competitive advantage to any one firm. Then too many companies introduce new products even after a simulation suggests—or in some cases, guarantees—failure. We described a number of these cases earlier. A powerful champion for the new product is able in many organizations to push the idea into the marketplace even when research is screaming, "Don't do it!"

For these reasons and others (e.g., too many line extensions, bad advertising, decreasing innovation as a result of declining R&D budgets, among others), new product failure rates continue to climb. As we discussed in chapter 1, the failure rate for new packaged goods is currently hovering between 90 percent and 95 percent. New financial products and services, television programs, new fast food menu items, Hollywood movies, and business-to-business products and services expire, as best as we are able to determine, 80 percent–90 percent of the time.

THE CASE OF THE UNRESPONSIVE AD AGENCY

One reason for the high rate of failure is that marketing managers test too few plans before introducing a new (or repositioned) product. Not long ago, a client asked us to simulate the performance of a single marketing plan for their soon-to-be-restaged flagship brand. Concerned, we asked to see the advertising. It was bad. We were especially troubled because it didn't communicate the essential positioning strategy we had worked so hard to develop.

The client asked for a recommendation. We suggested a half-day meeting with the advertising agency. We would present the positioning research for half the time, and would offer ten alternative creative ideas just to get the agency's imaginative juices going. The client's CMO said, "That can't work. You guys don't want to be pushing creative on the agency."

We said there was no sense going ahead with the simulated test market with such weak advertising. The product would be doomed from the start. After considerable more discussion, she agreed with our suggestion for a meeting.

We actually came up with fifteen ideas and put them on boards. For the meeting, the advertising agency sent an executive vice president, the most senior account executive, the senior creative director, and the agency's executive vice president for planning.

We talked about the targeting and positioning research we'd done, and then we began to show alternative creative approaches. While the client was a little anxious, the agency people became more and more enthusiastic. They wanted to know more: "What about this idea? What about that idea?" We had to say repeatedly, "We're not the creative types. Your job is to do the creative. All we're trying to do is show that the targeting and positioning strategy in the brief we gave you can be executed in a lot of different ways. And we'd like to see you come back with a bunch of different ideas."

We spent two hours discussing alternative creative. The client became so excited by this, she said, "Here's an idea! Why can't we take the creative group at the agency, and break it into two? Give both groups the brief, the research, and if a consulting company can come up fifteen creative ideas in a few weeks, then surely each of the groups could come with fifteen to twenty ideas, right? We could be sitting here in a month from now with thirty or forty ideas!" Everyone agreed that was brilliant.

Then, because everybody seemed so energized, we said, "While you're thinking about ideas, we've got to run the simulation with a planned media schedule. Why can't we come up with some alternative media schedules to test as well?"

Universal agreement around the table. "Yeah! Right! Great!" The meeting broke up with everyone pleased as can be.

We met again a month later. To our amazement the agency brought in one idea. They said they had actually "ideated for weeks and had in fact developed many ideas, but this one stood out head and shoulders above the rest." Unfortunately, that one idea wasn't any better than the one we started with. And the media plan was unchanged. We were back to square one.

As we noted in chapter 2, most marketing executives do not even realize how many plans they could test. Some executives believe that if they provide the simulated test market (STM) company with three alternative plans and pick the winner in terms of a volume forecast, that that's about as far as they can go. But simulated test marketing research can go beyond pure volume forecasts to provide managers with the tools they need to diagnose (and, if needed, improve) a new product's targeting, positioning, and pricing—indeed, the entire marketing plan. This chapter shows how and discusses such issues as line item distribution and cannibalization, issues that a simple volume forecast does not address.

A SIMULATION OFFERS TARGETING GUIDANCE

When introducing a new product, a line extension, or a restaged product, company executives have determined (or should have determined) the prime market target. But sometimes the planned market target is not the group that actually tries and continues buying the product when it is introduced. Then, too, as we discuss in *Counterintuitive Marketing*, some companies don't have a fix on the market target at the beginning of the project.[1] Not enough time is spent studying this critical business decision.

The marketing manager can spend the marketing budget more efficiently by scheduling the media and the promotion that reaches the most profitable target group. Moreover, the advertising agency can improve the creative and copy's effectiveness when it is tailored especially for this target because the agency will know (or can know) the target market's wants, needs, hopes, desires, fears, and more.

STM research results can help answer targeting questions. A comparison is done of trial and repeat rates by different need-states, behavioral patterns, and demographic and geographic groups to see if differences in behavioral appeal exist.

To show how a marketer can use trial rates for targeting, consider the example of a new, solid antiperspirant deodorant formulated from only natural ingredients, Naturally Dry. Figure 7.1 shows the strong appeal of this new

Awareness-to-Trial of *Naturally Dry*
by Selected Demographic Groups

Total	**29.9%**
Gender	
Female	43.7%
Male	15.2%
Age	
18-34	42.5%
35-44	33.5%
45-54	27.7%
55 or Older	16.9%
Marital Status	
Married	33.1%
Not Married	23.9%
Education	
College Graduate	24.1%
Not College Graduate	32.5%
Total Household Income	
Under $25,000	37.4%
$25,000-$34,999	30.0%
$35,000-$49,999	26.7%
$50,000 or over	26.6%
Presence of Children	
Have Children Under 18	30.8%
No Children Under 18 at Home	28.2%

FIGURE 7.1.

product among women (a 43.7 percent trial probability) compared to the appeal among men (a 15.2 percent trial probability). Moreover, the concept performs best among younger, downscale consumers, a very different target than the one the marketer intended. This suggests either that the concept or advertising copy or media plan—or all three—need to be "fixed" to better position the new entry and bring performance back in line with objectives.

A problem with Naturally Dry was clearly evident when STM research was called upon to show the appeal of the concept among different types of users. This research discovered that the new entry had its greatest appeal among very light users who would buy the product primarily for special occasions when they feel a need for a different kind of deodorant. This disappointing discovery contributed to the low projected usage level for the new brand and anticipated marketplace failure.

Diagnostics also showed the marketing manager that a potential exists for additional volume if the company can increase trial appeal among prospects who use a solid antiperspirant deodorant regularly, that is, heavy users. Conversely, the company could position Naturally Dry as the special antiperspirant deodorant by taking advantage of its higher trial among those consumers who buy it for special occasions. This is a classic marketing problem: the manager must choose between dominating one segment or broadening appeal among several segments. Often, by broadening the appeal and thereby diluting the impact in the most responsive segment(s), a company's attempt to expand fails on both fronts. Additional marketing research can help the marketing manager to determine the best alternative.

A SIMULATION PROFILES NEW PRODUCT BUYERS VS. NONBUYERS

Simulated test marketing research can also provide a behavioral profile of the new product's buyers. To illustrate the type of consumer profile data available, here is an example of a purchaser versus nonpurchaser profile generated by the simulated test market for Naturally Dry.

A comparison of brands purchased in the past twelve months by purchasers of Naturally Dry versus nonpurchasers indicated that the purchasers (i.e., the triers) were more likely to purchase Brands A, B, C, and G than nonpurchasers (figure 7.2). Since the company was positioning Naturally Dry as a premium product and Brands D, E, and H are positioned as premium brands (and priced accordingly), these results were not encouraging.

A SIMULATION PROFILES THE FRANCHISE

A profile of the ultimate franchise, the loyal repeaters, provides the marketing manager with additional targeting guidance. To segment the franchise in the STM research, the researchers define the franchise as those who purchased in the laboratory environment and who report they would "definitely" or would "probably" repurchase Naturally Dry after using it at home for two weeks.

Brand Profile of *Naturally Dry*
Purchasers vs. Non-Purchasers

Bought in Past Year	Purchasers (328) %	Non-Purchasers (769) %
A	83	62
B	77	59
C	44	20
D	23	16
E	29	29
F	10	11
G	29	12
H	6	12
I	5	8

FIGURE 7.2.

Researchers examined customer loyalty to a single brand. That is, are there brands that customers tend to buy all the time versus brands they buy occasionally? Or are there brands to which customers show little loyalty; they are among a cluster of brands customers buy with equal frequency? In this research, we found only one brand that loyal Naturally Dry customers buy significantly more often others. These consumers are more likely to have bought Brand A in the past 12 months (figure 7.3). Brand A tends to be a less expensive brand that dominates the mass merchandiser channel in this market. This was more bad news for the new product manager who was expecting the brand to take business away from premium entries.

A SIMULATION OFFERS POSITIONING GUIDANCE

Although this study provided insight into the characteristics of triers of the new product and the likely franchise, many questions and hypotheses remain regarding *why* consumers buy the new product and which product attributes and benefits from the dozens available the marketer should stress. For example, should the marketer assert

Behavioral Profile of Repeat Buyers (i.e., The Franchise)

Share in Past Year	Naturally Dry Franchise (211) %	Naturally Dry Rejectors (910) %
A	43	27
B	27	28
C	6	7
D	4	4
E	1	3
F	5	14
G	2	3
H	4	3
I	–	2

FIGURE 7.3.

"Naturally Dry has no harsh chemicals," or

"Naturally Dry is a sexy, erotically charged product," or

"Naturally Dry doesn't stain clothes," or

"Naturally Dry smells fresh and clean," or something else entirely?

Researchers generally take a direct approach to finding out what is important to consumers in a marketing research study. Unfortunately this is more likely to lead you to the wrong strategy than to the correct one.

This approach is to ask consumers what is important. Researchers give the respondents a list of characteristics of the product or service and ask them to rate each characteristic on a five-point scale. For example, "When you are in the market for a deodorant, how important is it to you that the deodorant has no harsh chemicals? Would you say it is extremely important? Very important? Somewhat important? Slightly important? Not important at all?"

This self-reported importance methodology is exactly what you do *not* want to do. It is unlikely to tell you what is really motivating in the product category, because people will give you the most rational, expected, socially acceptable answers. They will tell you that great taste and refreshment are very important characteristics of a soft drink, even though most Americans can not differentiate between Pepsi and Coke in a blind taste test. They will tell you that security in an e-commerce site is key, even though buyers rarely know anything about a site and its backers. They will tell you that safety is what they want in an automobile when most of what they know is based on advertising-driven perceptions, not hard data.

People will never admit that sexual magnetism is important to them, even though for some segments of the market it is highly motivating. And we have observed that in an increasingly price-driven world relatively few consumers will tell you that price is one of their most important considerations. Who wants to admit they're cheap?

The approach we recommend is based on breaking developments in marketing science using a three-component theory of attitudes as a starting point: dream detection, problem detection, and brand preference detection.

Psychologists and human behaviorists have argued for three decades that attitudes are formulated through these three components. Marketing science uses the three-component theory of attitude as a starting point.

Because a product attribute can be strong in one component but weak in others, it's important to evaluate it on each of the three dimensions. That way, you do not overlook potential strengths. Ideally, you'd like the product and its positioning to excel on all three components: people say they want what the product offers, don't get it with the products they currently use, and they'd buy a product with it if they could get it.

Dream detection, the affective component of motivating power, assesses the interest level of each attribute and benefit. What do consumers truly want in the category—no matter how unrealistic or preposterous? Example: "It's very desirable to have a deodorant that makes me more attractive to the opposite sex."

We use a desirability scale rather than an importance measure because people tend to report intangible attributes and benefits as being more appealing when they answer on a desirability scale than on an importance measure. Ask, "How important is it that the next automobile you buy impresses your brother-in-law?" and people tend to say, "Not very important."

If you ask, however, "How desirable is it that the next automobile you buy impresses your brother-in-law?" and people (some people, anyway) will say, "Very desirable." Couple this phrase with a picture, and people may even say, "It's extremely desirable."

"Importance" implies rationality. People want to give a response they think researchers want to hear, a response they think will make them look good in the interviewer's eyes. "Desirability" is a less loaded word; add a visual and the combination encourages respondents to say whatever feels most true.

Before we expose respondents to the test product's advertising and the simulated store, we ask them to evaluate a list of product characteristics in terms of desirability. These characteristics include tangible attributes and benefits such as "easy to use" and "relatively inexpensive" and intangible attributes and benefits such as "make me feel very sexy," or "I feel I'm doing the most for my hair."

Problem detection, the difference between our dreams and reality, is the cognitive component. It measures what respondents want (desirability) versus what they are getting (or not) from their current brands. For example, virtually all automobile owners want high reliability; Lexus and Honda owners are getting it (according to *Consumer Reports*), Volkswagen owners are not.

You cannot identify a problem by asking people what is important to them. How important is it that your next car have four wheels? Extremely important. But all new cars have four wheels so this is not a problem. How important is it that a solid antiperspirant deodorant keep your underarms dry? Extremely important. But dryness in an antiperspirant is a cost of entry.

Many would agree with Procter & Gamble, which defines marketing as the discipline concerned with solving people's problems with products and services for a profit. And the way to measure this is by finding discrepancies between what people want and what they're getting.

Brand preference detection, the behavior component, determines which attribute ratings are correlated with, or predict, purchase behavior. In a typical study we have respondents rate each of the leading brands in their evoked set in terms of each the 30-plus attributes and benefits we are studying. Later in the interview we also ask a number of questions concerning purchase probabilities for each these brands.

It is also possible to use a constant-sum tool, where you ask recipients, "Out of the next ten times you make a purchase in this product category, how many times are you likely to make a purchase of these different brands?" The brands you ask about are the same brands respondents rated earlier. It is a simple matter then of doing correlation/regression analysis to predict the overall rating. You must do this analysis for each individual respondent separately, however, not the aggregate.

This leverage analysis illustrated in figure 7.4 correlates, on an individual respondent basis, degree to which the respondent perceives brands to offer a specific attribute or benefit with actual preference or behavior. In other words, if a woman sees a product to have a valuable benefit, it is more likely she will buy the product in the future. The analysis supplements what consumers say they want (that is, "desire") with what appears to drive their actual preference or purchasing behavior.

For example, in an analysis of a new credit card service a bank planned to offer, one respondent said that "Makes me feel very smart when I use it" is only

Illustration of a Leverage Anaylsis
For a New Credit Card

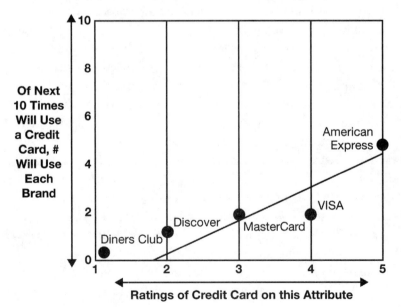

FIGURE 7.4.

slightly desirable. Leverage analysis, however, revealed a strong positive relationship with overall preference, a correlation of 0.9 (figure 7.4). The same respondent rated the bank's new credit card service very high on that attribute, *and* said she planned to use more of this service in the future.

As other illustrations, characteristics having to do with automotive performance (e.g., acceleration) are highly correlated with overall preference for BMW. Characteristics having to do with youthfulness are highly correlated with preference for Pepsi-Cola. Characteristics having to do with being good for children, fun for children, a place children like, are highly correlated with preference for McDonald's.

In contrast, old fashioned and stodginess are negatively related to a choice of a BMW. Authenticity and nineteenth-century Americana are negatively related with preference for Pepsi. And an extensive menu and table service are negatively related to the choice of McDonald's.

The next step is to rescale all three of these dimensions *for each respondent* from −100 (extremely demotivating) to +100 (overwhelmingly motivating) and to take a weighted average of the three components to establish the motivating power of each attribute. Motivating power, as we have discovered, is not just about dreams, problems, and preference, but a composite of all three. See figure 7.5 for an illustration of this three-dimensional model of consumer motivations.

A Three Dimensional Model of Motivations

Affective Component	Cognitive Component	Behavioral Component
Dream Detection Self-reported in the questionnaire using a 9-point symmetric scale	**Problem Detection** Desires versus satisfaction with preferred deodorant	**Brand Preference Detection** Correlation between brand ratings and likelihood of purchasing

New Deodorant Motivating Power
Weighted Average of the Three Components
(Computed for each attribute/benefit for each respondent)

FIGURE 7.5.

One simple way to do this is to weight each dimension equally for each respondent and average them. Our experience has shown, however, that the desirability component for new products should be ratcheted up and the brand preference estimate ratcheted down. For established products and services the problem scores are more important than simple desirability ratings.

But the job is not finished, because while characteristics can be critical to consumers, they may not actually drive behavior because every competitor offers the benefit (four wheels, brakes) or no one does. For example, two decades ago, you would have found that people who liked and wanted to buy a new two-seater roadster had a problem: they couldn't get one. The "two-seater" attribute, while motivating, would not have been a good predictor of purchase behavior because at the time no company offered small sports cars. Consumers may want a laptop computer that runs for a year on a single charge, but, at this writing, it does not exist.

In an STM study, researchers interview respondents to learn their background habits and practices—an interview that includes the desirability question. They expose respondents to an advertisement or a concept, depending on the stage of development. This exposure includes competitive and clutter ads or competitive concepts to simulate the marketplace environment. When a product is available, the researchers show the actual item and competitive products in a simulated store.

Following exposure to the test stimulus, the researchers administer a post-exposure evaluation questionnaire. This portion of the interview contains the brand rating question, asking respondents to evaluate the test brand and key competitors according to the same attributes and benefits they rated in terms of desirability.

Assume that in the Naturally Dry simulation study, 30 attributes and benefits were included and 1,000 respondents were interviewed. For every respondent there are 30 A/B desirability ratings, 30 problem scores, and 30 correlation/leverage calculations. In total, that's 30 times 3 times 1,000 separate computations, or 90,000 individual-level calculations combined into 30 different motivating-power scores for each respondent, one for each of the attributes and benefits.

We then examine these motivating-power scores among the total sample, among purchasers versus nonpurchasers of the new product or service (in this case, Naturally Dry) and for the franchise. This enables the marketing manager to understand the elements that influence consumer purchasing behavior in the product category as well as to assess similarities and differences between buyers and nonbuyers.

The research found that, for the total sample, the category's highly motivating characteristics were "all-natural ingredients," "quality," "prevents odors," "will not stain," "a brand I trust," and "reasonably priced." The category characteristics low in motivating power were "long lasting," "easy to use," "easy to open," and "overall strength."

When we look at the motivating power of these characteristics among people who do not buy Naturally Dry, we immediately see an important difference. Naturally Dry buyers rate "all natural" as a highly motivating attribute while people who did not buy Naturally Dry rate it as having low motivating power. Further, buyers rate "reasonably priced" and "value for the money" as high in motivating power while non purchasers are hardly motivated by these characteristics at all.

Although comparing motivating power by purchasing group is useful in assessing a new product or service's positioning, comparing brand ratings by attributes and benefits as is shown in figure 7.6 explicitly shows the product's strengths and weaknesses in the competitive environment.

Brand Strategy Matrix

Naturally Dry vs. "Brand B"

		Naturally Dry Superior	Parity: Excellent: Could Not Be Better	Parity: Acceptable But Could Be Better	Unacceptable	Naturally Dry Inferior
Motivating Power	**High**	No Chemicals	Keeps You Dry	Reasonably Priced	No Stains	Stops Perspiration
	Mod	Degradable	Long-lasting	Brand I Trust	Easy to Open	Easy to Close
	Low	Natural Ingredients	Cylindrical Shape	Right Size	Recyclable	Well-known Brand

FIGURE 7.6.

For a new product or service to generate trial, prospects must view it as having a comparative advantage over the competitive products for at least some of the highly motivating characteristics. Those attributes and benefits that consumers consider the product having a comparative advantage represent an immediate positioning opportunity. Those highly motivating characteristics the consumers consider the test product to be at parity compared to other brands represent the category's price of entry. In other words, "stops wetness" in an antiperspirant, "great taste" in a soft drink, or "financially reliable" in an insurance company are all highly motivating, but every product in the category has them.

Parity is not enough to generate trial in a highly competitive marketplace (which is why "me-too" products fail). A company must combine parity with a comparative advantage for at least some highly motivating characteristics. When consumers believe that a new product is at a comparative advantage for highly motivating factors, the positioning should reflect it.

Comparing brand ratings between the new product, Naturally Dry, and an existing product, Brand B, shows that among purchasers, Naturally Dry is at a comparative advantage for its pricing and environmental characteristics. However, consumers rate it at parity or at a comparative disadvantage for the remaining highly motivating factors. This finding helps explain the disappointing performance of the new brand among upscale demographic targets. Marketing management hoped to imprint premium imagery, yet this analysis shows that people perceived it as low priced.

Nonpurchasers rated Naturally Dry at parity with Brand B for all motivating attributes. Although they rated Naturally Dry at parity for its highly motivating characteristics, that provides no incentive to switch their buying from Brand B to Naturally Dry. To foster trial, Naturally Dry needs a positioning that generates a comparative advantage for more of the highly motivating characteristics. It needs a positioning in the upper left-hand corner of the Brand Strategy Matrix (figure 7.7).

A SIMULATION OFFERS ADVERTISING GUIDANCE

One of the great mysteries to marketing consultants is how few advertising campaigns marketers develop and test for a new product launch. In many cases, they test one or two commercials and compare the results to the copy-testing norms of the research service. If the copy testers declare that the new

A Blueprint for Action

<u>The Brand Strategy Matrix</u>: Your Brand vs. Brand X

		Your Brand Superior	Excellent: Could Not Be Better	Acceptable But Could Be Better	Unacceptable	Brand X Inferior
				Both the Same		
Motivating Power of Attribute/Benefit	High	Key Positioning Opportunity	Price of Entry — Maintain	Possible Opportunity	New Product	Serious Weakness — Try to Fix
	Mod	Secondary Opportunity	Secondary Price of Entry	Possible Opportunity	Probable Opportunity	Secondary Weakness
	Low	Potential Opportunity — Increase Importance?	Cut Costs	Cut Costs	No Action	No Action

FIGURE 7.7.

spot performs "significantly better" than the norm, it's given a green light to be used in the simulation exercise and, later, the real world.

Marketers need to know however, that the average ad campaign today yields a return on investment (ROI) no greater than 3 percent. Some analyses for established products and services suggest a return hovering around negative 40 percent. That is, if you invest $1 million, you get back $600,000 in revenue. Super Bowl spots perform even more poorly, with an estimated ROI of negative 80 percent. And this is advertising that actually runs in the real world. It's frightening!

And it gets worse. If real-world advertising is pitiful, consider the quality of the advertising that represents the overwhelming majority of commercials in copy-testing databases throughout the land. Thus, if you say your commercial performed better than the copy-testing norm, all you're really saying is that your commercial is not awful, but probably has something close to a zero return on investment. What companies need is advertising that performs at two or three sigma or more above the norm—advertising that is truly extraordinary.

The more different advertising campaigns that marketers encourage their agencies to develop and test, the more likely they will find a campaign on the right-hand side of the advertising performance bell curve. That is a remarkable effort, which really moves the needle in a significant direction. Consider figures 7.8, 7.9, and 7.10.

Figure 7.8 illustrates a typical performance of a 2,000-GRP (gross rating point) prime-time campaign over a six-month period for a new product or service. Awareness starts at zero and six months later ends up at a shade under 50 percent. This performance is based on an average advertising campaign in the middle of the bell curve in terms of generating awareness.

But what would happen if a marketer chose an advertising campaign that was one standard deviation (sigma) above average (see figure 7.9) or, better yet, two standard deviations above average? In the latter case (illustrated by figure 7.10), 825 GRPs produced the same effect as the average campaign with 2,000 GRPs behind it.

Now, considering the 2,000-GRP campaign today costs approximately $25 million and 825 GRPs costs approximately $10.3 million, this suggests a con-

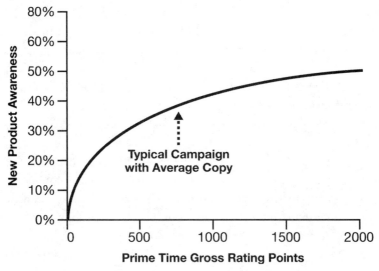

Effects on New Product Awareness
of 2000 GRPs with Average Copy

FIGURE 7.8.

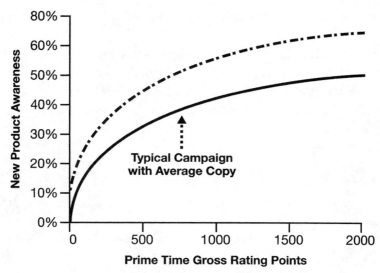

Effects on New Product Awareness
of 2000 GRPs with Two Sigma Copy

Typical Campaign
with Average Copy

FIGURE 7.9.

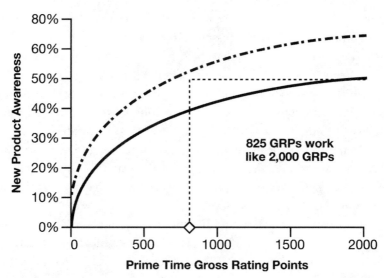

Effects on New Product Awareness
of 2000 GRPs with Three Sigma Copy

825 GRPs work
like 2,000 GRPs

FIGURE 7.10.

siderable savings—$14.7 million, or 59 percent of the original investment—by going with the more powerful advertising.

Some people might argue that the costs of developing and producing a powerful advertising campaign are very high, and, in most cases, are not warranted. This turns out not to be true for most major marketing efforts. In fact, the cost to create and test enough campaigns to find one well on the right-hand side of the bell curve is often modest compared to the potential payoff.

A SIMULATION CAN EVALUATE A LINE OF ITEMS

Often, a marketer will want to use STM research to evaluate a new or restaged line of items that differ in flavor, size, form (liquid versus powder, for example), or some combination of these. Since retail shelf space is limited, few companies are able to distribute all items in a line. Retailers choose the varieties they believe will be the most popular among their customers, but a supplier can influence that choice with convincing research.

Simulated test marketing research systems have two procedures to deal with the problem of how to deal with distribution in forecasting. One procedure assumes that the company will accomplish full distribution and that consumers will find any items in the line they want. In this case, the system bases the volume forecast on the "any item" all commodity volume (ACV) distribution for the line. In other words, the "any item" ACV distribution represents the probability that the consumer can find any item.

When the marketer assumes that the consumer will not be able to find the exact item he or she seeks (because not every retailer will stock every item), an STM can employ a second procedure. This accounts for the divergence of line and item ACV distribution in generating a volume forecast; the customer's probability of finding a particular item is lower than her finding any item in the line. To model the line item's impact on the forecast, a smart STM can account for actual expected distribution and for consumer preference for specific items and generate three separate forecasts with maximum, minimum, and moderate ACV distribution levels.

The first forecast is a maximum distribution forecast using the "any item" of the entire line's ACV distribution. This forecast assumes that the consumer will find the item he or she wants. (This is the same forecast that the first procedure produces.)

The second forecast is a minimum distribution forecast based on the extremely conservative assumption that no consumer will buy an item other than the size, flavor, or form he or she prefers. The model calculates a minimum distribution by weighting the anticipated ACV distribution by the item purchase share on an item-by-item basis.

Finally, a smart system can turn out a moderate distribution forecast based on the average number of acceptable brand choices among loyal buyers. The research determines the average number of acceptable choices through a constant sum question that interviewers ask the loyal buyers: essentially, how many acceptable brand choices does the line contain? The system assumes a linear relationship between effective distribution and the average number of brand choices.

Figure 7.11 indicates that if a marketer is unable to achieve full distribution of a five-item line—not every consumer can find the exact item he or she wants—the failure affects Year 1 sales significantly. The forecast based on "any item," or maximum distribution, is 8 percent higher than the moderate distribution forecast. In this case consumers indicated that the average number of acceptable choices among the five items was 2.8.

The most conservative assumption—that consumers will buy only the one item they prefer—results in a forecast 16 percent lower than the one based on the maximum distribution.

A SIMULATION DIAGNOSES CANNIBALIZATION

After learning a new product's projected volume, marketing managers usually want to know where the sales will come from. Volume source is important because managers want to know who they are competing with. Moreover, they want to know if the volume represents sales the new product will take from the company's existing brands. In short, they want to know how much (if any) a new product will cannibalize the firm's own brands.

An STM research system computes a new or restaged product's volume sources by analyzing and comparing the share of requirements among the product's target market (or franchise) at two stages of the simulated test market research: 1) before prospects see the advertising or the product, and 2) after customers use the product.

The shift in the share of requirements provides insight into the contribution different brands make to the new (or restaged) product's sales. If, for example, the leading brand had a 75 percent share of market before the

STM Forcast for a New Five-Item Line

	Minimum Distribution	Moderate Distribution	Full Distribution
Effective Distribution			
Month 1	67%	73%	80%
Month 2-12	72%	78%	85%
Awareness			
Range – Year 1	21-27%	22-29%	23-31%
Average	25%	27%	29%
Penetration			
% Ever Tried at End of Year 1	15.6%	16.8%	18.1%
Volume			
(MMs of Cases)	3.78	4.07	4.38
(MMs of Units)	45.36	48.90	52.62

FIGURE 7.11.

company introduces a new brand, and if the leader's share falls to 72 percent after the introduction, the 3 percent loss is considered the new brand's effect.

When the new or restaged product is a line extension or competes with the company's other products, the system estimates the impact on existing or parent brands. To increase the measurement validity (because it can be difficult to gauge cannibalization) the model employs a multiphase approach. The STM system can take as many as four separate actions to capture cannibalization's impact:

1. Share disaggregation
2. Disproportionate draw
3. Constant sum
4. Test cell versus control cell comparison

One system, for example, finds the mean of the four approaches to estimate the new product's cannibalizing impact on the parent brands. Researchers have been able to validate the system's ability to estimate cannibalization in 34 cases. Looking at the impact of a new or restaged product on a current brand's sales, the forecast was within 10 percent of the actual impact in 29 of the cases.

To illustrate the four convergent methodologies, take a hypothetical example. Assume the parent brand enjoys a 38 percent current market share, the parent brand has had a past three-month penetration of 44 percent, and an STM model has projected a 2.6 percent share for the new product.

Share Disaggregation

The share disaggregation approach parallels the approach the system employs to forecast the sales of any new or restaged brand or line extension. Instead of coupling the market response data for the entire sample with the marketing plan, however, this approach couples the market response data of the current brand buyers with category data for this group (in terms of size and volume). With this data the model forecasts this group's share of the new brand's sales. The system follows the same procedure for those outside the current franchise (figure 7.12).

Share Disaggregation Approach

| Model Inputs | Current Parent Brand | | |
	Purchases	Non-Purchases	Total
Trial	35%	28%	33%
Repeat	30%	34%	31%
Usage (Units/Yr.)	87.6	72.7	83.3

FIGURE 7.12.

To disaggregate the new entry's forecast share, researchers reweight the forecasts for the current franchise and nonbuyers of the current brands by the actual penetration of brand buyers and nonbuyers in the market. In this case, brand buyers represent 44 percent of the market and nonbuyers 56 percent. This reweighted forecast is then employed to allocate the anticipated share between the parent brand's current buyers and nonbuyers.

In the example, although the model forecasts the new entry achieving a 2.6 percent share of market, 52 percent of the volume will come from current brand users, or a cannibalizing share of 1.35 percent. The remaining 1.25 percent share will come from people who do not now buy the parent brand. Thus, based on the share disaggregation approach, the incremental share achieved by the brand is only 1.25 percent.

Disproportionate Draw

To calculate the (dis)proportionate "draw" from the existing brand's franchise, researchers develop a buyer and repeat buyer profile in terms of past brand and category behavior. They then contrast that against the total sample. Profiling people who first try the product and the people who subsequently repeat their purchases by past three-month purchasing (figure 7.13) reveals that people who buy the product for the first time (members of the new entry franchise) are no more likely to be users of currently available parent brands than nonfranchise members. Therefore, we can expect a proportionate draw from the franchise.

Since we expect a proportionate draw and since the current share of parent brand products is 38 percent, this methodology suggests that 38 percent of the

Disproportionate Draw Approach

	Total Sample	New Entry	
		Purchasers	Franchise
Purchased Any Parent Brand (Past 3 months)	63%	69%	63%

FIGURE 7.13.

new entry's sales, or 1 share point, will be taken from the parent brand(s). The other 62 percent, or 1.6 share points, will be incremental to the parent brand's sales.

Constant Sum

The constant sum approach examines pre-/postshifts in brand purchasing. This is obtained by investigating the ways customers shift their brand purchases by a constant sum approach at three interviewing points: pre–product exposure, post–product exposure, and post-usage (figure 7.14).

The constant sum share of purchases reveals that the share of the brand family including the new entry increase by 3.4 percent due to the new entry's introduction. Increasing the brand family's actual current share, 38 percent, by the increase of 3.4 percent means that the company's overall market share will grow to 39.3 percent. The model attributes an incremental 1.3 share points to the new entry. Since the projected share for the new entry is 2.6 percent, the new entry will take 1.3 share points from the existing brand, and generate an incremental 1.3 share points.

Constant Sum Approach

	Pre-New Entry	Post-New Entry	Share Point Increase	% Increase
Parent Brands (Based on Constant Sum)	40.8%	42.2%	+2.4%	+3.4%

FIGURE 7.14.

Test Cell versus Control Cell Comparison

Researchers often incorporate a control cell into the study design when they are testing a line extension or a restaging, or when the company must know the new entry's impact on existing brands to decide whether to introduce the product or not. They use the control cell to observe the current brand's performance in a simulated store setting. It generates a measure of the incremental trial, repeat purchase, purchase cycle, and ultimately sales over those the current brand enjoys (figure 7.15).

Control Cell Approach

	Across All Parent Brands	
	Control	Test
Lab "Trial" (Penetration) of Any Parent Brand	9%	19%
Lab "Trial" Units per Transaction	13.8	10.8
Repeat	67%	55%
Total Parent Brands' Share of Category Requirements	88%	90%

FIGURE 7.15.

In this case, when we compare the control and test cell's share of requirements the forecast indicates that the parent share will increase by 2.8 percent
from 88 percent to 90.5 percent. Applying this increase to the current parent
38 percent share yields a new share of 39.1 percent—a gain of 1.1 share points
and a loss of 1.5 share points for existing brands.

Convergence of Four Approaches

The results of the four separate methodologies for cannibalization fall
within one half of a share point of each other (figure 7.16).

The incremental share points resulting from the launch range from 1.1 to
1.6 share points. Averaging the four approaches indicates the company will enjoy approximately 1.3 incremental market share points by launching the new
entry. With this information, management can decide whether this increment
is worth the manufacturing and marketing investment. Without it, management makes a decision based on flawed information—the projected gross
share of the new product without considering the impact on existing products.

A SIMULATION CAN PROVIDE PRICING GUIDANCE

In the past, marketers have given minimal attention to the role of pricing in
developing marketing strategy. The marketing drama's starring roles went to

Comparison of the Four Approaches

	New Entry Unit Share	−	Net Parent Unit Share Cannibalization	=	Incremental Parent Unit Share Points
Share Desegregation	2.6	−	1.35	=	1.25
Disproportionate Draw	2.6	−	1.0	=	1.6
Constant Sum	2.6	−	1.3	=	1.3
Control Cell	2.6	−	1.5	=	1.1

FIGURE 7.16.

product development and advertising. Of course, marketers have paid lip service to the four Ps—product, price, place, and promotion. But in practice, most companies have used pricing only tactically, to support promotional strategies or to launch new products.

STM research companies have employed STM technology to provide marketing managers with the answer to the key marketing question: what is the optimal price? The manager can base an optimal pricing strategy on a combination of a trade-off analysis (either conjoint measurement or choice models) and the STM experiment.

Here is how trade-off analysis was used to find the optimal price-feature combination for a new Internet service provider (ISP). A major American telephone company was interested in launching a new service that would extend its business beyond local and long-distance calling. Although company management felt that telephone customers would pay for the service, executives were not sure what features the service should have or how to price it. The firm's challenge was to engineer the optimal combination of features and price. The more features the system included, the more it would cost to set up and maintain. Thus, management wanted to include only those that customers saw as having value and were willing to pay for.

To undertake the trade-off analysis, the research company randomly selected 500 prospective users from a master list of all the telephone company's Web-connected customers. Researchers conducted interviews that averaged approximately 40 minutes. During the interview, respondents viewed 18 different combinations of possible features and prices. These 18 combinations represented a carefully selected mix of six different factors: special subscriber-only content, 24-hour customer service support, online file storage, antispam/antivirus protection, special phone/broadband packages, and the service's monthly charge.

Respondents rated each configuration, then later in the interview rated the individual factors and levels using simple purchase intent rankings. The system then used these data to develop a "micro-model" of the potential market, which enabled the research firm to estimate the number of consumers who, once they became aware of the service, would sign up for each of the more than 500,000 possible feature combinations. The trade-off analysis showed that price was a critical determinant of interest for this new ISP. Averaging across the different combinations of features, figure 7.17 shows the impact of price on the predicted awareness-to-trial (the example assumes 100 percent awareness and an opportunity to buy the service).

Given the importance of price, company management wanted to ensure that the service included only those features that justified their value to potential users. Consequently, management paid particular attention to the utilities attached to various attributes. Figure 7.18 shows the utilities associated with online file storage and with price.

How Price Affects Trial

Monthly Service Charge ($)	Predicted % of Customers Who Would Sign Up (Assuming Awareness and Opportunity)
$15*	49%
20	37%
25*	23%
30	15%
35*	9%
40	4%

* These three levels were included in the tradeoff experiment.
The other levels were estimated using Monadic Ratings.

FIGURE 7.17.

How On-Line File Storage and Price Affect Utilities

On-Line File Storage	Utility	Monthly Service Charge	Purchase Likelihood
None	+11	$15	36%
100 Megabytes	+22	$25	49%
200 Megabytes	-9	$35	14%
500 Megabytes	-24	$50	1%

FIGURE 7.18.

These showed that customers would find an ISP that offered 100 megabytes of storage and cost $25 a month far more attractive than one that offered no online storage at all but cost only $15. Further, the smaller utility increases for the 200 and 500 megabyte storage features indicate that customers would be unwilling to pay an additional $10 for them.

Marketing scientists were able to estimate utilities and purchase probabilities for more feature price levels than the trade-off questionnaire actually included using micro-modeling technology. As a result, brand management was able to observe the forecasted gain (or loss) in sales at any price change that accompanied a change in features. By evaluating the sales gains and losses associated with various combinations of features, the telephone company management was able to select an optimal combination of price and features.

When a company has chosen a product's optimal features and pricing is the final marketing decision, STM researchers can design a study to observe the effect of price on product trial and repeat purchase in the laboratory environment. Such research uses multiple cells to test alternative prices and, coupled with trade-off analysis, to estimate the optimal price.

One case used multiple cells to test two to four different prices, as figure 7.19 shows, for a super premium Bourbon. The model can use multiple cells coupled with trade-off analysis to test three to ten prices. Figure 7.20 depicts the results of such an analysis for a microwave entree.

A SIMULATION MEASURES PRODUCT OR SERVICE PERFORMANCE

The callback questionnaire researchers administer during the in-home use phase of the STM research includes an additional rating of the test product on

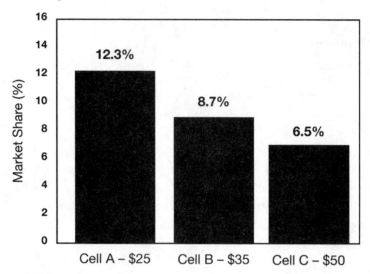

Pricing for a Super Premium Bourbon

Product: Super Premium Bourbon
Budget: $4.8MM

FIGURE 7.19.

the attributes that consumers rated during the pre-usage phase. Comparing the ratings before and after use allows the model to assess the product's or service's fulfillment against the consumer's expectations that the advertising created.

Comparing attribute ratings shows a significant change in the ratings of ten attributes after consumers have used the product (figure 7.21). Naturally Dry performed better than they expected for six attributes: "all-natural ingredients," "quality," "prevents odors," "will not stain," "a brand I trust," and "reasonably priced." The product did not perform as expected for four other attributes: "overall strength," "easy to open," "easy to use," and "long lasting." This information tells the marketing manager that, to compete successfully over the long run, the company must improve the characteristics on which it did not perform as well as expected and to stress those that performed better than expected.

SENSITIVITY ANALYSIS CAN IMPROVE A PLAN

Since marketing managers tend to test few marketing plans, STM researchers have developed sensitivity analysis methods to diagnose a plan's

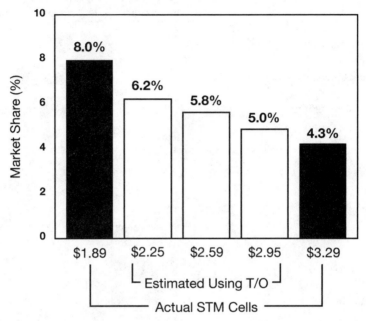

FIGURE 7.20.

various elements. Sensitivity analysis allows marketing management to explore the effect each element in the marketing plan has on sales, on profits, or on both.

The Discovery algorithm approaches the problem by running the model many times for each component in the marketing mix, increasing and decreasing the component's value by 10, 20, 30, 40, and 50 percent (or more) while holding all other plan elements constant. This analysis provides managers with insights into the relative cost-effectiveness of every component in the marketing mix.

Figure 7.22 illustrates the type of information the system provides to show what would happen to sales if the marketer increased and decreased spending on each marketing ingredient.

This example illustrates a $43 million marketing plan. The company has allocated 52 percent of the marketing dollars to coupons and 48 percent to

Pre/Post Usage Rating of *Naturally Dry*
on Ten Selected Characteristics

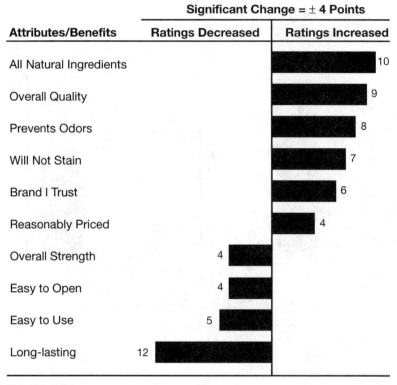

Attributes/Benefits	Significant Change = ± 4 Points	
	Ratings Decreased	**Ratings Increased**
All Natural Ingredients		10
Overall Quality		9
Prevents Odors		8
Will Not Stain		7
Brand I Trust		6
Reasonably Priced		4
Overall Strength	4	
Easy to Open	4	
Easy to Use	5	
Long-lasting	12	

FIGURE 7.21.

advertising. Sensitivity analysis shows that it is inefficient to allocate such a large proportion of the budget to coupons; such spending has reached the point of diminishing returns. If the company reduces the coupon budget by $3,855,000 (a 20 percent reduction), the model forecasts the reduction will cut sales by 290,000 units. If the firm shifts $3,291,000 of that reduction to 30-second daytime television advertising (a 50 percent increase), the model forecasts an increase in sales of 672,000 units—a net increase of 380,000 units while saving $564,000.

Similarly, if the company shifts $222,000 out of prime-time 15-second television spots (a 10 percent reduction), it will reduce sales by 27,000 units. If it adds $225,000 to daytime 15-second spots (a 40 percent increase), however,

Example of a Sensitivity Analysis for Selected Marketing Components

	% Change in Marketing Plan Element									
	-50%	-40%	-30%	-20%	-10%	+10%	+2%	+30%	+40%	+50%
Prime :15 Second ($738.6M)										
Change in Sales (000s of Units)	-115	-97	-71	-44	-27	+27	+44	+71	+88	+115
Cost (000s of $)	-369	-295	-222	-148	-74	+74	+148	+222	+295	+369
Prime :30 Second ($4,351.6M)										
Change in Sales (000s of Units)	-920	--725	-531	-345	-168	+168	+327	+476	+628	+779
Cost (000s of $)	-2,176	-1,741	-1,305	-870	-435	+435	+870	+1,305	+1,741	2,176
Day :15 Second ($187.5M)										
Change in Sales (000s of Units)	-52	-44	-35	-27	-9	97	+27	+35	+44	+53
Cost (000s of $)	-94	-75	-56	-38	-19	+19	+38	+56	+75	+94
Day :30 Second ($2,193.2M)										
Change in Sales (000s of Units)	-779	-610	-451	-301	-150	+142	+284	+416	+549	+672
Cost (000s of $)	-1,079	-877	-658	-439	-219	+219	+439	+658	+877	1,097
Couponing ($6,426M)										
Change in Sales (000s of Units)	-725	-584	-434	-292	-142	+142	+292	+434	+575	+717
Cost (000s of $)	-3,213	-2,570	-1,928	1,285	-643	-+643	+1,285	+1,928	+2,570	+3,213

FIGURE 7.22.

that will increase sales by 44,000 units. That is, the $3,000 cost increase results in a 17,000 unit sales increase.

Discovery uses the sensitivity analysis information to construct a marginal cost relationship for each marketing plan element. The marginal cost represents the incremental dollars a company needs to generate one additional unit of sales while holding all other spending constant. The lower the marginal cost, the more efficient the media, couponing, or sampling.

The marginal cost is the change in cost divided by the change in sales. The marginal cost varies as sales vary. The average marginal cost for all expenditure levels, therefore, shows the relative efficiency of each vehicle in figure 7.23

As the sensitivity analysis showed earlier, coupons are the least efficient vehicles in this $43 million plan because they have the highest marginal cost. In this example, if the marketer adds additional coupons to the plan, an incremental unit will cost $4.45 in coupons; by contrast, an incremental unit will cost only $1.51 in incremental daytime 30-second commercial expenditures.

Sensitivity analysis clearly shows the marketing manager that for this product and spending level, the promotion plan is less efficient than every element of the advertising plan. Since the system can test more than one marketing plan, the sophisticated marketing manager will test additional plans that incorporate the efficiencies the sensitivity analysis reveals, thereby improving the final plan's potency.

We have long felt that more simulated test marketing researchers should employ sensitivity testing technology. At professional meetings where we have presented this approach we've been asked, "How is it possible to do this kind of analysis?" Or, "Sensitivity analysis takes STMs well beyond their capabilities!" We respond that every STM firm in the industry will tell clients that it can accurately, validly forecast new product sales if the advertiser changes media weight, promotional plans, or other components in the marketing mix.

Marginal Cost of Marketing Elements
Based on a $43,000,000 Marketing Plan

Marketing Vehicle		Average Marketing Cost
Coupons		$4.45
Prime time	:15 Commercial	$3.13
Prime time	:30 Commercial	$2.59
Daytime	:15 Commercial	$1.72
Daytime	:30 Commercial	$1.51

FIGURE 7.23.

But how can it do so and not have a model that incorporates the effects of these changes on marketplace response? If the model exists, then it can be programmed to do sensitivity analyses. After all, a sensitivity analysis only represents the coupling of a valid STM model with some automated intelligence programming to produce the type of output shown in figure 7.22. Any marketer or service that can't provide a detailed sensitivity analysis does not have a sophisticated model of the marketing process.

MANAGEMENT IMPLICATIONS

This chapter has described a variety of tools and approaches that simulated test marketing researchers are using to go well beyond the volume forecasting capabilities of current STM models. Today, as we have said repeatedly, most new products and services introduced in the real world are failures and, not surprisingly, most STM research projects should forecast failure. What managers need to know is not simply how the new product can be expected to perform but what needs to be done to make it a success.

A properly designed simulated test marketing experiment can research and analyze targeting, positioning, advertising, line extensions, cannibalization pricing, and product/service quality to build better marketing plans. Indeed, in this age of marketing failure when 90 percent or more new products and services, packaged goods and durables, consumer and industrial are forecast to be failures, technology that builds better plans has become an imperative.

The better simulated test marketing services today can tell you not just how you will do (i.e., how the new or restaged product will perform) but what to do (i.e., what changes need to be made) to insure a successful introduction.

Our dream, as we'll discuss in chapter 12, is to provide management with a marketing instrument panel—a navigation station, if you will—that provides the best possible insights into what will happen to a new product or service, consumer or business-to-business, if the company introduces into the world the plan being simulated. In that world, managers will answer questions about the target, the positioning, the media types used, the media schedule, the advertising effectiveness, couponing, promotion—every element of the marketing mix by month—and the model will provide guidance.

Then it is not a complicated matter to vary the inputs and run the model over and over again until the model's output approaches something that might be called an optimal plan.

NOTE

1. Kevin J. Clancy, and Peter C. Krieg, *Counterintuitive Marketing: Achieve Great Results Using Uncommon Sense* (New York: The Free Press, 2000), 87–107.

8

The First Door to Success: Forecasting Awareness[*]

Marketing managers—and their bosses—want to know whether a marketing program will succeed and to what degree it will improve sales, market share, and profitability. They believe that consumer awareness measures will help tell them. Many marketing managers and almost all new product/service models assume that if consumer awareness increases, sales and market share gains will follow.

Most of the time, this belief is correct. It is true in theory, and true in fact. There needs to be a certain level of awareness or familiarity with your product before you get any trial or interest.

On the other hand, the notion that the company needs *only* awareness is a mistake. During the Internet bubble in 2000–2001, it was widely believed that if you spent $30 million building awareness of your brand on the Internet—such as Boo.com, Living.com, eToys.com, and many more—that was all you needed. We are particularly fond of the 2001 spot for Agillion, which helped popularize the song "We Are the Champions." We've seen that commercial at least 20 times and still have no idea what the company does—it communicates awareness of the name and nothing else. The thinking behind this school of advertising is that you don't need a raison d'etre, you don't need a positioning, you don't need an extraordinary product, you don't need to do anything

---

[*] This chapter is based on work by Joseph D. Blackburn, Vanderbilt University; Kevin J. Clancy; and R. Dale Wilson, Michigan State University.

other than tell people "Here I am." And it does not work. Awareness is not enough, but awareness is the first step in everybody's process.

Marketing executives like awareness measures because these seem to provide a convenient and inexpensive way to track market performance in situations where it is more difficult (or more costly) to obtain other measures, such as changes in consumer buying intentions or in actual behavior.

But there are many different kinds of awareness measures and they are not all equally valuable. Indeed, as we will see, some are not valuable at all.

THE FAILURE OF AWARENESS MEASUREMENT STUDIES

Most awareness measurement studies are not guided by a comprehensive conceptual model of how advertising works in a particular product category. Not only are there the obvious differences between products and services and between new and established products, there are differences between related products and services. For example, advertising works one way for home insurance, another way for car insurance. This calls for different types of awareness measurement.

Few awareness measurement studies compare results to specific, measurable, and realistic objectives. Most measure an incomplete set of variables or, worse, the wrong variables. Most do not capture all forms of communication, including not only advertising, but public relations, event marketing, direct mail, and special promotions.

Usually awareness studies do not use measures that are sensitive to small changes—indeed, nothing significant changes over time—and top management questions the value of both the study and research generally. At one time we were consulting to American Express to help improve their tracking system. American Express and its competitors, Visa, Master Card, and Discover, were doing the same things year after year with the same budgets and nothing was changing. But management was unhappy. They wanted to see changes in awareness and perceptions to reduce their discomfort with "flat numbers" quarter after quarter. We did make recommendations, but it was easier to kill the study than to make dramatic changes in their marketing efforts, changes that might yield shifts in tracking study numbers.

Interestingly, brand equity studies, the kind we talked about in chapter 1, find the credit card category turning into one big commodity. Credit cards lead our list of products that are no longer differentiated. This was true in the

Copernicus/Synovate study cited earlier, and it's true in proprietary brand equity work we completed recently where the different brands looked like peas in a pod.

Marketing executives often design marketing campaigns—especially advertising campaigns—to increase brand awareness among the target consumers. Marketers like awareness measures as a way to suggest communication effectiveness because consumers must be aware of a product before they will buy it.

Because established products tend to resist immediate changes in other attitudinal and behavioral criteria, awareness as a measure of communication effectiveness offers convenience and cost savings. With established products, corporate management may be hesitant to measure the small changes a campaign produces—such as a 0.3 percentage point increase in market share or a 4 percent change in the proportion of consumers who include the test brand in their evoked set—because the research requires a large and expensive sample. Instead, the company can use awareness measures as an inexpensive "leading indicator" of campaign success.

While awareness information is important for established products, it may be even more important for new products because managers use awareness measures in forecasting, tracking, and diagnosing results before, during, and after test marketing. In most simulated test market methodologies, estimated awareness shows a linear effect on the eventual market share forecast; as awareness rises, so does share. New product marketing managers, moreover, invariably include awareness measures in research studies designed to track campaign performance. These are awareness, trial, and usage studies—or simply ATU studies.

Finally, new product managers routinely diagnose marketing campaign results. They look for ways to improve their campaigns and investigate the factors they believe are critical to brand success. Brand awareness is one critical factor. (Others include distribution, pricing, and competitive activity.) Most managers seek opportunities to improve campaign performance by producing and maintaining higher awareness levels than industry averages.

Because awareness is so important in evaluating marketing and communication program effectiveness, it is crucial to understand what determines awareness, the most useful measures of awareness, and how simulated test market research can predict the level of awareness a new (or established) product will achieve.

Drs. Joseph Blackburn, R. Dale Wilson, and the present authors have done empirical research to investigate these issues and this chapter incorporates their findings.

HOW TO MEASURE AWARENESS

Contemporary research commonly uses a variety of specific measures of brand and campaign awareness. Our experience suggests that two consumer awareness measures are most appropriate; the choice of measure depends upon the marketing situation. For *new* products and services, we have found total brand awareness to be the most appropriate measure.

For new campaigns for *established* products and services, we have found campaign penetration to be the most appropriate measure. We'll discuss how to measure campaign penetration in a moment.

Figure 8.1 shows a number of different awareness measures in widespread use and illustrates the way the questions would be asked in an advertising research study of luxury cars.

Not all awareness measures, however, are equally valuable. As figure 8.2 shows, "first brand awareness" is generally useless—it's relatively insensitive to changes in the marketing mix—while campaign penetration, a relatively new measure, is much more sensitive.

Our experience with *new* product introductions suggests that total brand awareness—the combination of unaided and aided brand awareness—strongly correlates to consumer trial purchase. It is quite sensitive to changes in various marketing mix elements and, happily, can be forecast accurately with a sophisticated model of the awareness-generating process.

For new campaigns for *established* products and services, however, total brand awareness is inappropriate because the figure tends to be stable over time and is not very sensitive to marketing mix changes. Trying to change brand awareness for an established product is like trying to move a ping pong ball in a jar of peanut butter. Since marketing program changes seldom alter this relatively immutable measure significantly, total brand awareness for established products is a relatively poor performer in predicting changes in future consumer behavior.

Awareness Measures in Widespread Use

First Brand	"When you think of luxury automobiles, what is the first brand that comes to mind?"
Unaided Advertising	"Which brands of luxury automobiles have you seen or heard advertised during the past 90 days?"
Aided Advertising	"Have you seen or heard of any advertising for Lexus during the past 50 days?"
Theme and Related Ad Recall	"What do you remember seeing and hearing in Lexus advertising?"
Partially Aided Tracer Penetration	"Which brand of luxury automobile... ...advertises 'The Passionate Pursuit of Perfection'?" (slogan example) ...advertises 'Enter a new world of luxury'?" (message example) ...uses Chuck Goldsborough to advertise their product?" (spokesperson or dominant visual example)
Fully Aided Tracer Penetration	"Have you seen or heard any advertising for Lexus during the past 90 days that uses the slogan 'The Passionate Pursuit of Perfection'?"
Unaided Brand	"What are all the different brands of luxury automobiles you can think of."
Aided Brand	"I'm going to read you a list of luxury automobile brands. For each one I name, please tell me if you ever heard of it."
Total Brand	The combination of aided and unaided brand awareness.
Campaign Penetration	A weighted combination of all the above measures.

FIGURE 8.1.

Tracer penetration refers to consumer playback of some aspect of the advertising unique to the particular campaign. The tracer—or signaling—element is something unique to a particular advertising campaign. This may be a message, a slogan, a dominant visual, a spokesperson, or a musical score. There are two separate measures of tracer penetration: partially aided tracer penetration and fully aided tracer penetration. We measure both because the combination is more sensitive than either alone.

Tracer element penetration is a useful measure of awareness for established products because it is more sensitive to marketing mix changes, and, for strong, successful advertising campaigns it correlates positively with purchase behavior.

But how do all the various awareness measures relate to changes in the marketing mix? Figure 8.2 shows the differences.

For products that have been around for years and are massively promoted—like Pepsi, Crest, American Express, or FedEx—the total brand awareness number (aided and unaided) is bumping against a real-world ceiling of about 96 percent, which represents the percentage of the population who know the name of our president on an aided basis, that is, "Have you ever heard of George W. Bush?" Thus, this is a dysfunctional measure to track the performance of a campaign for this kind of product.

Other measures as shown in figure 8.2 have their pros and cons. For a new product, total brand awareness works well. For a re-staged established product, campaign penetration is particularly useful. This is a new measure, and it requires several steps to develop:

1. Select all realistic, specific, and measurable advertising recall criteria. These include elements such as a slogan, message, spokesperson, unique visual, or musical theme.
2. Rank them from low to high in terms of "value" as "true" measures of advertising penetration.
3. Assign weights to each one from 0 to 90 percent probability of a particular measure indicating "true" advertising penetration, the theory being that no single measure gives you more than 90 percent certainty.
4. Create all possible combinations of measures, add up the individual weights, and calibrate them so that the highest score is 100 percent.

Common Awareness Measures and Their Sensitivity

First Brand	Very close to market share	Behaves much like market share; resists change; tend to be insensitive to changes in the marketing mix.
Unaided Advertising	Approximately two times the brand's share of voice	Behaves like attitudinal measures; closely correlated with the evoked set measures for product category; relatively insensitive to changes in the marketing mix.
Unaided Brand	Approximately two to three times the brand's market share	
Partially Aided Tracer Penetration	The same to as much as twice the brand's share of voice	Highly sensitive to changes in advertising but without observing the "advertising impact" of the new campaign, can be difficult to predict. After observing new campaign's impact over the course of 4 weeks, it is possible to predict tracer penetration measures later in the year.
Fully Aided Tracer Penetration	Approximately two to four times the brand's share of voice	
Aided Advertising	Approximately two to four times share of voice	Improves only with major changes in various aspects of the advertising program.
Total Brand (Aided and Unaided)	Extremely high, often in the 80 to 90 percent range	Improves only with massive changes in the marketing mix.
Campaign Penetration	Approximately two times share the brand's share of voice	The single best measure of the true awareness; sensitive to changes in advertising strategy and media weight; indicates current rather than past campaign performance.

FIGURE 8.2.

The resulting measure of campaign penetration is extremely powerful. It ranges from 0 to 100 percent, is sensitive to changes in media weight and ad copy, and relatively unlikely to reflect the effects of past advertising efforts.

Here is an example of how awareness criteria can be weighted to reflect the probability of proven campaign penetration:

A. Proven advertising recall   90

B. Partially aided awareness of campaign slogan/theme
    and three or more specific messages   70

C. Partially aided awareness of slogan/theme and one or
    more specific messages   60

D. Partially aided awareness of slogan/theme only   50

E. Message only   40

F. Related recall (nonproven)   30

G. Aided recall of slogan/theme and one or more messages   25

H. Aided recall of slogan/theme only, no messages   20

I. Aided recall of messages only   15

J. Unaided ad awareness   5

K. Unaided brand awareness   2

L. No recall   0

Taking these weighted measures it is possible to calculate campaign penetration. For example, adding together A, proven advertising recall; B, partially aided awareness of campaign slogan/theme and three or more specific messages; J, unaided ad awareness; and K, unaided awareness, equals 167 (90 + 70 + 5 + 2). This is calibrated to 100 percent, and the 167 becomes the divisor for other calibrations.

To suggest how this applies, assume that a respondent is aware of the slogan or theme (D), plays back something about the campaign that would be considered related recall (nonproven; F), and gets the theme and ad messages on an aided basis (G). Add these together (50 + 30 + 25) and divide the 105 total by 167. These three elements result in a campaign penetration measure of 63 percent.

One more example. What is the penetration of aided recall of messages only (I); unaided ad awareness (J); and unaided brand awareness (K)? Add the three weights (15 + 5 + 2), divide the total, 22, by 167 for a campaign penetration measure of 13 percent.

HOW WELL DOES AWARENESS FORECASTING WORK?

To examine and improve simulated test marketing research's ability to forecast new product introduction awareness, Drs. Joseph Blackburn, Kevin Clancy, and R. Dale Wilson analyzed awareness forecasts for 21 products and four services.[1] They compared awareness forecasts made at the simulated test market (STM) stage with the awareness levels the products and services achieved in the marketplace following their introduction (figure 8.3).

To generate the "original forecast" figures, they used data from the marketing plan as well as marketing and consumer research studies as inputs in the STM awareness model. This resulted in 25 different awareness forecasts over a 12-month period.

Figure 8.3 contrasts the forecasted awareness with the actual awareness the marketing achieved at the end of the 12-month period for each product or service introduction. Actual awareness was measured using standard unaided and aided awareness questions combined into a measure of total awareness among large representative samples of the target market.

One would expect errors in these forecasts. Differences between forecasts and reality result from—among other reasons—the differences between the marketing plan used in the STM forecast and the plan the company actually implemented. Competitive effects is another major reason why forecasts and reality differ. Marketers today are increasingly savvy and sometimes attempt to poison a competitor's test market results. In addition, a three-to-six point variation at the 0.10 level of statistical significance occurs in the actual awareness measurement due to sampling error alone.

Following the launch of a new product or new campaign, tracking study data may be used to help calibrate the model and improve forecasts of awareness, trial, and purchase. Sometimes the research company doing the STM

Awareness Forecasts for New Product/Service Campaigns

	Actual Year-end Awareness	Original Forecast			Forecast After Calibration		
		Forecasted Awareness	Difference	Percent Error[a]	Forecasted Awareness	Difference	Percent Error[a]
Products:							
1	35	39	-4	11.4%	37	-2	5.7%
2	57	66	-9	15.8	65	-8	14.0
3	70	72	-2	2.9	70	0	0.0
4	76	83	-7	9.2	79	-3	3.9
5	79	72	7	8.9	76	3	3.8
6	32	34	-2	6.3	34	-2	6.3
7	45	48	-3	6.7	48	-3	6.7
8	70	62	8	11.4	70	0	0.0
9	32	30	2	6.3	36	-4	12.5
10	18	12	6	33.3	15	3	16.7
11	30	24	6	20.0	26	4	13.3
12	43	45	-2	4.7	43	0	0.0
13	54	51	3	5.6	52	2	3.7
14	57	52	5	8.8	54	3	5.3
15	65	57	8	12.3	57	8	12.3
16	57	63	-6	10.5	58	-1	1.8
17	49	49	0	0.0	49	0	0.0
18	53	48	5	9.4	51	2	3.8
19	54	47	7	13.0	48	6	11.1
20	56	58	-2	3.6	57	-1	1.8
21	37	51	-14	37.8	35	2	5.4
Services:							
1	28	22	6	21.4	25	3	10.7
2	12	16	-4	33.3	17	-5	41.7
3	45	41	4	8.9	42	3	6.7
4	30	37	-7	23.3	32	-2	6.7
Overall Mean[b]	47.36 (17.66)[c]	47.16 (17.88)	5.16 (3.00)	12.19 (10.05)	47.04 (17.46)	2.80 (2.18)	7.76 (8.56)
Products Mean[b]	50.90 (16.26)	50.62 (16.85)	5.14 (3.23)	11.33 (9.25)	50.48 (16.47)	2.71 (2.33)	6.10 (5.19)
Services Mean[b]	28.75 (13.50)	29.00 (11.92)	5.25 (1.50)	21.73 (10.02)	29.00 (10.61)	3.25 (1.26)	16.45 (16.94)

[a] Percent errors are calculated as: |(actual awareness – forecasted awareness)|/actual awareness.
[b] Absolute values are used in calculating the means.
[c] Standard deviations are given in parentheses for each mean.

FIGURE 8.3.

does these tracking studies; often, however, the marketer hires an independent research company to collect the awareness data.

Figure 8.3 shows the level of accuracy achieved in the total brand awareness forecasts for each case and for the totals. For products and services combined, the mean error is only 5.16 points with a standard deviation of 3.00 points. Calibration reduces the error to 2.80 points with a standard deviation of 2.18 points. The overall percentage error for all 25 cases is 12.19 percent (with a standard deviation of 10.05) before launch; this drops to 7.76 percent (with a standard deviation of 8.56) using awareness, trial, and usage data to calibrate the model.

The numbers in figure 8.3 indicate that, although the original forecast experiences a 12.2 percent error with a 5.2 point mean difference, calibrating the model with awareness, trial, and usage data results in a more accurate forecast of total brand awareness. For all 25 introductions, after calibrating the model with ATU data, the forecasting error, as measured by the mean absolute difference, tumbles 46 percent—from 12.2 percent to 7.8 percent. In 6 of the 25 cases (products number 6, 7, 9, 15, 17, and service number 2), the original forecast was as good as or better than the postcalibration forecasts.

ADDITIONAL VARIABLES INFLUENCE AWARENESS FORECASTS

As we discussed in chapter 5, adding variables concerning the marketing plan improves the awareness forecast's accuracy. We examined the 21 new products mentioned earlier (figure 8.3) to assess the impact of adding variables on awareness modeling.

We used six different versions of the model to investigate the impact of adding marketing plan variables. The simplest model, represented by X_1, uses only gross rating points, an expression for initial awareness, a ceiling effect, and a forgetting effect to generate an awareness forecast. We built five additional versions of the model by adding variables—media schedule, media impact and share of voice, advertising impact, promotion (coupons and samples), and distribution and product category effects—to the simple model. The results are shown in figure 8.4.

Variable set X_6 represents a very sophisticated model used to forecast awareness. Experience indicates that reordering the sequence in which the variables were added would not significantly alter the incremental effect of each on the forecast's accuracy because the predictor variables show low levels of redundancy.

The Effect of Adding Variables on Awareness Forecasts
for New Product Campaigns

	(x_1) GRPs Only	(x_2) x_1 plus Media Schedule	(x_3) x_2 plus Media Impact and SOV	(x_4) x_3 plus Advertising Impact	(x_5) x_4 plus Promotion	(x_6) x_5 plus Distribution and Product Category Effects
Variables Used in LITMUS Forecasts[a]						
Mean Difference[b]	13.52 (12.40)[d]	9.90 (13.27)	5.62 (3.37)	4.00 (2.57)	3.24 (2.21)	2.76 (1.70)
Mean % Error[b]	28.98 (31.51)	20.00 (32.85)	12.71 (10.84)	8.99 (7.47)	7.35 (6.93)	6.20 (5.41)
Percent Reduction in Mean Error[c]	—	30.99	56.14	68.98	74.64	78.61
Correlation with Actual Year-end Awareness	.81[e]	.80[e]	.92[e]	.96[e]	.98[e]	.98[e]

a In addition to the variables indentified in the column headings, the Litmus model also includes
   terms representing initial awareness, a ceiling effect, a forgetting effect, and a ghost
   awareness factor.

b Absolute values are used in calculating these means.

c Calculated as: (mean percent error for Model x_1 - mean percent error for any Model x_2
   through x_6)/mean percent error for Model x_1.

d Standard deviations are given in parentheses for each mean.

e $p < .001$

FIGURE 8.4.

Figure 8.4 demonstrates that adding variables to the STM research improves accuracy substantially. The mean differences, calculated by using the absolute difference between the actual year-end awareness and the awareness forecast for each variable set, X_1 through X_6, decreases monotonically as the awareness model includes more variables.

In addition, the mean percentage error decreases from 29.0 percent for variable set X_1 to 6.2 percent for variable set X_6. (We calculate these for each product by dividing the absolute difference by the actual year-end awareness measure.) Each correlation is significant at the 0.001 level. The Pearson correlation coefficients for awareness based on X_1 increases from 0.81 for X_1 alone to 0.98 for the full battery of factors expressed as X_6; they have, therefore, a strong correlation.

To determine the degree of variability among the six means in figure 8.4, we ran a one-way analysis of variance (ANOVA) on the data. The result, which tests the null hypothesis that these six means are equal, yields an F-value of 2.27, where $p = 0.0519$. This suggests that at the 90 percent level of confidence, the hypothesis of equality across all six means is rejected.

We ran t-tests for each pair of means to examine the differences across all six mean awareness forecasts. J. Scott Armstrong discusses this procedure in *Long-Range Forecasting: From Crystal Ball to Computer*.[2] He suggests comparing model forecasts using t-tests that incorporate Tukey's HSD (Honestly Significantly Different) procedure to control for statistical effects of multiple comparisons.

The multiple comparison test results, summarized in figure 8.5, suggest the relative contribution of adding variables to the model when we use it to forecast new product awareness. Figure 8.5 indicates that the mean level of actual awareness, Y, is significantly different at the 0.05 level for a two-tailed test from the mean awareness forecast for the simple model X_1 and variable X_2. However, it is not significantly different from X_3.

The mean projected awareness levels for the most simple forms of the awareness equation, using variables X_1 and X_2, are significantly different for each paired comparison. Therefore, the awareness generated using only gross rating points plus the media schedule yield mean forecast awareness levels significantly different from the mean actual awareness levels and the awareness levels generated with additional marketing variables.

Differences Between Means for Awareness Forecasts[a]

	x_1	x_2	x_3	x_4	x_5	x_6
y	13.53[b]	9.34	0.76	0.47	0.38	0.10
x_1		4.19[b]	14.29[b]	14.00[b]	13.91[b]	13.43[b]
x_2			10.10[b]	9.81[b]	9.72[b]	9.24[b]
x_3				0.29	0.38	0.86
x_4					0.09	0.57
x_5						0.48

a Differences between means are presented as absolute values.
b $p < .05$ Using Tukey's HSD method of multiple comparisons (cf. Armstrong 1985, pp. 462-7).

FIGURE 8.5.

The mean for X_3 is significantly different from X_1 and X_2. However, the mean for X_3 is not significantly different from Y, actual awareness, or any other of the awareness forecast means. Thus, the addition of media impact and share of voice to the gross rating points (GRPs) and the schedule significantly improves the awareness forecast.

These comparisons suggest that, on average, a sophisticated model which includes a combination of GRPs, media schedule, media impact, and share of voice provides an extremely powerful awareness forecasting tool. The incremental value of adding the variables in X_4, X_5, and X_6—advertising impact, promotion, and distribution and product category effects—is smaller than the incremental value of adding media impact and share of voice.

More recent work reveals that variables not included in our original model, but captured in Discovery, can in some cases add to forecasting accuracy. Six of these variables are direct marketing, outdoor (including new electronic billboards), public relations, a website, Internet advertising, and word-of-mouth. This is particularly true when these marketing investments represent a significant share of the overall marketing budget.

Take for example a new product supported by a large direct-mail campaign that is integrated with other marketing activities. One question increasingly asked today is how does such a direct-mail program work when it's enhanced by television advertising? Should it always be supported by TV? Or, in stark contrast, is TV an unnecessary expense? In one recent study for an energy company, the State of California was divided into 20-plus geographic areas. An experimental design was employed to vary these areas in terms of different levels of direct marketing and television. Results showed a clear interaction effect: market response was far greater and return-on-investment higher when DM and TV worked together. This finding could have been simulated using STM models without investing $35 million in a single state.

The same is true for public relations and websites. A well-designed public relations campaign can have a surprising effect—sometimes greater than that of advertising—while websites are becoming increasingly important as sources of information for new products and services, particularly in higher-involvement categories where the buyer is looking for information about new things in the marketplace. Both public relations effects and website investments can be simulated in a manner similar to other marketing components.

We are especially intrigued by applications of simulation to issues involving outdoor advertising including sports sponsorships and celebrity endorsements. We have in our database four new cigarette brands supported by a first-year advertising budget of approximately $50 million each, which are unique because they employ no television advertising.

The lack of television, combined with a budget level that most other product categories would consider quite high, forced us to experiment with methods for forecasting new brand awareness as a result of outdoor and print alone. The results have been relatively satisfying, convincing us that outdoor, too, can and should be simulated prior to a major real-world investment.

THE IMPLICATIONS FOR MANAGEMENT

The research this chapter reports has suggested that total brand awareness is a reasonable awareness measure for most new products and services. Campaign penetration (based on a composite of many different indicators of campaign elements) is a more appropriate awareness measure for established products and services. Fall-back measures would be unaided and aided tracer penetration and total advertising awareness.

Moreover, the research reveals that a sophisticated awareness forecasting submodel can be used successfully to forecast awareness of a new product or a new campaign and that these forecasts can be generally improved by calibrating the model based on early returns from an in-market tracking survey.

Finally, this and other research we have done shows that the addition of media impact, share of voice, advertising impact, packaging, point-of-sale materials, distribution, direct marketing, buyer involvement in the category, public relations, outdoor, a website, Internet banner ads, and word-of-mouth significantly improve the awareness forecast relative to a forecast that includes only television, print, and radio gross rating points and media schedule.

Stated differently, a more complete model works better than a parsimonious model. Awareness forecasting methods based on GRPs and even a complete media schedule will not perform as well as those that include a larger number of advertising/marketing elements. Since most STM models employ relatively unsophisticated awareness forecasting submodels, this finding is disturbing. If it takes a sophisticated model to produce an accurate forecast of awareness, and if awareness is linearly related to sales, then unsophisticated models have built-in handicaps that attenuate the validity of their forecasts.

NOTE

1. This chapter is based on the work of Joseph D. Blackburn, Kevin J. Clancy, and R. Dale Wilson as reported in chapter 8 of *Simulated Test Marketing* by Kevin J. Clancy, Robert Shulman, and Marianne Wolf (New York: Lexington Books, 1994).

2. Scott J. Armstrong. *Long-Range Forecasting: From Crystal Ball to Computer*, 2nd ed. (New York: John Wiley & Sons, 1985) 135ff.

9

How to Find the Best Media Weight and Schedule

Marketers inevitably want to know, How much should we spend on advertising and when should we spend it?

Since research has proven the validity of simulated test marketing models to forecast everything from brand awareness to sales and return-on-investment, companies can apply this technology to help answer these questions. This chapter, based on the work of Clancy, Blackburn, and Wilson, will show how a smart simulated test marketing model can be employed to answer media expenditure and timing questions.[1]

We use a simulated test marketing model to explore the relationship between media weight and timing and consumer awareness and market share for new and established products. We examined this relationship using prototypical new-product-marketing-plan parameters and prototypical new campaigns for established products. The chapter explains the methodology employed to evaluate media weight and timing and the research's results.

HOW WE SET MARKETING PLAN PARAMETERS

To examine the effects of differences in media expenditures and media timing patterns, we examined three different levels of media weight, three types of media timing patterns, four different purchase-cycle lengths for both new and established products (that's 72 different combinations). While systematically varying these four different factors, we assigned "average" values based on historic experience to all other marketing plan and market response parameters necessary to run the model.

The marketing plan parameters included all aspects of the media mix, the advertising's attention-getting power, media impact, share of voice, and all commodity volume distribution.

The market response parameters included an initial level of consumer awareness and forgetting, a ceiling on awareness, the average package size the consumer buys the first time and on repeat occasions, the annual consumption rate, the awareness-to-trial rate, and the multiple repeat buying rates.

To develop variants for each of the base cases, the same historical experience was drawn upon to detail the "typical" new and established product. We accomplished this by systematically altering six of the key market response parameters the model manipulates as inputs:

1. The advertising's attention-getting power
2. The media impact
3. The ACV (all commodity volume) distribution percentage
4. Awareness-to-trial conversion estimates
5. The probability of first repeat purchase
6. The probability of multiple repeat purchases

We then picked values for each of these six parameters to reflect the approximate quintile score for each parameter observed while applying our evolving simulated test market model during the course of the last decade. Of the total set of 15,625 possible combinations, eight were randomly selected, which, with the two base cases, yielded nine new product plans and nine established product plans.

Media Weight and Media Timing

For each of these 18 different marketing plans, we then systematically varied the media timing patterns and media weights. We selected three different media timing patterns and three different media weight levels. The three different media timing treatments were 1) a front-loaded schedule; 2) a flighted schedule; and 3) a sustained schedule.

The front-loaded schedule allocated the entire media budget to the first three months of the product's introductory year. This schedule assigned 30 percent of the budget to the first month, 40 percent to the second, and the 30 percent to the third.

The flighted schedule allocated the budget equally to every other month—16.67 percent to the first month, 16.67 percent to the third month, 16.67 percent to the fifth month, and so forth.

The sustained schedule divided the media budget equally between every month.

The three spending levels for media weight were 1) a light media plan consisting of 600 gross rating points (GRPs); 2) an average budget of 1,200 GRPs; and 3) a very heavy budget of 2,400 GRPs. These three different GRP levels correspond to advertising spending for 30-second commercials on prime time television of approximately $9 million, $17 million, and $32 million, respectively. Since we did not examine media mix, we chose prime time so that the plans would be comparable.

Purchase Cycle

Media planners have long recognized that the purchase cycle—the average time between buys—for various products influences the effectiveness of various media schedule and weight combinations. If a consumer buys the product every other week and the advertising runs weekly, she has the opportunity to see the advertising two times before buying the product. If she buys the product once a month, however, and the advertising runs once every six months, she may not see any advertising at all during a period in which she buys the product five times.

For this reason, we incorporated four different purchase cycles into each of the nine media schedules and weight combinations to determine whether the purchase cycle affects the media weight and schedule combination effectiveness. These purchase cycle lengths were twice a month, once a month, once a quarter, and once every six months.

Marketing Parameter Combinations

The database development process yielded a total of 648 different variable combinations. These product scenarios resulted from the combination of nine marketing plan variations for each of three media weight variations (heavy, average, and light), three media schedule variations (front-loaded, flighted, and sustained), four purchase cycle variations (twice a month, monthly, quarterly, and twice a year), and two product types (new and established). Thus we employed a $3 \times 3 \times 4 \times 2$ experimental design, each cell containing nine observations. We then used each of the resulting 648 combinations as simulated test market model inputs.

Measures of Consumer Awareness and Market Share

We used two different measures of consumer awareness and two different measures of share as the model's output as the dependent variables in the simulation study to see how the model's predictions would vary as a result of media weight and media timing variations. For the purposes of making predictions from the model, we employed a one-year period. The study examined four dependent variables: 1) average awareness, 2) end-of-year awareness, 3) average market share, and 4) end-of-year market share.

Since media timing was one of the independent variables the study investigated, consumer awareness and market share for two different time periods—the average for the year and the forecast for Month 12—were used.

Because the appropriate definition of product awareness depends upon whether the product is new or established, the study retained this distinction to maintain a high degree of realism in the research. As we discussed in chapter 8, experience shows that total brand awareness serves as the most appropriate consumer awareness measure for a *new* product or service; tracer element penetration is the most appropriate awareness measure for an *established* product or service.[2]

HOW WE ASSESSED MEDIA WEIGHT AND TIMING

We employed an analysis of variance (ANOVA) to determine the influence of media weight, media timing, purchase cycle, and product type on the model's predictions of awareness and market. To identify important trends in the data, we used the 0.05 level of statistical significance, and as a measure of each experimental factor's importance, we also used the percentage of the total sum of squares contributed by each main and interaction effect. In those instances in which the ANOVA identified statistically significant main or interaction effects, we also analyzed the cell mean figures.

Consumer Awareness and Market Share

The results of the ANOVA runs indicated that several different main and interaction effects were statistically significant. Figure 9.1 shows that the study

Summary of Analysis of Variance Results

Source	df	Average Awareness		End-of-Year Awareness		Average Market Share		End-of-Year Market Share	
		F-Value	Percent of Total Sum of Squares	F-Value	Percent of Total Sum of Squares	F-Value	Percent of Total Sum of Squares	F-Value	Percent of Total Sum of Squares
Media Weight (W)	2	163.83[c]	29.37	129.22[c]	21.30	28.69[c]	5.51	31.69[c]	6.45
Media Timing Pattern (T)	2	12.92[c]	2.32	29.58[c]	4.88	9.07[c]	1.74	0.59	0.12
Purchase Cycle (C)	3	1.15	0.31	4.93[b]	1.22	0.19	0.05	0.88	0.27
Product Type (P)	1	94.36[c]	8.46	217.56[c]	17.93	331.49[c]	31.83	312.70[c]	31.80
W x T	4	0.58	0.21	3.13[a]	1.03	0.25	0.09	0.26	0.11
W x C	6	0.43	0.23	0.23	0.11	1.00	0.57	0.23	0.14
W x P	2	22.78[c]	4.09	27.88[c]	4.60	0.81	0.16	2.21	0.45
T x C	6	0.58	0.31	0.37	0.18	1.97	1.13	2.22[a]	1.35
T x P	2	7.08[b]	1.27	2.80	0.46	2.26	0.43	0.24	0.05
C x P	3	1.56	0.42	1.36	0.34	1.74	0.50	1.33	0.40
W x T x C	12	0.38	0.41	0.11	0.11	0.63	0.72	0.13	0.16
W x T x P	4	0.56	0.20	0.35	0.11	0.47	0.18	0.60	0.02
W x C x P	6	0.43	0.23	0.24	0.12	0.88	0.51	0.83	0.05
T x C x P	6	0.36	0.19	0.08	0.04	0.64	0.37	0.40	0.02
W x T x C x P	12	0.33	0.35	0.09	0.09	0.75	0.87	0.03	0.04
Error	576		51.64		47.47		55.32		58.57

[a] $p < .05$
[b] $p < .005$
[c] $p < .001$

FIGURE 9.1.

found significant main effects for media weight and type of product on all four dependent variables. Therefore, media weight and type of product each affected average and end-of-year consumer awareness, and average and end-of-year share of market. The media timing pattern influenced average awareness, end-of-year awareness, and average market share. The length of the purchase cycle affected the end-of-year awareness figure.

The research also found statistically significant interaction effects. There were interactions between media weight and type of product on both awareness measures, between the media timing pattern and type of product on average awareness, and between media timing and purchase cycle on end-of-year market share.

Examining the percentage of total sum of squares explained by the independent variables indicates that media weight and media timing exert, as one might intuitively expect, more influence on awareness than on market share. The main effect of media weight explains 29.4 percent of the total sum of squares for average awareness and 21.3 percent of the total sum of squares for end-of-year awareness. Media weight, however, explains only 5.5 percent of the total sum of squares for market share and 6.5 percent of the total sum of squares for end-of-year market share.

Similarly, the main effect of media timing explains 2.3 percent of the total sum of squares for average awareness and 4.9 percent of the total sum of squares for end-of-year awareness. Yet the media timing pattern explains only 1.7 percent of the total sum of squares for market share and 0.1 percent of the total sum of squares for end-of-year market share.

Comparing the relative importance of media weight and media timing in determining consumer awareness and market share indicates that media weight was considerably more important than media timing. Across all four measures, media weight explained 62.6 percent of the total sum of squares for awareness and market share, while media timing explained only 9.1 percent of the total sum of squares.

The main effect of media timing had no effect on end-of-year market share since it was not significant at the .05 level. Thus, media weight was nearly seven times more important in explaining the total sum of squares for the four dependent measures of market response than was media timing.

Or, to put it another way, the *amount* of media dollars is more important than *when* the company spends them. This is not all that surprising in light of the whopping differences in media weight tested in the study. The high level of spending was four times greater than the light level.

HOW MEDIA WEIGHT AFFECTS AWARENESS AND MARKET SHARE

An analysis of cell mean figures provides a more complete interpretation of the influence of the various determinants of market response. Figure 9.2 presents the means for each of the four dependent variables for each media weight level. These data indicate a monotonically increasing trend for each measure of market response as the level of media weight increases from a light budget

Effects of Media Weight on Measures of Market Response

Dependent Variable	Level of Media Weight		
	Light	Average	Heavy
Awareness:			
Average	15.4%	23.2%	36.2%
End-of-Year	16.7%	26.0%	37.4%
Market Share:			
Average	6.2%	7.3%	9.3%
End-of-Year	5.7%	7.1%	8.8%

FIGURE 9.2.

(600 GRPs), to an average budget (1,200 GRPs), and finally to a heavy budget (2,400 GRPs).

For example, as we increase media weight, the mean forecast of average awareness rises from 15.4 percent to 23.2 percent and then to 36.2 percent. For average market share, the mean forecast rises from 6.2 percent to 7.3 percent to 9.3 percent as media weight increases. As GRPs increase, the mean forecasts for end-of-year market share show similar rises.

Figure 9.3 shows the means for each type of media timing pattern. These data confirm that timing's influence is not as great as that of media weight. For example, the front-loaded pattern realizes average and end-of-year awareness mean forecasts of 28.3 percent and 21.1 percent, respectively; the flighted pattern produces means of 23.3 percent and 28.5 percent; and the sustained pattern turns out means of 23.2 percent and 30.5 percent.

The average and end-of-year market share forecasts are 8.6 percent and 6.9 percent, respectively, for the front-loaded pattern, 7.2 percent and 7.3 percent for the flighted pattern, and 7.0 percent and 7.3 percent for the sustained pattern. Figure 9.3's results illustrate that a front-loaded media pattern is likely to generate the highest average awareness levels and market shares. On the other

Effects of Timing Pattern on Measures of Market Response

	Type of Media Timing Pattern		
Dependent Variable	**Front Loaded**	**Flighted**	**Sustained**
Awareness:			
Average	28.3%	23.3%	23.2%
End-of-Year	21.1%	28.5%	30.5%
Market Share:			
Average	8.6%	7.2%	7.0%
End-of-Year	6.9%	7.3%	7.3%

FIGURE 9.3.

hand, a sustained pattern is likely to generate the highest end-of-year awareness levels and market shares.

These findings are consistent with historical research, including that reported by Hubert A. Zielske and Walter A. Henry in the *Journal of Advertising Research* and discussed by Julian Simon in the *Journal of Marketing Research*.[3] They found that a front-loaded pattern causes large market response increases early in the year, but subsequent market response trails off rather drastically later in the year.

Purchase Cycle and Media Timing

Figure 9.4 presents end-of-year market share forecasts for the three media patterns by purchase cycle length. These show that for a product consumers buy frequently (twice a month or monthly), the front-loaded approach is the most effective.

For a product consumers buy quarterly, the flighted media pattern produced the highest end-of-year market share forecasts. For products the consumer buys twice per year, the sustained media pattern overwhelms the other two patterns with an 8.4 percent mean end-of-year market share forecast; the flighted pattern obtained a 7.1 percent share; the front-loaded pattern a 5.6 percent.

Effects of Purchase Cycle and Media Timing Pattern on End-of-Year Market Share

	Type of Media Timing Pattern		
Purchase Cycle Length	Front Loaded	Flighted	Sustained
Twice per Month	7.3%	6.9%	6.5%
Monthly	7.9%	7.6%	7.2%
Quarterly	7.1%	7.6%	7.3%
Twice per Year	5.6%	7.1%	8.4%

FIGURE 9.4.

This study's results suggest that purchase-cycle length can affect the media timing pattern's effectiveness considerably. For products that turn rapidly—that have short purchase cycles—companies want to motivate consumers to try the product and then repeat their purchase soon after the campaign's launch. For products consumers buy infrequently, a front-loaded campaign is a large advertising expenditure when consumers may not be in the market to buy and have forgotten about the brand when they are next in the market.

These findings are consistent with two decades of in-market testing undertaken by package goods marketers to assess the effects of different media variables on advertising performance. The inconsistency of the findings from study to study are revealed to be partially a function of purchase cycle. Given the finding here that purchase cycle has a clear effect on the measured effects of advertising, and that purchase cycle has rarely—if ever—been systematically taken into account in designing and analyzing in-market test results, the bewildering, seemingly inconsistent patterns of past research findings should have been expected.

Product Type and Media Timing

Figure 9.5 shows that for new products, a front-loaded media pattern produces a higher average awareness level, 35.4 percent, than either the flighted or sustained patterns, which achieved 26.4 percent and 26.8 percent, respectively.

Effects of Product Type and Media Timing Pattern
on Average Awareness

| | Type of Media Timing Pattern | | |
Type of Product	Front Loaded	Flighted	Sustained
New	35.4%	26.4%	26.8%
Established	21.2%	20.1%	19.6%

FIGURE 9.5.

For new campaigns for established products, the effects of media timing are not statistically significant. Thus, while this analysis suggests that a front-loaded media schedule produces a significant advantage in generating above-average awareness for new products, no media timing pattern produced a comparable advantage for established products.

For end-of-year consumer awareness, the interaction effect between the type of media timing pattern and the type of product did not meet the .05 criterion for statistical significance. It was significant at the .06 level, however, which suggests that these results are "significant" from a managerial perspective. Here, the front-loaded pattern showed a smaller mean forecast of end-of-year awareness for new products than either the flighted or the sustained patterns. The front-loaded pattern's mean end-of-year awareness levels were 27.2 percent, the flighted pattern's were 37.5 percent, and the sustained pattern's were 38.7 percent.

For new campaigns of established products, the end-of-year consumer awareness mean scores were 15.1 percent, 19.4 percent, and 22.4 percent, respectively. These results confirm figure 9.3's results that the front-loaded media pattern produces some early advantages in building awareness, but the high levels diminish over time unless the media schedule maintains the high awareness level.

Product Type and Media Weight

For both consumer awareness levels, media weight demonstrates a powerful effect on new product awareness, as well as a strong effect on new cam-

Effects of Product Type and Media Weight Pattern
on Average and End-of-Year Awareness

Dependent Variable	Product Type	Level of Media Weight		
		Light	Average	Heavy
Average Awareness	New	16.6%	27.0%	45.0%
	Established	14.3%	19.4%	27.3%
End-of-Year Awareness	New	19.8%	33.5%	50.1%
	Established	13.7%	18.5%	24.7%

FIGURE 9.6.

paigns for established products as suggested in figure 9.6. For example, the mean level of end-of-year awareness for new products increased 153 percent as media weight increased from 600 GRPs to 2,400 GRPs. For established products, end-of-year awareness increased 80 percent.

As media weight increases from light to heavy, the average awareness measure also follows this pattern, showing a 172 percent increase for new products and a 91 percent increase for established products.

Media Weight and Media Timing

Increasing media weight generates the largest gains in end-of-year consumer awareness from the sustained media pattern as figure 9.7 shows. Increasing media weight from light to heavy produces a 105 percent rise in end-of-year awareness for the front-loaded media pattern, a 121 percent rise for the flighted pattern, and a 140 percent rise for the sustained pattern.

Further, when we compare end-of-year consumer awareness for each media weight level, we find the sustained media timing pattern accomplishing the strongest results. The sustained pattern yields the most productive results as the advertiser increases media weight. When a marketer believes it important to have strong year-end consumer product awareness, the sustained timing pattern is most productive.

Effects of Media Weight and Media Timing Pattern
on End-of-Year Awareness

	Type of Media Timing Pattern		
Level of Media Weight	Front Loaded	Flighted	Sustained
Light	14.0%	17.9%	18.3%
Average	20.7%	28.0%	29.4%
Heavy	28.7%	39.5%	44.0%

FIGURE 9.7.

MANAGEMENT IMPLICATIONS

The effects of media weight and timing are clearly more complex than was previously thought and than most marketers would want to believe. Basically, this study found that media timing and media weight effects depend largely on whether a product is new or established and whether consumers buy it frequently or infrequently. Further, the effects depend on what metric is used to measure success—consumer awareness or market share—and whether we report the metric as an average over the course of a year or simply focus on what is happening at year's end.

Some readers may question this research's relevance. After all, the research purports to analyze data from 648 different simulations, not real-world cases. The results, one could argue, are simply a reflection of the model used to make the forecasts. And there is some truth to this line of reasoning.

On the other hand, the modelers did not create a model to produce the outcomes presented in this chapter. Rather, we developed a model to describe the reality of the world and tested model validity by comparing model performance against reality in hundreds of cases, improving it annually as discrepancies between forecast and real world performance appeared. Litmus was used in this application, a model that evolved into the current Discovery.

If Discovery uses exactly the same and somewhat limited input variables as Litmus, and makes the same assumptions about the effects of theses inputs as Litmus, the results produced by both models will be the same. Thus, we think of the current Discovery model as being similar to the physical models used in wind-tunnel experiments to investigate the effects of different automobile or aircraft designs. These models are designed to capture current knowledge and predict the future. Similarly, the Discovery model, like its parent Litmus, has been designed to do the same. Therefore, since Discovery/Litmus has been fire-tested over years, we feel very comfortable using the model to draw inferences about what will happen when different parameters in a marketing program are modified.

Perhaps the best testimony to the validity of this simulation exercise came from a senior management science executive at Procter & Gamble, a company that has probably done more in-market testing than any other. His response to an earlier draft of this work was simply, "This study does more to explain decades of in-market tests at Procter & Gamble than anything else I've seen. The main effects and interactions reported here are right on with our experience. Indeed, if we'd had the results of this simulation earlier, we would have undertaken far fewer tests and designed them very differently."

Management can use these findings (and models such as those reported here) to improve the media budget's effectiveness on a case-by-case basis. For example, we found that for a given media weight, a front-loaded plan generates the highest *average* consumer awareness and market share. However, a sustained media plan generates the highest *end-of-year* consumer awareness and market share. Management objectives for average and end-of-year awareness targets dictate which media timing pattern is best for a given situation.

Most importantly, the results clearly demonstrate the need to take the product purchase cycle into account in planning and implementing marketing campaigns for new and established products and services. Front-loaded schedules always seem to work best for *fast turnover* new products (one to four or more purchases per month).

They invariably fail for *slow turnover* brands (those purchased twice a year or less frequently), whether the products are new or established. The reason is simple: a front-loaded campaign will fire up awareness when people are not yet ready to buy. It's like heating the furnace on a warm day. When people are ready to buy because they've used up whatever the new product is designed to replace, they've already forgotten that the new brand exists. The fuel burned in summer does nothing to warm the house in winter.

NOTES

1. This chapter is based on the work of Joseph D. Blackburn, Kevin J. Clancy, and R. Dale Wilson as reported in chapter 9 of *Simulated Test Marketing* by Kevin J. Clancy, Robert Shulman, and Marianne Wolf (New York: Lexington Books, 1994).

2. Joseph D. Blackburn, Kevin Clancy, and R. Dale Wilson, "Forecasting Awareness of New Products and Penetration of New Campaigns for Established Products," in *Simulated Test Marketing*, p. 200.

3. Hubert A. Zielske, and Walter A. Henry, "Remembering and Forgetting Television Ads," *Journal of Advertising Research* 20 (April 1985), 7–13; Julian L. Simon, "What do Zielske's Real Data Really Show about Pulsing?" *Journal of Marketing Research* 16 (August 1979), 415–20.

10

Measuring the Effects of DTC Campaigns[*]

Direct-to-consumer (DTC) pharmaceutical advertising is one of the hottest areas in marketing today. In August 1997, the Federal Drug Administration relaxed its rules on television and radio advertising of prescriptions drugs, allowing companies to promote specific products without having to include all the patient information (potential side effects, warnings and precautions, etc.) that they must include in newspaper and magazine ads.

As a result, pharmaceutical companies spent more than $2 billion on DTC advertising for prescription drugs in 2000 and they spent more than $6 billion in 2004. As drugs go off patent, companies want to protect their brands from generic alternatives. And new drugs such as Levitra and Cialis for erectile dysfunction will be trying to take a large piece of that $1 billion (and growing) market.

Pharmaceutical company managements have concluded that if they advertise directly to consumers, people will identify with the medical problem, understand the solution and what's different and better about the advertised drug compared to competitors, and remember the brand advertised. These people will then make an appointment with their physicians to ask for the drug by name.

---

[*] This chapter is coauthored by Dr. Steve Tipps of Copernicus Marketing Consulting, a codeveloper of Discovery and an authority on STM applications to DTC campaigns.

Bases, NFO FYI, Assessor, and Discovery have all developed methodologies to examine consumer and physician responses to DTC advertising in the pharmaceutical industry. These are all spin-offs of their basic simulated test market (STM) models. All have been developed to reduce the risks of launching DTC campaigns.

Pharmaceutical executives look at a few high-profile products—Allegra and Viagra, to name two—and assume that many, or perhaps most, such marketing efforts can be equally successful. They are usually mistaken. Consider the following.

HOW TO BLOW $38 MILLION

Not long ago, a major pharmaceutical marketer hired our firm to forecast the incremental effect its planned $35-million, first-quarter consumer advertising campaign would have on the year's product sales. That is correct; the corporation planned to spend $35 million in three months. This was in addition to the professional campaign directed against physicians.

The client wanted to know whether DTC advertising would pay its way. Would enough prospective users—or, as they are called in the pharmaceutical world, sufferers—ask their physicians about the new drug to make the advertising investment a sound one?

Our marketing mix simulation model, Discovery, found in a simulated test that the $35 million would produce a share gain of 1 percent but yield a negative return on the investment. Consumers, the simulation research discovered, were unlikely to remember this product's difficult name (let's call it Plutonixerion) or any reason for its superiority—let alone remember the name and the benefits long enough to request a prescription on a visit to the doctor weeks, if not months, later.

The company's executives were, to put the best possible face on it, distressed by our report, a distress intensified by their experience with another consulting firm, which we were surprised to learn had been retained to do a forecast in parallel with our own. That firm had projected a significant gain in share and a positive return on investment (ROI). Why couldn't we use the other firm's model? Perhaps it would project a better outcome than our negative ROI. We asked the client to send us the report and said we would try to uncover the discrepancy between our forecast and the other firm's.

Before we could complete our analysis, however, the client elected to launch its campaign anyway. The corporation spent not $35 million but $38 million over four months in television and print to advertise Plutonixerion. Although we had provided a unsatisfactory (i.e., bad) forecast, the client continued to work with us to help monitor the performance of the DTC campaign. They hired a research tracking company to interview both sufferers and physicians on a continuous basis and compared the results of the tracking study to the output of the Discovery model and a competitive model with actual prescriptions of Plutonixerion.

The most common first step in most new product forecasting models is to establish brand awareness. Awareness measures are popular indicators of communication effectiveness because consumers must be aware of a product before they buy it. Researchers may use any one (or a combination) of the eight awareness measures we showed in chapter 8 in figure 8.1.

For new package goods products, as noted earlier, we have found total brand awareness—the combination of aided and unaided awareness—to be the most effective measure. A typical total brand awareness number for a major introduction might be 30 percent from the advertising, promotion, and public relations; that is, 30 percent of the population knows something about the product within 6 to 12 months after the company introduces it to the marketplace.

One justification for using total brand awareness for a consumer package good is that when the customer is in the supermarket, pushing a cart down the aisle, and sees the brand on the shelf, the sight triggers memory. She's seen the product before in a television commercial or in a magazine ad or in a newspaper insert (or in all three). Ideally, she remembers something positive about the product message and adds the product to her cart based on what she recalls.

In contrast, DTC pharmaceutical advertising requires that consumers actually remember the (often strange) brand name and the message strategy because they must make an appointment with their doctors and remember to ask for the product by name during the appointment. Because DTC advertising is so different from ordinary package goods, we had told our pharmaceutical client that in our DTC modeling we would use "proven awareness" as the criterion for awareness, not total brand awareness—proven awareness being awareness of the brand name and something about the product.

The company's tracking research showed a 5 percent proven awareness by the end of four months, a poor showing for a $38-million advertising effort. Among the people who remembered something about Plutonixerion and its message, only 20 percent asked their doctors about the medication, which was 1 percent of all sufferers. These are disturbingly low numbers, but not very different from those the Discovery model had predicted.

The tracking research among physicians told the same bottom-line story. Doctors said that fewer than 1 percent of their patients had asked for a prescription for Plutonixerion. The tracking research among physicians and sufferers and the Discovery model all pointed in the same direction: campaign failure.

After a period of convalescence, our client asked us to help explain the discrepancy between the competitive firm's model (that they wanted to believe) and the marketplace results. We regarded this as an interesting R&D exercise.

WHAT WENT WRONG WITH THE FORECAST

The first thing that we learned is that other firm forecast a 44 percent advertising recall in contrast to our 5 percent proven recall. Moreover, the other firm forecast that 35 percent of the aware sufferers would ask their physicians for a prescription versus our 20 percent of the proven recallers or 1 percent of all sufferers.

But a 44 percent ad recall figure is unrealistically high. We haven't seen this kind of number since Lever Bros. was torturing consumers with the late Jim Jordan's very successful "Ring Around the Collar!" campaign. How was it possible that the other research company and the client had expected a recall number so extraordinary?

The other firm had used a recognition-based measure in which the researchers gave respondents copy points from the television and print advertising and asked if they remembered them. The firm counted people who claimed to remember two or more copy points as having recall, which it is not. Indeed, if you ask people about ads that never ran or copy points never used, recognition scores are surprisingly high. People have a tendency to overstate what they remember, perhaps in the hope of pleasing the interviewer.

Another issue was the number of people who, recalling the advertising, would ask their doctor for a prescription—35 percent according to the other firm's research. This would be a good number for a new package good, but to think that 35 percent of the people who see a pharmaceutical commercial on television or in a magazine advertisement note the brand name, remember its message, make appointments with their doctors, and request the drug during the appointment is to believe that you can still buy the Brooklyn Bridge.

It turns out that the other firm had accepted sufferers' self-reports of what they would do as fixed truths rather than adjusting those reports downward to compensate for overstatement.

We put together a presentation unraveling the research mystery, and presented our results to about 20 people, expecting the worst. The client marketing and research people asked good questions as we waited for the attacks, because basically we were saying that the company had blown $38 million in one quarter based on an overly optimistic forecast.

But the attacks never came because, we learned for the first time, the company had launched other, similar DTC campaigns over the past three years with equally disappointing results and without learning anything from the experience. This time, at least, they learned something about the factors that drive DTC success, including the need to imprint the product name and its message and to find new and creative ways to motivate people to request the drug from their physicians.

We have investigated more than 35 DTC advertising campaigns in depth and found only five for which the advertising and marketing produced a clear return on the investment. We have, however, learned at least nine things about DTC campaigns that have helped improve the ROI of client pharmaceutical marketing efforts.

WHAT WE HAVE LEARNED ABOUT DTC CAMPAIGNS

1: The first thing we have learned is that DTC marketing communications—particularly print advertising and television commercials—usually fail to imprint the brand name and its raison d'etre (its reason to exist, its essential selling message) in the minds of doctors and prospective users. Awareness numbers under 12 percent are commonplace. This represents one fundamental reason underlying the high DTC failure rate.

2: Sufferers—even if they become "aware" of a medication's name and usage—are far less likely to contact their physicians and ask for a pharmaceutical by name than pharmaceutical marketers commonly believe.

While many DTC marketers believe that this conversion from awareness to behavior hovers around 30 percent, it is, in fact, usually under 10 percent. Of all sufferers who become aware and can play back something about the DTC campaign, only 2 in 10 will actually contact their doctor and only half of those, 1 in 10, will specifically ask for the advertised medication.

3: The probability that aware sufferers will make appointments and request the medication varies considerably depending on sufferer "involvement" in the product category. The more sufferers are involved in the category (and we'll talk about "involvement" in a moment), the more likely they will ask their doctors about a medication. This has implications for marketing strategy, tactics, and simulated test marketing estimating procedures.

The more a DTC marketer targets "highly involved" sufferers, the more likely is a marketing success. And the better a simulation technology takes involvement into account, the greater is its validity.

4: The task of a DTC ROI analysis is to estimate the number of prescriptions that are incremental, that is, due to the DTC campaign. How many patients would have gone to the doctor or received a prescription had the campaign *not* aired? Accordingly, to understand the benefit of a DTC marketing effort, a marketer must take into account the "base rate" of prescriptions—the annual number of new patients or new prescriptions that are generated without any DTC advertising.

The base rate value can vary considerably due to current category growth, maturity of the products, and the number and budgets of DTC competitors. In our experience, however, base rates range from 2 to 10 percent and average around 5 percent.

5: Physicians, because they are also exposed to consumer media, may be impacted even more by DTC campaigns than their patients. This explains why, in many cases, DTC marketers observe a sales increase for the advertised pharmaceutical without seeing significant shifts in sufferer awareness and behavior. The sufferers are either oblivious to the advertising or unaware of the medication's implications for their condition, while their doctors, sitting at home in their living rooms, are more attuned to the advertising and its implications.

STM systems, as a consequence, need to model the effects of the consumer campaign on both sufferers and physicians. A system that looks at only one is likely to ignore a significant element of the DTC campaign.

6: Doctors typically honor patient requests for a medication; the compliance rate is 75 percent or more. In spite of early fears that physicians would resent patients who were dangerous with a little knowledge, doctors tend to report that they value the initiative a patient has taken by researching and requesting a pharmaceutical. Furthermore, in most categories the leading drugs are similarly effective and safe, so doctors risk little in complying with patient requests, making the patient a partner in treatment decisions. Only in certain cases where doctors consider competing brands to have very different profiles can compliance drop to as low as 15 or 20 percent.

As a result of the high compliance rate, DTC advertising tends to have no effect on these rates. Practically speaking, most compliance rates can go no higher than they are, and DTC advertising neither helps nor hurts.

7: DTC advertising, moreover, often has an impact on the share of prescriptions physicians allocate to the advertised brand. In certain cases, DTC-aware doctors indicate that they prescribe a brand more frequently than nonaware doctors. This tends to occur for smaller share brands that have fallen off doctors' "radar screens" or for older brands that have been undeservedly eclipsed in the doctors' minds by larger, newer, and newsier competitors. The DTC advertising acts as reminder that the brand still exists and offers valuable benefits, and it serves to reinstate the brand into the physician's consideration set.

The result is that the advertised brand can increase its share among aware doctors by 7 to 15 percent, producing a net 0.5 to 1.5 share point gain.

8: Branded campaigns are usually more profitable than unbranded campaigns. Branded campaigns tie the product message to the brand name and provide a definite call to action for sufferers. Once in the doctor's office, the sufferer is clear about what brand it is that drove him or her there.

On the other hand, branded campaigns are twice as expensive as unbranded ones because they incur costs for the time/space dedicated to "fair balance" statements. In addition to being less expensive, unbranded ads are also commended for their noncommercial, soft-sell approach that can be considered more appropriate for pharmaceuticals.

While our database is not extensive, in our experience the branded version is often more profitable. It is true that in a very new category with few diagnosed sufferers, the market leader would benefit most from an unbranded campaign making sufferers and doctors aware of the medication. In more established categories, however—the ones that see most of the DTC activity—branded ads have an advantage despite their higher cost for at least two reasons:

- They are more effective, as one might expect, in driving current patients being treated into the doctor's office to discuss the medication.

■ Current patients, obviously, are more likely to receive a prescription than sufferers who are not being treated.

Unbranded ads are more effective in motivating the latter group to visit a doctor; however, the response rates of the two groups (diagnosed/treated, undiagnosed/untreated) are not as great as they are for branded ads. Branded ads perform better among the undiagnosed than unbranded ads do among patients currently being treated. Sufferers who go to their doctor's office because of a brand advertisement are far more likely to receive a prescription for the advertised medication than sufferers motivated by an unbranded ad.

The net result, taking into account differential sufferer response and prescription rates tends to be a higher ROI for the branded version of a campaign.

9: A company can predict the performance of most DTC programs well before the firm spends any money on a real-world, regional or national product introduction. This is what makes simulated test marketing such a theoretically useful tool.

Since real-world introductions (whether test markets or larger regional/national efforts) cost a great deal, take a long time, give away ideas, are susceptible to sabotage, and often the results cannot be projected anyway, market response modeling is an appropriate alternative in many cases.

This is particularly true when the DTC simulation forecasts marketplace failure. Some failures can be reversed. Market response modeling technologies, through diagnostic analyses, are sometimes able to transform an apparent failure into a success. A company can sometimes develop and launch a new marketing program, and/or develop and schedule new advertising that yields a very different outcome from the initial effort.

HOW TO IMPROVE DTC CAMPAIGNS

As we pointed out earlier, much traditional simulated test marketing research has serious limitations.

Sample Limitations

Research companies sometimes employ small (100 to 200), non-projectable groups of men and women willing to answer questions for the research.

Measurement Problems

Researchers often use purchase intention and other rating scale measures with unknown reliability and validity. The scales miscarry because researchers don't know a) if they repeated the study they would obtain the same results, or b) if the results actually reflect what they want to learn.

Alternative Possibilities

Few researchers are able to ask "what if" questions concerning variations in concept features and benefits efficiently. What if the pills are blister-packed? Come as capsules? What if the price is $8.73 a pill? $10.95?

Ignorance of Costs

In our experience, marketing managers seldom know the fixed and variable manufacturing and marketing costs, and researchers never know them. But without knowing costs, a manager cannot estimate profitability.

Limited Models

Finally, few researchers offer a valid model of the DTC marketing mix into which to feed concept scores to predict sales and profitability. Researchers present concept scores to management as if they were discrete pieces of information in themselves: "This one got a 33 percent top two box score, beating the control concept by almost two to one." That's nice, but will it sell? And if it sells, will it be profitable?

Companies can reduce these problems with several changes.

Larger Samples

Begin with a larger, more projectable sample of prospective buyers (300 to 500) in more locations than the ones traditionally found for such tests. These people should be serious respondents, people recruited via random digit dialing and then brought to a central location or interviewed over the Internet.

Full Descriptions

Expose this sample to the big idea—a full description of the new pharmaceutical, complete with the name, positioning, packaging, features, and price (it's surprising how many marketing tests ignore price). Present the pharmaceutical in its competitive frame, that is, with competing products sold in the market at their actual prices. The more a test simulates, models, or mirrors reality, the more accurate the forecast.

Measure the Probability of Behavior

Have "sufferers" rate the concept, on 11-point scales, in terms of the probability that they will make an appointment with their physician and request a prescription from their doctors. Of course, like all self-reported measures of consumer buying, these scales overstate actual sufferer behavior. Much of this overstatement comes about because the research environment assumes 100 percent awareness and acceptance by insurance carriers, two conditions the company never realizes. Researchers tend to assume all sufferers will be aware of the product (which never happens) and all those aware of it will ask their doctors about it (which also never happens).

Moreover, people are more likely to say they are "certain will ask physician" than in fact do ask. This is true in every pharmaceutical category we have ever investigated. We have also closely examined the relationship between people's reports on the 11-point scale and awareness-to-trial figures (among people who were aware of a product and for whom product was available to be purchased) for numerous consumer packaged goods. And we have looked at this relationship in durable goods/financial service cases including a hand-held microcomputer, a portable PC, an iPod analogue, long-lasting light bulbs, new car dealer visits, overnight messenger services, a new premium charge card, software for the home and business markets, and a new personal banking service.

Usually no more than 75 percent of the people who claim they "definitely will buy" or "certainly will ask" actually do buy or do ask. This figure declines as self-reported purchase probability declines, but the ratio is not constant. Indeed, the higher the level of self-reported behavior probability, the greater the ratio of reported-to-actual probability.

Also, depending on the product category and the situation, virtually none of the people at the low end of the scale—those who say there is some or a slight possibility they will ask their physician—will actually do so. This means all such intent figures must be adjusted downward.

By taking behavior probabilities and sufferer involvement into account, however, it is possible to produce a reasonably valid estimate of actual prescription volume (i.e., the percentage of sufferers who would ask their doctor and obtain the product at their pharmacy at least once).

HOW DTC MODELING WORKS

DTC modeling (like the "marketing mix modeling," "promotional modelings" and "simulated test marketing" we've discussed earlier) represents a set of equations that predict real-world *output* (including new and repeat prescriptions) from marketing-plan *input* (such as prime-time network television target rating points per month).

Figure 10.1 shows a DTC consumer model with the inputs on the left, the outputs on the right. Many of the inputs—the campaign media, share of voice; product concept; price, availability (distribution)—are common to other marketing mix models. Similarly, the outputs are familiar to pharmaceutical marketing executives—target universe, brand or campaign awareness, physician contact, physician compliance, pharmacy visit, and the like.

Discovery DTC Consumer Model

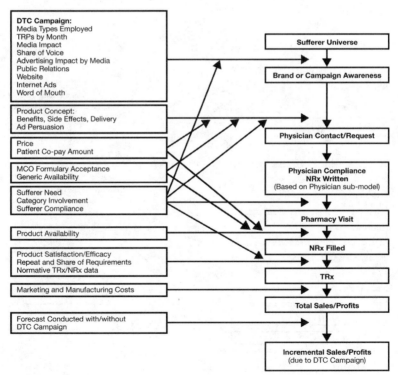

FIGURE 10.1.

What is not so common are the inputs of "sufferer need," "category in-volvement," and "sufferer compliance." As the illustration suggests, these af-fect brand awareness, physician contact, pharmacy visits, and prescription refills.

The illustration of the DTC physician model, figure 10.2, shows that while the inputs are similar to the consumer model, the outputs are less complex: Physician universe, brand awareness, prescriptions written, and incremental prescriptions written.

A DTC simulation is designed to forecast sales and further refine a reason-ably well-developed product concept and marketing plan. The consumer sample typically requires 200 to 300 suffers; the total depends on the number of subgroups to be analyzed. Based on a study's requirements, the research may also use split cells or a control cell or both. The sample geographically represents the product category and includes, where appropriate, sample weighting or covariate adjustments or both.

Discovery DTC Physician Model

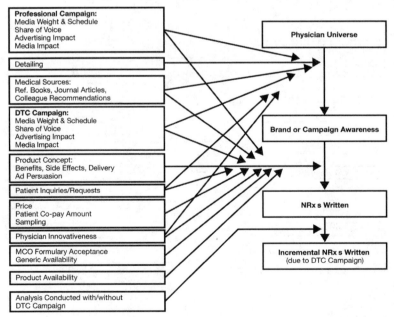

FIGURE 10.2.

The physician sample requires approximately 200 physicians, again depending on the number of subgroups to be analyzed. As with the consumer study, the research may also use split cells or a control cell or both. Split cells are common when the research studies different physician specialties and the client wishes to understand hypothesized differences in response (for example, primary care providers versus OB/GYNs).

Both the consumer and physician samples require a 35- to 50-minute interview done over the Internet, telephone, or in person, the length and methodology determined by the number of questioning areas and the types of stimuli required.

SUFFERER DATA COLLECTION METHODOLOGY
The sufferer data collection methodology has several steps.

Exposure to the Concept or the Advertising
If advertising is used (typically television or print), clutter ads are included and embedded in a half-hour television program or a forthcoming issue of a magazine.

Test Ad Recall and Communication Diagnostics
The ad recall is compared to norms to gauge the advertising's impact. Sometimes these studies are done in conjunction with an ASI copy test so that ASI norms are employed as well.

A Behavior Prediction Battery
This includes the sufferer's intent to contact the doctor and intent to request a prescription. In the Discovery model, a multiple item measure employs proprietary "weights" to calibrate self-reported behavior to estimate actual behavior.

Sufferer Treatment History
This includes the pharmaceutical brand awareness, past and current usage of the pharmaceutical, usage of over-the-counter medications, treatment satisfaction, and the type and number of physicians visited. The interviewers collect a detailed history of condition-related treatment and medication usage for each sufferer.

Category Involvement Measures

Used in the Discovery model, this includes a five-factor, 15-item propri-etary measure of "involvement" that is employed to calibrate behavioral mea-sures and to provide diagnostic information. The five factors include:

- overall health—general concern for health, proclivity to visit physician, ten-dency toward hypochondria;
- problem seriousness—severity of affliction, duration/frequency of the problem, degree to which onset of the problem is *not* predictable (for example, the pain of an ulcer is often predictable; an angina attack is not);
- information seeking—information gathering activities, word-of-mouth ac-tivities, interest in new treatments and drugs;
- brand differentiation—perceived efficacy available in the category, per-ceived pharmaceutical brand differentiation, degree to which over-the-counter to prescribed medication does *not* occur (the more the sufferers are willing to rely on over-the-counter medications, the less involved they are); and
- product risk—potential for adverse side effects, cost of the pharmaceutical to the sufferer, confidence in the physician prescribing correct/best treat-ment.

The more sufferers are involved in their condition—particularly when the onset of the problem is *not* predictable such as an angina attack, and when sufferers are willing to switch from an over-the-counter medication to an eth-ical drug—the more likely they are to acknowledge the advertising and talk to their doctors and ask about a prescription.

Conversely, when sufferers are not involved (or aware of their condition such as adult-onset diabetes), they tend to be oblivious to the advertising. Also, if sufferers believe that the drugs they are taking are just fine, they tend not to look for new medications.

As good as the weighted scale and the involvement adjustments may be, the model adds two other sets of measures to estimate whether consumers will visit their doctors to talk about and request a prescription. These are seven-point scales covering affective and cognitive reactions and are administered as part of the multidimensional "inventory." (These are different from the 11-point purchase intention scale we just discussed.)

Affective Measures

These include factors such as the sufferer's first impression of the medication; whether the medication is for people like me; whether it is for symptoms I experience; likeability—whether the sufferer likes the company or the advertising (or both); the overall impression conveyed; and whether the medication seems helpful at treating problems.

Cognitive Measures

These include factors such as the pharmaceutical's price; value of the product; clarity of the concept; whether the advertising and concept are believable; the pharmaceutical's uniqueness; and its superiority to other medications on the market.

PHYSICIAN DATA COLLECTION METHODOLOGY

The physician data collection methodology also involves a 35- to 50-minute Internet, telephone, or in-person interview conducted among condition-relevant specialties. The information gathered includes

A Profile of Current Practice

specialty; the number and types of patients; therapies employed; distribution of brands prescribed, frequency of prescription requests; and compliance by brand. The goal here is to obtain a detailed description of medical practice to estimate prescription volume and to provide measures of "pre-exposure" prescription habits.

Exposure to the Product Concept, the Test Advertising, or Both

Reaction to the Concept or the Advertising, or Both

expected distribution of new and refilled prescriptions, expected compliance with prescription requests, communication diagnostics, and brand perceptions/imagery. The research compares expected postexposure behavior to pre-exposure measures to gauge the impact of DTC campaign awareness.

Similar to the sufferer data collection methodology, the model employs a five-factor, 15-item proprietary measure of physician "innovativeness" to estimate behavior and to provide diagnostic information. The factors include

- innovativeness—willingness to try a new medication when it is approved, recognized as innovative by other physicians, self-perception as an innovator;

- knowledge—regarded as knowledgeable by peers, associated with a teaching hospital, considered an expert in treatment of a certain condition;
- professional development—works to keep up with breaking developments, attends conferences in the field, reads at least one professional journal during an average week;
- opinion leadership—advises other physicians on new treatments, often recommends new drugs and treatments to fellow physicians, receives referrals from other physicians with difficult cases; and
- diffusion potential—interacts with other physicians during a typical month, actively participates in professional medical associations, consults with other physicians.

Doctors rate each of these 15 items and the model averages the resulting scores for each respondent. Not unexpectedly, the more innovative doctors are more likely to respond favorably to a DTC campaign and to prescribe a new pharmaceutical than doctors who are less innovative.

With these (and other) inputs, the model is able to forecast several different performance measures, such as campaign penetration, also known as "real" awareness of the product and its raison d'etre. This is output from the model, not input from the marketer and takes into account the 21 factors that govern awareness.

It will forecast the percentage of target sufferers who will talk to their physician about the new product as well as the percentage of physicians who decide to prescribe because a patient requests a prescription or—a key point—because of their own response to the DTC campaign.

In addition, the model forecasts trial—the overall proportion of target sufferers who receive and use an initial prescription. And it forecasts new prescriptions, incremental prescriptions, total prescriptions, and revenues.

THE ADVANTAGE OF A DTC STM MODEL

The advantage of a simulated test marketing model to pharmaceutical companies, of course, is that it permits marketers to experiment with DTC inputs to see immediately their effect on the output. Will television advertising, for example, have the greatest impact on sales? More than direct marketing? Which day part will have the most effect? How much? At what cost?

To improve product positioning, it is critical for management to understand why sufferers are, or are not, interested in the pharmaceutical. What are the key appeals? Why do other sufferers *not* talk to their doctors about their condition? What are the key inhibitions? What positioning/communications strategy is best to overcome these reservations or inhibitions?

Why do some sufferers ask their physicians about the product? What are the key drivers? Why do others fail to make an appointment and ask? What are the key obstacles? What positioning or product refinements (or both) may be worth considering?

To obtain this positioning and product guidance, STM researchers and the company's management generate 15 to 25 tangible and intangible attributes and benefits that might be used to describe and position the product. These would include tangible attributes such as "easy to swallow," "relatively inexpensive," "minimal side effects," and the like. Intangible benefits are items such as "gives you security," "recommended by experts," "proud to tell your friends about," "soothing," and the like.

During the interview with sufferers, the researchers investigate these attributes/benefits using the same three-dimensional model of motivations described earlier. This intelligence, coupled with brand/product perceptions for the DTC-advertised product and its competitors, is then presented in the same brand strategy matrix also described earlier and shown in figure 7.7.

Again, one of the problems with survey research is that sufferers—consciously or otherwise—tend to overstate the importance of the rational or socially desirable attributes and to understate the importance of the intangible "imagery." To overcome this tendency, it is necessary to measure the motivating power of each attribute/benefit in terms of the three dimensions.

It is then necessary to examine consumers' perceptions of the new pharmaceutical vis-à-vis alternatives. What strengths and weaknesses are perceived in the product? How does this vary between sufferers who asked their doctors for a prescription versus those who did not? How does this change over time, from expectations to satisfaction? And relative to alternatives, how does the new product compare?

Finally, the STM model looks simultaneously at all three pieces of information: the motivating power of attributes/benefits, the consumer perceptions of the advertised medication, and consumer perceptions of competitive products. This analysis can identify those attributes/benefits on which to base a powerful positioning strategy. Among respondents who try the medication, the goal is to find attributes that are highly motivating, credible for the new product, and that the new product can preempt—alternative products are not as good on these attributes.

The research also wants to identify those attributes/issues that are the key hurdles for the new product to overcome. When analyzing those respondents who either do not try or who reject the new medication, we look for attributes that are highly motivating and whether these sufferers expect the new product to be inferior to the competing alternatives.

MANAGEMENT IMPLICATIONS

This chapter has noted that DTC marketing communications usually fail to imprint the brand name and its raison d'etre in the minds of doctors and prospective users. Even aware sufferers are less likely to contact their physicians and ask for a pharmaceutical by name than pharmaceutical marketers commonly believe. Of all sufferers who become aware and can play back something about a DTC campaign, only 2 in 10 will actually contact their doctors and only half of those will ask for the advertised medication.

We have found that as a result of these and other problems, most DTC campaigns fail to produce the ROI that pharmaceutical companies are looking for. It should be pointed out here that in contrast to most marketers who would be happy with a return of 30 percent, pharmaceutical marketers are often looking for 300 percent or more. It is difficult to achieve this high hurdle.

There are things we've learned, however, and steps that can be taken to improve the probability of achieving an acceptable level of ROI for DTC programs, many of which we have discussed in this chapter. For example, the more sufferers are involved in the category, the more likely they will ask their doctors about a medication. Therefore, the more a DTC marketer targets "highly involved" sufferers, the more likely the campaign will be a marketing success.

We have also reported that physicians, because they are exposed to consumer media, may be more impacted by DTC campaigns than their patients. Yet, most DTC pharmaceutical advertising agencies have not considered the effects of their consumer programs on physicians when developing their media plans. It is a rare case when a client comes to the table and says, "Here is the media plan for consumers, and here is the media plan for physicians."

We have also discovered that directing a campaign toward "involved" sufferers and "innovative" physicians is more likely to succeed than one that focuses on more generic targeting. In general, we should add, pharmaceutical marketers spend less time—and consequently waste more money—thinking through fundamental marketing decisions such as targeting and positioning than their counterparts in other product categories. We can name, as an illustration, only three pharmaceutical marketers who have expressed an interested in identifying the financially optimal target in their categories. Perhaps pharmaceutical companies are so profitable, inefficient marketing efforts are not a major concern.

One of the exciting developments in DTC simulations is the use of this technology to improve marketing programs, sometimes even resurrecting a moribund program. With such analyses it is often possible to turn an average pharmaceutical into a star, and to turn a winning one into a superstar.

11

Toward Marketing Plan Optimization[*]

Marketing managers want to know, Which marketing plan is best? Unfortunately, as we've noted several times, any product or service may have literally billions of possible plans. How is an executive to evaluate such a surfeit in a single lifetime? Most marketing managers, using traditional test marketing methods, develop and test only one or two plans among the possible billions—and they pick the few they decide to test based on experience and instinct. The usual result is new product failure.

Companies using simulated test marketing often fair no better. Many of the firms using the models described in this book invite their clients to provide up to three different marketing plans. Companies sometimes make the mistake of labeling the winning plan "the optimal one." In other words, the best of three is optimal. This, of course, is not close to optimal using the scientific sense of the word "optimization," which means "the most desirable or favorable."

In our view, testing two plans, three plans, even seven plans in either the real world or in a simulation is not enough. Marketers need to employ technology that allows them to evaluate a constellation of different plans to identify those likely to be marketplace winners, new product marketing programs which are far to the right on the Performance Bell Curve.

---

* The authors would like to acknowledge the invaluable contributions of Professor Joseph Blackburn of the Owen School of Management, Vanderbilt University, to this chapter.

Consider the hypothetical example of marketing planning for Vanilla Coke.

Because the manager was not sure what level of ad support was appropriate, he might have considered budgets that ranged from $5 million to $100 million in $250,000 increments. That's 380 advertising options.

Because Nielsen ACV distribution possibilities ranged from 10 (distribution in only one major market) to 90 percent (distribution in all chains that sold soft drinks), the manager had 81 distribution options.

Because the Coca-Cola Company can deliver coupons to any percentage of the population—from 0 to 100 percent—it had 101 coupon reach options. And because it can deliver as many as five coupons per household, it had six coupon frequency options (no coupon, to as many as five coupons).

Finally, because it might sample no one, everyone, or any percentage in between, it had 101 sampling options (figure 11.1). These options represent 1,883,920,680 possible plans[1] of which a typical marketer might evaluate 2. The expectation, as one might expect considering the 1 in 941,960,340 odds, is failure.

Another case we reviewed not long ago involved a new laptop PC. The corporation's marketing plan for this new product consisted of 15 strategic and tactical decisions, each one of which offered 2 to more than 100 possibilities.

Marketing Options for Vanilla Coke

Marketing Mix Component	Range	Options
Advertising	2-26 Million	250 (Hundreds of Thousands)
Distribution	10-90%	81 (Points)
Couponing (% Population)	0-100%	101 (Points)
Couponing (# of Coupons per HH)	0-5	6 (Numbers)
Sampling (% Population)	0-100%	101 (Points)

FIGURE 11.1.

The total number of possible plans was more than a trillion. The corporation assessed only a few—those that seemed to make the most sense in management's best judgment—and the new product failed.

DEVELOPING OPTIMAL MARKETING PLANS

Simulated test marketing research models offer marketing executives two different approaches to optimizing a marketing plan. In one, the modelers deploy a formal optimizing algorithm that seeks the best possible solution to the problem. We'll provide examples of this approach in a moment.

In the other approach, the marketing executives take the results of the simulated test market (STM) research and modify the plan to improve the predicted results. An STM, for example, can easily evaluate five different advertising spending levels, three different distribution levels, seven different prices, and so on. We'll conclude this chapter with a case showing how this approach can help make a better plan.

Since marketing mix models have proven that it is possible for a simulated test marketing study to evaluate a marketing plan (any plan) and forecast the probable results if the company takes that plan into the market, the success of a new product launch (or an existing product's relaunch) is limited only by the number of marketing plans the marketer tests.

In the following sections we will present case studies of how researchers have used modeling to address this optimization issue.

THE OPTIMIZATION PROCEDURE

In the Discovery and the Litmus models, there are two ways to guide the optimization procedure. With a budget optimization, the marketing manager fixes a budget level and the model produces a plan that maximizes share and profits within those financial constraints. With a share optimization, the marketing manager sets a market share objective and the model establishes the minimum marketing budget necessary to meet those share and profit goal.

In one sense, the optimal solution is the same for both problems. If the maximum sales for a $10 million budget are, for example, 100,000 cases, then the minimum budget necessary to attain sales of 100,000 cases is $10 million. Moreover, the marketing mix that generates the maximum sales is the same as the one that minimizes the budget.

The optimization procedure moves through four stages (figure 11.2). The first phase of the optimization procedure applies the sensitivity analysis we described in chapter 7 to the manager-prepared plan. This identifies the relationship between changes in each marketing tool (e.g., 30-second commercials, distribution level, couponing, etc.) in the manager-prepared plan and sales or profits or both. This phase identifies the plan's more and less cost-efficient vehicles.

The second stage applies sensitivity analysis to evaluate marketing vehicles that the manager's plan did not include. This allows the model to examine the effectiveness of all possible marketing vehicles—different advertising media, media schedules, coupons, samples, and their types and schedules.

The third stage develops a model-aided plan. A manual selection of a starting plan is based on the most efficient performance of media, media schedule, coupon type and schedule, and sample type and schedule subject to management constraints based on corporate policies and judgment. Management constraints may include rules like "no more than ten commercial spots a month in daytime television," "no more than one full page per monthly magazine per month"; or "no fewer than 80 total gross rating points per month during the campaign's last four months."

A Four-Stage Optimization Approach

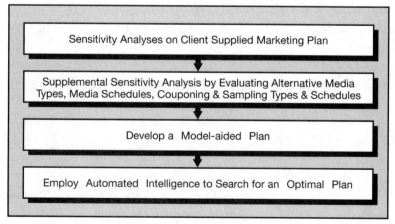

FIGURE 11.2.

The fourth stage is the formal optimization analysis that uses a hill-climbing procedure and manipulates four components in the marketing mix: advertising expenditures, coupon costs, sample costs, and distribution costs. The hill-climbing procedure is an adaptation of a standard mathematical algorithm in which the third stage defines the starting point. From the starting point, the model uses sensitivity analysis to determine the direction of most improvement in the marketing plan. After hundreds of small changes in the variables, and hundreds of runs, the model reaches the top of the hill—the optimal marketing plan.

Figure 11.3 depicts a view of a mathematical hill-climbing problem posed by optimization. Since the number of dimensions it can depict limits this figure, we assume for this example that the company has fixed sampling expenditures and distribution costs. Further, we assume that we want to optimize share with respect to a coupon and advertising budget. The goal is to search

Surface Mapping to Find an Optimal Plan

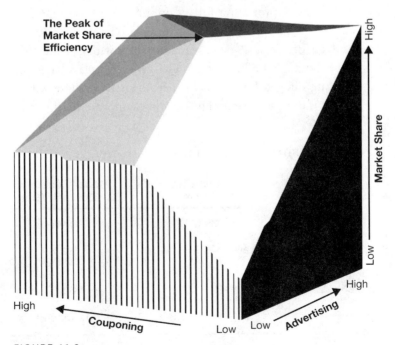

FIGURE 11.3.

along the two dimensions—advertising and couponing—seeking the maximum share point. The share values form a surface as the figure shows. The objective is to find the highest point on the surface.

CASE HISTORIES OF OPTIMIZATION AT WORK

To understand the benefits of optimization, we will examine two case histories, each a new food product. The first case shows the result of guiding the optimization procedure by minimizing cost based on a share goal constraint—a share optimization. In this case, management imposed no constraints on the optimization process.

The second case shows the result of maximizing share subject to a marketing budget constraint—a budget optimization. Although these examples show that optimization's benefits are great, the number of optimization applications remains small because they are time-consuming, costly, and because many marketers are unnerved by advanced technology.

A Share Optimization

Figure 11.4 shows a projection for an optimization case guided by cost minimization. The original manager-prepared plan, based on a $39 million marketing budget, forecast a 5.9 percent market share with an expected loss in the first year of about $20 million. The model-generated plan, based on a $28 million marketing budget, forecast a 7.2 percent market share with an expected profit of more than $1 million—a much more efficient marketing

Optimization Case for a New Beverage

	Manager-Prepared Plan	Model-Generated Optimal Plan
Cost of Plan	$39 Million	$28 Million
Forecasted Share of Market	5.9%	7.2%
Expected Gains/Losses (End of Year 1)	-20.5 Million	+1.6 Million
Pay Out Period	45 Months	12 Months

FIGURE 11.4.

plan. Instead of a first-year loss, the system projected the product to finish the year in the black, an unusual result for a new product.

Figure 11.5 indicates the ways in which the optimal marketing plan for a new food product differs from the manager-prepared plan. Neither plan allocates funds to samples. The model-generated plan allocates $1 million to distribution, which increases the average all commodity volume distribution in Year 1 to 78 percent, up from 65 percent in the manager-prepared plan.

The manager-generated advertising and coupon strategies are significantly different from the model-generated plans. The model pared advertising by $5 million; it recommended spending less on television and adding magazine advertising. Moreover, it increased the front-loading of the gross rating point pattern. With coupons, the model changed the pattern slightly and recommended spending 30 percent less than the manager's plan. The net result was a more efficient use of promotion dollars to achieve a slight share gain.

Constrained and Unconstrained Budget Optimization

The second optimization case is a budget optimization. In this case, the model produced two optimizations because management set media constraints, and we based one on these; the other had no constraints. Constraints limit the optimization procedure by eliminating marketing plans that could generate potentially higher sales. In this case, management chose to keep distribution expenditures constant and optimize media and consumer promotion expenditures.

Figure 11.6 shows the media constraints, the allocations in the constrained optimal plan, and the allocations in the unconstrained optimal plan. The constrained optimal allocation of gross rating points by the model is the management constraint for cable television and daytime television. However, the unconstrained optimal allocation of gross rating points by the model is above the management constraint for the relatively cost-efficient cable television and daytime television vehicles. Both the constrained and unconstrained optimal plans are under management's limit for gross rating points allocated to the first four months and for 15-second ads, which are relatively less cost-efficient media choices.

The budget optimization yielded significantly better results than the manager prepared plan. The constrained plan forecast a 14.8 percent sales increase over the manager-prepared plan's forecast; the unconstrained optimization forecast an 18.2 percent sales increase (figure 11.7).

Manager-Generated vs. Model-Generated Plan

	$27 Million Manager-Generated Plan	$19 Million Model-Generated Plan
Marketing Plan		
Media/Promotion	**$27.2MM**	**$19.0MM**
Advertising	13.9MM	8.8MM
Couponing	13.3MM	10.2MM
Distribution		1.0MM
Selected Plan Characteristics		
Advertising		
Media Types		
TV	Early Morning, Prime Day, Early/Late Fringe	Prime, Day, Early/Late Fringe
Magazines	None	*Good Housekeeping, Ladies Home Journal, Woman s Day*
Total GRPs	**3,778**	**3,021**
April	611	330
May	1,234	1,371
June	244	990
July	508	330
Aug	342	
Sept	242	
Oct	454	
Couponing		
Promotion Types	On Pack, FSI, Contact BFD	FSI, Contact wtih Fill-in, BFD (Newspaper)
Households Reached	**306%**	**283%**
April	56	47
May	71	67
June	35	53
July	48	62
Aug	48	27
January	48	
Sampling	None	None
Distribution	65% ACV April 72% Peak August 71% Off Season	78% ACV April Max 88% Aug/Sept Dropping to 84% Off Season

FIGURE 11.5.
*FSI stands for freestanding insert, the collection of coupons enclosed with a newspaper. BFD stands for best promotional advertising in the newspaper.

Media Constraints and Optimal Allocations

Parameter	Parameters for Management Constraints Optimization Maximum Allocation	Allocation Based on Constrained Optimization	Allocation Based on Unconstrained Optimization
GRPs Allocated to Months 1-4	69%	66%	55%
Broadcast GRPs Allocated to :15 Ads	43%	35%	30%
Broadcast GRPs to Daytime TV	35%	35%	45%
Percent of Total Dollar Spending Allocated to Cable TV	10%	10%	12%

FIGURE 11.6.

The allocation of dollars between advertising and consumer promotion is about the same in all three plans. Reallocating advertising vehicles for the constrained optimization increased the relative proportion of day, syndication, and cable GRPs; (figure 11.8). The optimal plan reduced early morning, prime, late fringe, and print's allocation of GRPs as a percentage of total GRPs.

The unconstrained optimal plan further increased the relative proportion of day, and cable gross rating points (figure 11.8). Moreover, the allocation of GRPs in late fringe was increased relative to the constrained plan, where fringe was excluded. This plan further reduced prime-time and print advertising, and cut the proportion of GRPs allocated to syndication as well.

USE STM TO BUILD THE BEST PLAN

The other way to improve the marketing plan is to take the simulated test marketing research's results and adjust weak elements of the marketing mix to

Baseline, Constrained, and Unconstrained Forecasts

	Baseline Forecast*	Constrained Optimization Forecast	Unconstrained Optimization Forecast
Total Expenditures	$10.3MM	$10.3MM	$10.3MM
Media Expenditures	7.4MM	7.4MM	7.4MM
Promotion Expenditures	2.9MM	2.9MM	2.9MM
GRPs	**1,687**	**1,901**	**2,066**
Awareness			
Year/Range	18 —38%	26 —41%	30 —43%
Average	32%	36%	38%
Penetration			
% Ever Tried at End of Year 1	10.0%	10.6%	10.7%
Volume			
Units (MM)	25.02	28.75	29.68
Cases (MM)	2.09	2.40	2.47
Percent Change			
In Cases from Baseline Forecast		14.8%	18.2%

*In 92% of cases, sales are within +/- 10% of forecasted levels.

FIGURE 11.7.

improve the product's chances for success. This is not optimization in its true, mathematical sense, but rather represents a common lay interpretation of the word. It means using the results of the simulated test market to help build the best possible plan, the objective of the work we described in chapter 7.

The following, based on an actual consulting project for a major multi-national client, illustrates that kind of optimization. We report this case in

Baseline and Optimal Marketing Plans
$7.4MM Media Spending

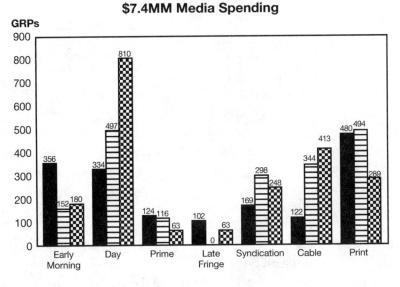

FIGURE 11.8.

considerable detail to show how new wrinkles in simulated test marketing can help improve a marketing plan.

The client corporation had developed a new product in a category that was still growing but in which the corporation did not currently have a product. The new product was a line extension; the corporation was taking its existing brand name into a different category of personal product.

The advertising agency developed four alternative television commercials, A, B, C, and D.

The corporation wanted to test six very different "premium" prices. For the research, we split the sample into separate price cells and each consumer interviewed saw only one price level.

Price Index
(relative to category average)

Price Cell 1	110
Price Cell 2	118
Price Cell 3	125
Price Cell 4	133
Price Cell 5	140
Price Cell 6	148

In other words, the product's price in Cell 1 was 10 percent higher than the average price in the category (average = 100), the price in Cell 2 was 18 percent higher, and so on.

The study's main objectives were to answer three questions:

1. How much was the new product's sales potential, and how did this vary by price and advertising execution?
2. How did the performance of each element in the marketing mix contribute to overall sales potential?
3. How could the corporation maximize the new marketing mix's potential?

The study was done among a random sample of women, the sample controlled for age and product category usage so that it represented the potential target audience. The sample contained about 60 percent product users. Because the parent corporation's distribution is greater than 95 percent, virtually all of the 40 percent nonusers were aware of the company's brand name.

During the field work, the researchers interviewed respondents concerning their current product usage habits and the brands with which they were familiar. Respondents watched one of the four ads for the new product in a clutter of competitive television commercials. They then had an opportunity to buy the new or competitive products with a voucher, and those who bought the new product were interviewed after they had used it in their homes.

What were the results?

Addressing the first question—how much?—we developed three sales forecasts: sales from advertising without sampling; sales with a sampling campaign without advertising; and sales with a combination of advertising and sampling. The best commercial (A) and best price (an 18 percent premium over the market average) with moderate advertising support (2,300 GRPs with commercial A²) and 76 percent distribution gave the following results:

Trial rate	17.5%
x	
Long term repeat	38.7%
= Sales potential (at full awareness and distribution)	6.8%
x	
Awareness	37.0%
x	
Distribution	76.0%
= Sales potential (at expected awareness and distribution)	1.9%

The best case involving a large sampling campaign—a 19 percent hit and use—with the same distribution gave the following results:

Hit and use	19.0%
x	
Distribution	76.0%
x	
First repeat after sampling	41.0%
x	
Nonoverlap with advertising	93.2%
= Additional penetration	5.5%
x	
Long-term repeat	38.7%
= Additional share from sampling	2.1%

The overall sales forecast (users and nonusers) under the best case scenario shows the following:

Users	
Share from advertising	1.9%
Share from sampling campaign	2.1%
Nonusers	
Share from advertising	0.4%
Share from sampling campaign	1.0%
Total share	5.4%

The best case, in other words, showed that the new product's total sales potential was only a 5.4 percent category share. Over half of all sales (3.1 percent) would come from the large sampling campaign. Around a quarter of this small sales volume was represented by current nonusers drawn into the category.

It is very rare for a new product to attract a significant number of new users into a product category. Most of the buyers of any new product are already buyers in the category. This finding is generally alarming to new product managers who expect their brands to not only take share away from existing brands, but to create new users at the same time. In our experience, 10 percent new users is a remarkably high figure, although marketers frequently make the unfortunate assumption that it can be dramatically higher. An exception to this rule is a breakthrough new product category where users don't come from existing brands because existing brands do not exist.

Take, for example, the new floor mop category that Procter & Gamble established when it introduced the Swiffer, "a long plastic stick attached to a swatch of cloth," in June 1999. There was nothing like it on the market and within three months the Swiffer had taken 25 percent of the mop and broom market. By the end of year, 72 competitive "wipe" products and accessories had appeared on the market. In mid-2000, Procter & Gamble responded with a jumbo-size Swiffer, and one that uses wet wipes in place of the original dry cloths. Today, supermarkets and discount stores have entire displays of Swiffer-style products, accessories, and competitors—a category that did not exist before 1999.

In the case of the new food product line extension, however, target category penetration was still growing, and the response among the research sample's nonusers showed that the new product would indeed gain significant volume by attracting new users.

In considering the second question—why the new product would obtain such a relatively small market share—consultants looked at several issues: product quality, advertising originality and relevance, advertising content, brand identification, trial rate, and price elasticity.

Product Quality

The new product's formulation was significantly better than consumers' usual products, showing well above "average" performance for a new brand. It obtained a new product usage score of 31 percent. This score equals the percentage of the sample who rated the product "better" or "much better" than their usual brand minus the percentage who ranked it "worse" or "much worse." This performance could be understood by its strong post-use image on two key perceptual dimensions of the market (numbers 1 and 3 in figure 11.9). Due to this good in-use performance, a sampling program was shown to be very efficient.

Advertising Performance Generally

Marketers often test two or three commercials and pick the one that performs best compared to each other and to the copy-testing firm's normative database. The marketer was somewhat unusual insofar as they tested four different commercials. It's worth noting, however, that comparing a commercial against a normative database is a serious mistake, despite the fact that companies do it all the time.

The average commercial aired in the real world is a failure. Its return on investment in late 2005 is 0 percent and sophisticated marketers know why. Relatively little advertising today provides buyers with a reason for preferring the advertised brand over competitors. Now, if the average aired commercial is a failure, and if the average aired commercial has tested better than the average of commercials in the copy-testing database, what does this say about the potential return on investment of ads in the database? They are disasters.

Therefore, comparing a new spot to a disaster and declaring it a winner ready for prime time invites new product failure. This argument aside, this is what we discovered for the four commercials tested here.

Price Index (Relative to Category Average)

Price Cell 1	110
Price Cell 2	118
Price Cell 3	125
Price Cell 4	133
Price Cell 5	140
Price Cell 6	148

FIGURE 11.9.

Advertising Originality and Relevance

The best performing television commercial projected average on originality (with an index of 115, i.e., 15 percent better than average) and slightly above average in relevance (103 index). The index is calculated relative to the category leader's advertising performance. Respondents rate the advertising's uniqueness and relevance on a seven-point scale. The other three commercials did not achieve above-average scores.

Advertising Content/Takeout

Consumers' content recall (the themes they could remember spontaneously after viewing the commercials) focused on an aspect shown to be of only minor importance (dimension number 6 in figure 11.9). Analysis of the market showed that this dimension explained only 8 percent of consumers' preference between brands. Given the strength of the product after use, our recommendation was to focus much less on this area and more where the product actually delivered better performance. These areas also corresponded to more important consumer needs (dimensions 1 and 3). Figure 11.9 shows respondent perceptions of the test product before and after use on the key dimensions consumers use to differentiate brands.

Brand Identification

The test product's second clear weakness related to its "stretch" from the parent category. The difficulty in establishing its own identity away from the parent brand was a weakness both in the advertising and in the packaging. Only half the respondents were able to identify the brand name correctly after viewing the commercials. The packaging obtained a low level of shelf identification compared to Discovery's standards.

Trial Rate

Even for the best advertisement, the average trial rate was a very low 17.5 percent at full awareness. This was much lower than the expected trial for the average new entrant into this category, which, based on the system's norms, would be 24.7 percent. These norms are grounded on 20 years of experience—over 4,000 STM projects—to show the expected trial and repeat levels for an average new entrant to the market.

Price Elasticity

It is not uncommon for the lowest price cell to correspond to the highest level of trial for a new product. All other factors held constant, consumer and industrial buyers are looking for the best deal. At the same time, however, price is often correlated with perceptions of quality, and, all other factors held constant, people also want the product with the highest level of perceived quality. For these reasons, it is dangerous to make assumptions about the relationship between any new product and alternative prices. If you want to know the effect of price, you have to test it! This calls for separate price cells, as were employed here.

The optimal price for the new product was in price cell 2. Above this cell (18 percent above the category average), trial for the new product fell off rapidly, as illustrated in figure 11.10. The change in repeat rate as the price increased was much less; the repeat declined from slightly under 40 percent in price cell 1 to just over 30 percent in price cell 6.

This research led us to make several recommendations to the client corporation's management to improve this new product's sales potential and profitability:

Improve Perceptions of the Product Before Trial

Eliminate the mismatch between the advertising communication and product reality. Focus on communicating the now-discovered strengths of the actual product, which are also more important to consumers than other features. Simulations showed that a trial increase of as much as 40 percent was possible if the pre-use perception of the product could be made to match that achieved post-use.

Improve Product Identification

This is a frequent weakness of brand extensions into different categories. We have, however, seen many cases in which companies overcame this weakness. In this case the specific areas to improve included packaging design, labeling, package shape, and better identification of the new brand name and product type in the advertising. Simulations showed that the product could achieve up to three extra market share points through these changes.

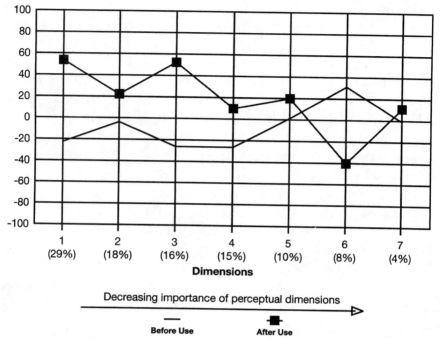

FIGURE 11.10.

Watch Price Elasticity

Researchers knew from their experience that the brand's inability to differentiate itself perceptually (that is, dominate a perceptual dimension pre-use) meant that price was relatively sensitive; without understanding the brand's value, customers were unwilling to pay a premium price. After customers used the product, however, the brand was in a very different situation. With its strong after-use performance, it was then far less price sensitive. If the corporation could successfully implement improvements, it could hope for a better trial price response.

Expand the Sampling Program

The effectiveness of any sampling program led us to simulate the effect of, and to recommend even higher, sampling levels than those the client had been considering.

The research concluded that while the new product had shown a strong in-use performance, its disappointing advertising did not support it. Elements of the packaging were also questionable. We warned the client about the vulnerability of such a brand to any changes in the competitive environment and recommended that rather than launch the product with the tested marketing program, the corporation improve the mix to increase the sales potential and to improve the "robustness" of the mix relative to competitive reaction.

The corporation did make several revisions to the marketing mix. These included two new television commercials (F and G) and revised packaging. We conducted a second study that included three price points, corresponding to Cells 2, 3, and 4 of the first study (indexes of 118, 125, and 133 relative to the average market price). The sample definition was the same, and the question flow was similar but without product placement.

The best case now included advertising F (the other spot did not present a significant improvement); a higher price level (price cell 3 with an index of 125); a large sampling campaign (39 percent hit and use); moderate advertising support (sampling was still more effective than increased advertising); and 76 percent distribution.

Under this scenario, the new product's sales potential rose to 8.1 percent at a higher price.

Why the improvement? The revised television commercial was more successful in conveying its message to consumers on the first key perceptual dimension of this market, although it did not manage to improve on the other dimensions.

Product identification, however, remained a weakness. The client managed to improve correct name recall and shelf visibility levels only marginally by package and advertising changes, but they were still below standard for a new brand. This is a common problem with line extensions of this type, and the client had not found a full solution.

The trial rate improved 26.5 percent in price cell 3 (a 25 percent premium). The previous trial rate in this cell had been 14.6 percent. The new rate was better than the average successful new product introduction in the category—24.7 percent.

Trial response to price improved, and the brand now supported a premium of up to 25 percent. Sales predictions for the three price cells (under the same assumptions as previous) became 8.4 percent for price 2 (an 18 percent premium); 8.1 percent for price 3 (25 percent premium); and 6.3 percent (33 percent premium).

Considering the third question—how to maximize the marketing mix—STM consultants knew from the first study that the product's high quality justified the use of sampling to increase penetration. The forecast showed even greater sales by doubling the sampling levels:

	19 percent hit and use	38 percent hit and use
Price 2	8.4%	11.9%
Price 3	8.1%	11.3%
Price 4	6.3%	9.5%

It would be very difficult, however, to reach 38 percent of the population with a sampling program effectively.

The new product now represented a very strong opportunity for the client. With high sampling levels, the client could anticipate an 8 to 11 percent share of category volume. One of the two new ads was significantly better than all others and offered the most robust mix and lowest price elasticity. The new mix would now support a price premium of 25 percent over the market average. The new brand's identification in both the advertising and the packaging still needed improvement, and the consultant made some suggestions to help both. And finally, the client could obtain very strong brand leverage from an efficient sampling program.

The client launched the product nationally shortly after the second study. Sales tracked very closely to the study's predictions. Shortly after the launch, a competitor introduced a similar product, but because the test product had been "optimized," the new entry did not affect its sales and the competitor was not a success.

MANAGEMENT IMPLICATIONS

This chapter discussed the benefits of an optimization approach to marketing planning. Using new and evolving tools like those discussed here and chapter 7, marketers are learning that simulated test marketing firms can go far beyond conventional volume forecasts to help improve marketing plans significantly.

This chapter reported two different approaches the industry uses to accomplish this end. The first is the type of formal, mathematical optimization modeling developed by Blackburn and Clancy and published in academic journals beginning in the mid-1980s. The second is the less technical but valuable approaches of the more sophisticated STM modeling organizations today. Both approaches show the marketing manager how best to allocate a marketing budget based on the market response the product generates and on the cost and effectiveness of the marketing vehicles available to launch the product.

We have found over and over that applying optimization modeling leads to forecast increases in profitability ranging from 20 percent to 400 percent over manager-prepared plans. It can also mean the difference between a successful new product launch and a likely failure. The edge that optimization provides a marketing manager varies by case. Also, as marketing managers use the system and learn from the optimization results, the system's superiority over manager-prepared plans declines.

Optimization's margin of superiority over the first plan submitted by a marketing manager has averaged 25 percent. In one application for a new food product, a case presented and discussed at two different management science conferences, optimization identified a $19-million marketing plan that performed slightly better in terms of market share than the product manager's $27-million plan and overwhelmed the manager's plan in terms of forecast profitability.

We have found that marketing managers and their advertising agencies usually concur with the optimization recommendations after they have had time to discuss, debate, and digest them. Sometimes this digestion process becomes charged with tension, even acrimony. In one case involving one of the country's largest advertising agencies, the optimization procedure recommended *against* the agency's spot television plan as part of a new product launch. The agency's reaction was a declaration of war. Diplomacy, however, averted actual combat.

The diplomatic efforts showed there was no difference between spot and nonspot markets in terms of advertising response as measured by the STM research. Moreover, while product usage was 30 percent greater in spot markets than in nonspot markets, spot television costs 40 percent more per GRP. The optimization sensibly recommended against the spot schedule and, in time, the agency not only concurred but happily adopted our discoveries.

NOTES

1. Nancy Einhart, "Clean Sweep of the Market," *Business 2.0*, March 2003, 56.

2. Simulations showed that a large sampling campaign was more effective than high advertising expenditure.

12

From the Back of an Envelope to a Marketing Navigation Station

Earlier in this book we talked about the back-of-the-envelope forecasting tools. Marketing consultants used these tools widely in the late 1960s and early 1970s, and, in some cases, they use them today. In fact, prior to running the Discovery model in a simulated test marketing engagement, the authors routinely use a back-of-the-envelope approach to estimate roughly where a forecast is likely to come out.

After all, if experienced marketing scientists know how much money a company is spending on advertising, they can estimate the level of media exposure (usually measured in terms of gross rating points, or GRPs) the budget can purchase. If they know the GRPs for a given time period, say, a year, they can estimate approximate consumer awareness level for a new product or service at the end of the year.

If they know the awareness level and if, through concept testing, they know what percentage of the prospects exposed to the concept are likely to buy it, and if they temper those numbers with an understanding of the relationship between self-reports and actual behavior, they can then estimate trial (that is, first purchase) assuming the product was distributed everywhere.

Once they have a ballpark figure for trial, they can take an estimate of ACNielsen's all commodity volume distribution at the end of the year (the percentage of total product category sales in those stores in which the product is distributed) and approximate trial in terms of units. They do this by simply multiplying the trial score by the distribution percentage.

If they then go on to estimate repeat purchase (the percentage of customers who will buy the product two or more times) and how frequently these repeaters buy products in the category and how much they buy on each purchase occasion, they can roughly estimate share of units. If they know the new product's price relative to other prices in the category, they can estimate share of market in dollars.

In short, an experienced marketing scientist, simply by using the back of an envelope, may say, "I forecast that the market share for this product in dollars will be about a five" and be in the ballpark much of the time. Clearly a simulated test market (STM) model can do much better than that; it will tell you that the dollar share will be exactly 3.2 percent or 7.5 percent, and that is what a manager really wants to know.

But on the other hand, sometimes a back-of-the-envelope modeler will sit in a meeting where people are presenting forecast results, and, before the forecast numbers are put up, will say, "Based on what you've told us, it is going to be a five." When the number comes in anywhere around the five, the others look as if the modeler were clairvoyant.

If back-of-the-envelope forecasting was cutting edge in the late 1960s, and sophisticated STM models are cutting edge today, what's next?

What we like to call "marketing instrument panels" or "navigational stations." Or, as our friend Randy Stone, CEO of MMA (Marketing Management Analytics)—our nation's premier consulting firm dedicated to teasing return-on-investment (ROI) insights out of sophisticated econometric analyses of large databases that capture both marketing investment inputs (such as advertising expenditures) and outputs (including sales, market share, and profitability)—likes to call it, "a marketing dashboard."

HOW TO VISUALIZE A MARKETING INSTRUMENT PANEL

To imagine what a marketing instrument panel might be like, think of sitting in the pilot's seat of, say, a Cessna Skyhawk, a single-engine aircraft with a view such as the one in figure 12.1.

You have a throttle to control the engine speed and therefore the propeller's rpms. You have a yoke to control elevators and ailerons, which controls how fast you climb, descend, and bank. You have rudder pedals to change the airplane's direction in level flight. These are your inputs.

On the instrument panel you have, among other dials, an rpm readout, a rate-of-climb indicator, an altimeter (how high you are above sea level), air

A Cessna Skyhawk Instrument Panel

FIGURE 12.1.

speed and ground speed displays, a turn/bank indicator (shows when you're flying straight and level), a compass, and a fuel gauge. These translate your inputs into information about the aircraft's performance.

For example, move the throttle forward, the rpms increase, release the brakes, and the ground speed begins to increase. When your ground speed is high enough, pull back on the yoke and the rate-of-climb needle and altimeter show how fast you are climbing and your altitude. Turn the yoke and the plane begins to bank. Ease back on the throttle and the number of rpms drops. Ease back enough and the rate-of-climb needle drops into the "descend" side of the dial.

The point is that the pilot, by changing the inputs, changes the aircraft's course and the instrument panel allows the pilot to see these changes. This is particularly critical at night over water and in overcast weather. Once in the air, the pilot may not be able to see the ground or the horizon and therefore have no visual reference on which to depend. She will have to rely on her instruments to tell her how fast she is going, how high she is, where she is headed, and how much fuel she has left to get there.

Wouldn't it be valuable if brand managers had analogous tools on their desk PCs? Wouldn't it be great if every brand manager had her own navigational station? They already have a budget (fuel) and a number of inputs they can control: advertising, couponing, sampling, distribution, direct marketing, public relations, pricing, and more.

What they need are a number of gauges that indicate how the brand is doing in the marketplace: absolute sales (units and dollars), share of market (units and dollars), sales by type of store (mass marketer, supermarket, convenience), and sales by time period (last week, last month, month-by-month, by quarter, etc.). What if the manager had gauges to show, virtually minute by minute, the changes the inputs have on these outputs?

It would be like taking off in a plane: launch the brand with heavy spending on advertising and promotion and watch the sales figure gauge change. Throttle back on the advertising and watch sales level off. Increase couponing and sampling and sales resume their climb.

Of course, the analogy is not perfect. Increase throttle in a Cessna and the propeller's rpms increase immediately; push the yoke forward and the plane begins to descend at once. The brand manager does not have such immediate, real-time control. Increase ad spending and it *may* take a month or more for the advertising to appear in the marketplace, although with large media buying companies such as our own parent Carat, this time lag is growing shorter over time. It may take another month before any effect can be seen, although more and more research has begun to indicate that the effects of advertising and other marketing mix components are more immediate than advertising practitioners previously thought, particularly in fast-turnover product categories.

Nevertheless, the goal is to give brand managers the tools to "fly" their brands higher and safer than they can do today.

THE NEED TO KNOW WHAT IS HAPPENING

What we have today is, at best, a series of snapshots. The company commissions an STM study and provides all the marketing input information we've described earlier. In time, the research company returns a month-by-month forecast of how the new or restaged product or service will perform in the real world—assuming the company spends the advertising dollars it said it will spend, obtains the distribution it says it will obtain, and holds all the other variables constant. The report may have sensitivity analyses and it may tell the company something about targeting and positioning.

Currently, many firms are using an alternative approach for established consumer products—marketing mix modeling. Such modeling became popular in the 1990s in package goods companies, but firms in many industries are beginning to investigate or to employ its capabilities. Package goods giants such as Procter & Gamble and Kraft are on board with the technology, but so are sophisticated marketers in other industries, including RadioShack, Nissan, and Gillette.

A marketing mix analysis starts with detailed data on a company's marketing investments, typically on a weekly or monthly basis. This goes down to how many 30-second spots the firm purchased on "Cold Case Files" in the first week in March, the gross rating points achieved by this buy, and the cost. The analysis enters sales data in units and dollars for the same time period(s). The company then runs time series regression analyses to relate investments and GRPs with dollar sales to calculate estimates of ROI. Companies customarily run these by brand and by individual media type within brands (for example, the ROI of 30-second television spots versus full-page ads in news magazines for Kraft's Cheez Whiz or for the Nissan Maxima.)

But suppose the manager wants to change the ad budget or ad copy, or the promotion budget, or the product's price, or the distribution channels. The research company can do another STM or marketing mix analysis and run another report. But the output remains a series of snapshots, usually depicting what happened in the past. In the case of an STM, it's a snapshot of what's happened when the study was done four to six weeks ago. In the case of marketing mix analysis, it's a snapshot of what happened last year. Moreover, STM reports are predictions of what will happen in the market while marketing mix analysis is history (i.e., again, what happened as long as a year ago); they are not reports of what is happening in real time—current spending and current sales. Wouldn't the following (hypothetical) situation be dramatically more useful?

Midway through the sales year, you pull the product's current monthly unit sales up on the computer screen: 310,000 cases—a market share of 4.2 percent of units. A few keystrokes and you pull up the current monthly dollar sales figure, $12.4 million—a dollar share of 4.8 because the product is priced at a premium relative to competitive items. A few more keystrokes and you can tell how you're doing in mass merchandisers, in supermarkets, in convenience stores.

You have at your fingertips, not only these results in absolute terms, but also a trend line generated by an econometric model built into the software driving the workstation. It shows sales are leveling off in mass merchandisers, but continuing to grow in convenience stores.

What about seasonality? How do the sales this week/month/quarter compare to sales last week/month/quarter? And how do they compare to the same week/month/quarter a year ago? In a flash the answers to all these questions appear on the screen.

You now pull up another screen showing marketing investments: a $27 million advertising budget, a $14.3 million promotion budget, and a $7.6 million sports sponsorship budget. You are halfway through the year, how much money do you have left? The screen says you've spent 66.2 percent of the advertising budget; you have 33.8 remaining or $9.1 million. It is like saying your fuel tank is a third full; how far will it carry you?

In real time, you can take another nonlinear regression analysis of the relationship between advertising and any sales result you care to look at: units, dollars, distribution channel, time period, whatever. The analysis shows a sales curve that suggests incremental spending is probably not going to add much more lift. In fact, it might make more sense to spend less money on a week-to-week basis.

On the other hand, when you look at your promotion spending and sales, there's almost a direct relationship. Perhaps it makes sense to increase that spending. How about sports sponsorship? You have $2.1 million left in the budget, but sports sponsorships have had virtually no effect on sales. Stop that spending entirely. What about the Internet, public relations, direct marketing?

The idea is to put on the screen all the information a brand manager would like to have, including spending data and current sales, and a tool that connects one to the other and suggests what will happen if the manager makes changes. What if you increase advertising by 10 percent, 20 percent, 30 percent? What if you decrease promotional spending by 10 percent, 20 percent, 30 percent? The model would automatically do a forecast based on current performance.

This instrument panel provides the brand manager with everything she needs to know to make better decisions. But what if she doesn't want to make a decision? What if she wants her automated brand manager program to make the decisions for her? What if she wants to put her aircraft on automatic pilot?

Instrument panels of the future will have this capability. Just as it was inconceivable 20 years ago that electronic technology embedded in automobiles would be making recommendations to a driver as to where to turn next to find a McDonald's in a strange town, instrument panels of the quickly evolving future will be driven by the kind of optimization routines we discussed in the last chapter.

BEYOND MARKETING TACTICS TOWARD MARKETING STRATEGY

The instrument panels (also known as dashboards or navigation stations) currently being developed are focused on the manipulation of the inputs in order to help improve brand performance—everything we talked about in the preceding section.

Instrument panels currently at the conceptual stage at Copernicus and MMA, however, go well beyond questions about the relationship between marketing investment inputs, sales outputs, and ROI. Although these analyses are indispensable to developing a great program, only when a marketer can have at her touch-screen insights into the ROI of alternative strategic decisions will the Cessna become a Learjet.

Consider for a moment a dial which provides a readout of alternative market targets for a package good. The pointers reflect all Americans, all adult Americans, 18-to-54-year-old women, 25-to-49-year-old women, heavy buyers, nonusers of the category, teenagers, and, very importantly, a target group identified through sophisticated modeling to be financially optimal.

Consider further that this brand manager, like most package goods brand managers, has targeted her company's marketing efforts against 25-to-49-year-old women. Then all the analyses reported earlier assume this target group. But what if all men and women were the target? Or heavy users? If that were the strategy, what would the ROI be? And what about a financially optimal target? What would happen if our brand manager addressed her efforts to impacting that group?

Today there are relatively few brand managers in America who can answer that question and they're probably all working at companies that are exclusively wedded to direct marketing, through the mail, the Web, and the telephone. None of them can be found at the package goods companies that have pioneered the development of STM and marketing mix modeling technology. It's as if the package goods managers have been content to ride the

Canadian Pacific while their peers in other industries are building Cessnas and more.

Everything we've said with respect to targeting holds for positioning, the second most important component in the marketing strategy mix. Positioning, as we've said, represents the message we want to imprint in our target's head about our brand and why our brand is different and better. Yet, as we talked about earlier, today the average brand in the average product category is becoming a commodity—it has no positioning. Imagine another dial on your instrument panel that depicts the relative strength of the new product positioning compared to world-class standards. Is the positioning about average, meaning that for all practical purposes we have no positioning at all? Is it one sigma or two sigmas above average? Three?

What about six sigmas above average, which is the goal at many manufacturing companies today? Clearly, where you are on the positioning dial, just as where you are on the targeting dial, can and will have a dramatic affect on your brand's performance.

Everything said here about targeting and positioning applies to every strategic decision that a brand manager has to make: ad copy and execution, pricing, the Internet, public relations, direct marketing, outdoor, sports and event sponsorships—everything. We talked earlier about managers who typically choose ad copy and execution based on its performance relative to copy-testing norms. But as we pointed out, those norms can be dangerous to your brand. An instrument panel, consequently, that includes a dial that enables you to assess the effects of a six sigma copy or pricing or public relations strategy relative to current practice would be invaluable. As an aside, the cost may be more expensive than the benefit involved in developing a six sigma strategy, but that's to be determined.

THE DEVELOPMENT OF EXPERT SYSTEMS

The marketing instrument panels we've been describing will be based in part on highly sophisticated marketing mix and simulated test marketing models, sophisticated marketing research, and evolving expert system technology. Expert systems are computer programs that either recommend a course of action or make decisions based on knowledge gathered from experts in the field. Expert systems, which barely existed in 1985, are now being employed in agriculture, business, chemistry, communications, computers, education, elec-

tronics, engineering, environment, geology, image, information, law, manufacturing, mathematics, medicine, meteorology, military, science, and space.

Over the past three decades simulated test marketing and marketing mix
modeling technology have evolved from reliable and valid sales volume forecasting tools into a collection of processes that provide targeting and positioning guidance, cannibalization analysis, marketing plan diagnostics,
competitive response analysis, and even optimal marketing plans. Marketing
plan optimization is at the forefront of existing marketing intelligence, the
edge that leads to the kind of marketing instrument panel we've been describing.

Although simulated test marketing technology offers marketing managers
the tools they require to launch successful new products and new campaigns,
most fail to use the available tools to their full potential—one reason why
most new products do not achieve the company's sales and profit objectives
and why 9 out of 10 attempts to relaunch, restage, or turn around dying products and services fail to reverse share declines.

New developments, however, are pushing back marketing's frontiers, and
the development of expert systems are among the most important. This technology offers the promise of a transition to "expert managers," executives who
will pilot their brands to exceptional marketing programs. Because even if a
brand manager today had the kind of marketing instrument panel we've been
describing, it would still require human judgment and experience to use properly. Consider the following, not uncommon, situation.

Procter & Gamble was introducing Crest toothpaste line extensions, and in
response, Colgate increased its advertising to counter the move. Six months
later, Colgate's ad spending was up relative to both the budget and year earlier
figures, while sales were down. But sales were not down because the advertising was bad. Most likely its sales would have been much worse had Colgate not
increased the advertising.

In the analogous situation, you are in your Cessna and notice that your
ground speed is dropping while your air speed remains the same. Headwinds
are picking up. You can increase engine speed to compensate and burn more
fuel, try to find an altitude where the winds are not as strong, or resign yourself
to a longer trip with an unexpected fuel stop. The pilot must still fly the plane.

To imagine how an expert system works, think of how a skilled mechanic
makes a diagnosis of a car's problem. He asks questions to establish symptoms,

history, and indications: What kind of noise? When did it start? Do you hear it only on cold mornings? On the basis of experience, the mechanic runs the tests that seem indicated. He applies his accumulated expertise selectively and by trial-and-error, testing for one thing, then another to rule out possibilities. He may consult with other mechanics or refer to repair manuals to learn more. Out of all this comes a diagnosis.

Skilled mechanics at sophisticated dealerships and repair shops today employ electronic tools that did not exist a decade ago to help make this diagnosis even more reliable. Today the mechanic can plug the shop's computer into an outlet in the car to learn that a problem is with the third cylinder.

Expert systems typically follow a similar process. They capture knowledge in symbolic form, with numeric values reflecting the subjective probability of the information's likelihood, or its truthfulness. The expert system's general reasoning strategy (the so-called inference engine) is separate from the domain-specific trial-and-error attempts, models, and facts (the so-called knowledge base). The domain-specific knowledge includes some combination of facts—in a marketing system these might be something like, "All new product introductions must pay out within 36 months" or "Every introduction requires at minimum a level of 80 percent Nielsen ACV distribution."

This separation between inference and knowledge allows the system to use knowledge in a variety of ways. It can select particular elements in the knowledge base and request additional information to solve a specific problem. An expert system can explain the reasoning behind its questions and recommendations by reporting the trials it has attempted and the facts it used to investigate hypotheses and to draw conclusions.

Expert systems will, we believe, lead to expert marketing managers, managers who will design and manage exceptional marketing programs. The kind of marketing instrument panel we just described would be based on an expert system.

A whole new class of "knowledge engineers" captures the expert's knowledge—the skilled mechanic or experienced marketing executive. The knowledge engineer's contribution is to create a computer program that reflects the knowledge, experience, rules of thumb, insights, heuristics, and judgments of a particular field's experts.

A good expert system thinks through a problem or question—given the available intelligent program, expert knowledge, and data base—to arrive at a solution, an answer, or a decision. In an expert system, as in real life, the higher the intelligence of the program or person, the greater the expert's knowledge, and the more sophisticated the databases, the better the solution, answer, or decision.

Such a system can use automated intelligence to follow complex orders. They do what they're told to do. They manipulate words and numerical characters, using algorithms and equations written in mathematical languages.

Computerized marketing decision support systems (MDSS) are outgrowths of corporate sales databases. The technology matches near real-time sales tracking information, which means that marketing executives obtain sales data almost as fast as sales occur, with sophisticated market modeling. The complaint of many practitioners struggling to implement a MDSS is that they are drowning in data and have no information—which is why some companies have created expert systems on top of the MDSS systems. These can absorb the huge data stream pouring into corporate databases, winnow through the flood to find the critical trends and advertising sales effects, and emerge with recommendations for action.

Tools now exist, some in the form of expert systems, that vary considerably in terms of sophistication. A device that simply takes a load of data and analyzes it to ferret out the key findings is a very primitive version of automated intelligence technology. But the fact that a technology may be primitive does not make it uninteresting or useless. Something may be very useful without requiring a great deal of technological polish.

Consider the programs that have become increasingly widespread for scoring standardized tests that our children take in school or personality tests that many organizations employ as part of human resources development initiatives. Not only are these tests electronically scored, but individualized, personalized reports are written based on the patterns of response in the tests. Consider as another example the talking GPS systems now available in automobiles. Now wives can say, "Jeez, Wally, you didn't want to read the map or listen to me, but would you please pay attention to the damn machine? It's telling you to turn on your blinker and make a right at the next intersection."

The most advanced of these programs incorporates the best thinking of inspired analysts with the tireless patience of the computer. In the future, these systems will use sophisticated modeling and decision rules to identify marketplace opportunities, such as local competitive vulnerabilities, long-term share-gain opportunities, and optimal price/deal tactics.

We do not think the computer can ever become a "marketing department in a box." The world, human beings, and reality will remain too complex. We do believe, however, that an expert manager, like an experienced pilot, aided by a sophisticated marketing instrument panel will be a formidable competitor. Companies that adopt this emerging technology early will enjoy an edge over competition, an edge that will be difficult to overcome. Perhaps total product failure rates, on average, will remain the same. But they will certainly decline for the firms employing expert managers and systems, as they will increase for the companies that do not.

The previous chapters showed that STM technology has been evolving. A smart optimization system (chapter 11) combines expert judgments, proprietary databases, and automated intelligence algorithms to search through billions of possible marketing plans to find the one plan forecast to be the most profitable.

This new expert system would automatically undertake the targeting, positioning, pricing, sensitivity, and other analyses we discussed in chapters 7 and 11 to make sophisticated recommendations for improving the product and its marketing program. Conceivably, the output from such a program would be reengineered recommendations to the white coats in the R&D labs and detailed marketing recommendations for communications and promotional planners, packaging and sales managers, and everyone else responsible for making key decisions for the new product.

MANAGEMENT IMPLICATIONS

The purpose of this chapter was to describe the marketing instrument panels—the nav stations—of the future and the expert systems on which they are based. Expert systems, as we have described them, represent the integration of marketing databases, the judgments of marketing experts, the results of high-powered marketing mix and STM modeling analyses, and automated or artificial intelligence programs—the result of which is a tool like an instrument panel designed to make the manager's work easier. Today primitive versions of this rapidly evolving technology write research reports, help an interviewer work her way through a difficult questionnaire, and help design new products and more effective advertising.

In the years ahead, expert systems will be developed to address every marketing problem from targeting and positioning to media selection and scheduling to distribution and pricing.

From our standpoint, the most exciting application of expert systems will occur when they are designed to help marketers not only create more effective marketing plans but manage their brands on a real time basis. When this happens, it is hard to imagine that simulated test marketing of new and restaged products and services and marketing mix analyses will not play a major role. Earlier chapters have described the tools that STM systems currently offer for improving—if not optimizing—a marketing plan.

When these tools are integrated with the thinking of marketing experts and intelligent programming algorithms highlighted in this chapter and put on the desktop for marketing managers to employ, marketing will have reached a new era of efficiency. Flying a brand with simply a control stick, rudder pedals, and a compass will have been replaced with the instrumentation and controls akin to those of a modern aircraft, enabling the brand manager to fly her brand faster, higher, and more safely.

Technical Appendix

The following is designed to supplement chapter 5, "Mathematical Modeling Marries STM." It includes some of the assumptions and the formulas the Discovery system uses in making awareness and sales forecasts.

ESTIMATING AWARENESS

Assume exposure to the product by advertising or through couponing or sampling or distribution to be independent effects. We define the following probabilities:

$P_A(t)$ = unconditional probability of awareness due to advertising in time period t

$P_C(t)$ = unconditional probability of awareness due to couponing in time period t

$P_S(t)$ = unconditional probability of awareness due to sampling in time period t

$P_D(t)$ = unconditional probability of awareness due to distribution in time period t

In early versions of Litmus, the model used a simple exponential relationship between advertising gross rating points and brand awareness patterned after the function used in the News system:

$$P_A(t) = 1 - e^{\alpha GRP(t)}$$

The components of the awareness function are defined as

$P_A(t)$ = probability of advertising awareness generated in period t;

$GRP(t)$ = gross rating points, period t; and

α = a parameter to be estimated.

Including the media schedule, media impact, share of voice, and advertising impact significantly improved the system's awareness forecasting power, so the advertising awareness sub model was revised to include them. The relationship the system now uses to forecast advertising awareness is

$$P_A = 1 - \exp[\alpha\Sigma_i(\beta_i\gamma_i GRP_i(t))]$$

where

$GRP_i(t)$ = gross rating points in media type i, period t;

α = a parameter to be estimated;

β_i = attention-getting power of media type i , the norm = 1;

γ_i = w_i (attention-getting power of advertising) + (1-w_i) (sov) where $0 < w_i < 1$;

sov (share of voice) = test brand advertising spending in dollars divided by average category spending times 1.5.

SIXTEEN AWARENESS STATES

In Month 1, 16 awareness states result from the possible combinations of advertising, couponing, sampling, and distribution. These include advertising alone, advertising plus couponing, advertising plus sampling, and so on. (see figure 5.5, page 133, and the accompanying discussion). By Month 2, the number of possible awareness states has increased to 256. By Month 3, the number of possible awareness states has increased to 4,096 (16 x 16 x 16).

Determine the probability that a consumer is in a particular awareness category in Month 1 from the unconditional probabilities of awareness due to

Advertising, $P_A(t)$;

Couponing, $P_C(t)$;

Sampling, $P_S(t)$; and

Distribution, $P_D(t)$.

Using these unconditional probabilities and assuming independence, the probability of advertising awareness only is
$$P_1(t) = P_A(t) - P_5(t) - P_6(t) - P_{10}(t) - P_{11}(t) - P_{12}(t) - P_{13}(t) - P_{15}(t).$$
The probability of couponing awareness only is
$$P_2(t) = P_C(t) - P_5(t) - P_7(t) - P_9(t) - P_{11}(t) - P_{12}(t) - P_{14}(t) - P_{15}(t).$$
The probability of sampling awareness only is
$$P_3(t) = P_S(t) - P_6(t) - P_7(t) - P_8(t) - P_{11}(t) - P_{13}(t) - P_{14}(t) - P_{15}(t).$$
The probability of distribution awareness only is
$$P_4(t) = P_D(t) - P_8(t) - P_9(t) - P_{10}(t) - P_{12}(t) - P_{13}(t) - P_{14}(t) - P_{15}(t).$$
The joint probability of couponing and advertising awareness is
$$P_5(t) = P_C(t){}^*P_A(t){}^*(1 - P_{12}(t)){}^*(1 - P_{11}(t)).$$
The joint probability of sampling and advertising awareness is
$$P_6(t) = P_S(t){}^*P_A(t){}^*(1 - P_{11}(t)){}^*(1 - P_{13}(t)).$$
The joint probability of couponing and sampling awareness is
$$P_7(t) = P_C(t){}^*P_S(t){}^*(1 - P_{14}(t)){}^*(1 - P_{11}(t)).$$
The joint probability of sampling and distribution awareness is
$$P_8(t) = P_S(t){}^*P_D(t){}^*(1 - P_{14}(t)){}^*(1 - P_{13}(t)).$$
The joint probability of couponing and distribution awareness is
$$P_9(t) = P_C(t){}^*P_D(t){}^*(1 - P_{14}(t)){}^*(1 - P_{12}(t)).$$
The joint probability of advertising and distribution awareness is
$$P_{10}(t) = P_A(t){}^*P_D(t){}^*(1 - P_{13}(t)){}^*(1 - P_{12}(t)).$$
The joint probability of advertising, couponing, and sampling awareness is
$$P_{11}(t) = P_A(t){}^*P_C(t){}^*P_S(t){}^*(1 - P_D(t)).$$
The joint probability of advertising, couponing, and distribution awareness is
$$P_{12}(t) = P_A(t){}^*P_C(t){}^*P_D(t){}^*(1 - P_S(t)).$$
The joint probability of advertising, sampling, and distribution awareness is
$$P_{13}(t) = P_A(t){}^*P_S(t){}^*P_D(t){}^*(1 - P_C(t)).$$
The joint probability of couponing, sampling, and distribution awareness is
$$P_{14}(t) = P_C(t){}^*P_S(t){}^*P_D(t){}^*(1 - P_A(t)).$$

The joint probability of advertising, couponing, sampling, and distribution awareness is

$$P_{15}(t) = P_A(t)^*P_C(t)^*P_S(t)^*P_D(t).$$

In addition to the awareness probabilities defined, the probability of not being exposed in the current period is $P_{16}(t)$.

The probability of forgotten awareness is $P_{17}(t)$.

NEW AWARENESS

For each of the fifteen states in which the prospect is aware (in $P_{16}[t]$ the prospect is unaware; in $P_{17}[t]$ the prospect is no longer aware), the fraction of people who are newly aware in the current purchase period, $A_i(1)$, where $i = 1 \ldots, 15$, is the product of the unaware fraction in time period t, m, and the probability of new awareness in category i, $P_i(t)$:

$$A_i(1) = P_i(t)^* \mu(t).$$

To update the unaware fraction at the beginning of the next purchase period:

$$\mu(t+1) = \mu(t)(1-\sum_{i=1}^{15} P_i(t))$$

That is, reduce the pool of consumers who are unaware of the product by the fraction of those who become aware of it during period t.

TRIAL PROBABILITY OF NEW PEOPLE AWARE OF THE PRODUCT

Newly aware consumers have a trial probability τ_i where i denotes the consumer's particular awareness state:

τ_1 = awareness-to-trial due to advertising, or probability of trial given awareness due to advertising alone;

τ_2 = awareness-to-trial due to couponing, or probability of trial given couponing awareness alone;

τ_3 = awareness-to-trial due to sampling, or probability of trial given sampling awareness alone;

τ_4 = awareness-to-trial due to distribution, or the probability of trial given distribution awareness alone.

The probability of trial given advertising and couponing awareness is

$$\tau_5 = \tau_1 + \tau_2 - (\tau_1^*\tau_2).$$

The probability of trial given advertising and sampling awareness is
$$\tau_6 = \tau_1 + \tau_3 - (\tau_1 * \tau_3).$$
The probability of trial given sampling and couponing awareness is
$$\tau_7 = \tau_2 + \tau_3 - (\tau_2 * \tau_3).$$
The probability of trial given distribution and sampling awareness is
$$\tau_8 = \tau_3 + \tau_4 - (\tau_3 * \tau_4).$$
The probability of trial given distribution and couponing awareness is
$$\tau_9 = \tau_2 + \tau_4 - (\tau_2 * \tau_4).$$
The probability of trial given distribution and advertising awareness is
$$\tau_{10} = \tau_1 + \tau_4 - (\tau_1 * \tau_4).$$
The probability of trial given advertising, couponing, and sampling awareness is
$$\tau_{11} = \tau_1 + \tau_2 + \tau_3 - (\tau_1 * \tau_2) - (\tau_1 * \tau_3) - (\tau_2 * \tau_3) + (\tau_1 * \tau_2 * \tau_3).$$
The probability of trial given advertising, couponing, and distribution awareness is
$$\tau_{12} = \tau_1 + \tau_2 + \tau_4 - (\tau_1 * \tau_2) - (\tau_1 * \tau_4) - (\tau_2 * \tau_4) + (\tau_1 * \tau_2 * \tau_4).$$
The probability of trial given advertising, distribution, and sampling awareness is
$$\tau_{13} = \tau_1 + \tau_3 + \tau_4 - (\tau_1 * \tau_3) - (\tau_1 * \tau_4) - (\tau_3 * \tau_4) + (\tau_1 * \tau_3 * \tau_4).$$
The probability of trial given distribution, couponing, and sampling awareness is
$$\tau_{14} = \tau_2 + \tau_3 + \tau_4 - (\tau_2 * \tau_3) - (\tau_2 * \tau_4) - (\tau_3 * \tau_4) + (\tau_2 * \tau_3 * \tau_4).$$
The probability of trial given advertising, couponing, sampling, and distribution awareness is
$$\tau_{15} = \tau_1 + \tau_2 + \tau_3 + \tau_4 - (\tau_1 * \tau_2) - (\tau_1 * \tau_3) - (\tau_1 * \tau_4) - (\tau_2 * \tau_3)$$
$$- (\tau_2 * \tau_4) - (\tau_3 * \tau_4) + (\tau_1 * \tau_2 * \tau_3) + (\tau_1 * \tau_2 * \tau_4) + (\tau_1 * \tau_3 * \tau_4)$$
$$+ (\tau_2 * \tau_3 * \tau_4) + (\tau_1 * \tau_2 * \tau_3 * \tau_4).$$

These estimates of trial probability assume that the joint effects of different awareness forms act independently. For example, in the expression for τ_6, if the prospect is aware of the product because of the advertising and having received a sample, the model assumes trial to occur as a result of one of these two effects.

Let event A denote trial due to advertising awareness and event S denote trial due to sample awareness; then

$$\tau_6 = P(A \cup S) = P(A) + P(S) - P(A \cap S)$$
$$= \tau_1 + \tau_3 - (\tau_1 * \tau_3).$$

under the independence assumption. Derive the other trial expressions similarly.

The model assumes no interaction between the different forms of awareness and satisfies the following inequalities:

$$\max\{\tau_1, \tau_3\} \leq \tau_6 \leq \tau_1 + \tau_3.$$

Although it might hypothesized a positive interaction exceeding that suggested by τ_6, no empirical evidence supports the hypothesis. Experience with the Discovery simulated test marketing model and with consumer test marketing suggests that the interactive effect is negligible.

PEOPLE AWARE OF THE PRODUCT FOR MULTIPLE PERIODS

Two additional factors complicate computing trial probabilities for prospects who have maintained awareness for two purchase periods. Since these prospects have failed to try the product during one purchase period, their probability of trial should be less than those of newly aware prospects. In addition, the marketer has exposed these prospects to new advertising or a promotion in the current period and this will alter the degree of their awareness and, as a result, trial probability. To account for this latter factor, denote the awareness state by two components (i, j) where

$i =$ one of the 16 possible awareness states in time period t, including unaware, and

$j =$ awareness state in time period t-1.

For example, $(1, 6)$ is the initial awareness due to advertising (State 1) in period t, and initial awareness due to advertising and sampling (State 6) in period t-1 (see figure 5.5, page 133, for an illustration of these states).

State 16 indicates no new awareness in the current time period. So $(16, 1)$ indicates a consumer who was initially aware of the product due solely to advertising and then, since there was no new exposure, simply retained the awareness in period t.

State 17 indicates forgotten awareness. So $(2, 17)$ denotes a consumer who became aware in period t-2, forgot the product, then had renewed awareness achieved due to couponing in period t.

The model expresses trial probability as $(\tau_{ij})^2$ for consumers who are aware for two periods. The model squares the probability to show the failure to purchase effect during period t-1, the period of initial awareness

$$\tau_{ij} = \tau_i + \tau_j - (\tau_i * \tau_j),$$

where $\tau_1, \ldots \tau_{15}$ are prospects who are newly aware of the product, and thus τ_{ij} depends on the mix of exposures over the previous two time periods. Also, $\tau_{16} = \tau_{17} = 0$.

Three-period people who are aware of the product first achieved awareness in period t-2 and have failed to try the product in the two time periods prior to t.

Developing the consumer states analogously to the two-period people who are aware of the product, the model denotes this state by a triplet (i, j, k), where

i = awareness state in time period t;

j = awareness state in time period t-1;

k = awareness state in time period t-2; and

$$i, j, k = 1, \ldots, 17.$$

The trial probability is given by $(\tau_{i,j,k})^3$ for consumers who are aware for three periods and

$$\tau_{i,j,k} = \tau_i + \tau_j + \tau_k - (\tau_i * \tau_j) - (\tau_i * \tau_k) - (\tau_j * \tau_k) + (\tau_i * \tau_j * \tau_k).$$

As before, $\tau_1, \ldots, \tau_{15}$ are the awareness-to-trial probabilities for new people who are aware of the product and $\tau_{16} = \tau_{17} = 0$.

UPDATING AWARENESS AND NEW-TRIER FRACTIONS

Consumers who first achieve awareness in period t, $A_i(1)$, where i = 1, \ldots, 15, can be in one of three states in period t+1:

1. they are new triers;
2. they retained awareness, but did not try in preceding period; or
3. they have forgotten the product.

In calculating the fraction of new people who try the product, the effect of imperfect distribution in period t is to diminish the probability of trial by a factor, $D(t)$, which denotes the probability that the product is available to a prospective purchaser. The trial fraction from new people who are aware of the product in period t is

$$T_1(t) = \sum_{i=1}^{16} A_i(1)^* \tau_i^* D(t).$$

The expression, $(1-\lambda_i^* D(t))$, is the fraction of the newly aware prospects who did not try the product in period t. Of the prospects who do not buy the product (the nontriers), a fraction will retain awareness and the remainder will not.

is the fraction of the newly aware prospects who did not try the product in period t. Of the prospects who do not buy the product (the nontriers), a fraction will retain awareness and the remainder will not.

The retention coefficient, $r_c(i)$, denotes the probability that a consumer in awareness state i will retain awareness in the succeeding purchase period. The fraction of consumers in two-period awareness state (j, i) in period $t+1$ is given by

$$A_{ji}(2) = P_j(t+1)^* r_c(i)^* A_i(1)^*(1-\tau_i^* D(t)),$$
$$i = 1, \ldots, 15;$$
$$j = 1, \ldots, 16.$$

The fraction of consumers who fail to retain awareness is

$$\sum_{i=1}^{15}(1-r_c(i)^* A_i(1) \cdot (1-\tau_i D(t))).$$

These consumers can achieve new awareness states in period $t+1$:

$$A_{j17}(2) = P_j(t+1)[\sum_{i=1}^{15}(1-r_c(i)^* A_i(1) \cdot (1-\tau_i D(t))))]$$

where $j = 1, \ldots, 16$.

An analogous process will update two-period awareness in period t. The trial fraction $T_2(t)$ is given by

$$T_2(t) = \sum_{j=1}^{17} \sum_{i=1}^{17} A_{ji}(2)^* \lambda_{ji} D(t).$$

Awareness in t+1:

$$A_{kji}(3) = P_k(t+1) * r_c(j,i) * A_{ji}(2) * (1-\tau_{ji}^2 D(t)),$$

where $i = 1, \ldots 17; j = 1, \ldots 16; k = 1, \ldots 16$.

New awareness created from the pool of consumers who had failed to retain earlier awareness may be expressed by

$$A_{kji}(3) = P_k(t+1)\sum_{j=1}^{15}\sum_{i=1}^{15}[(1-r_c(j,i)*A_{ji}(2)*(1-\lambda_{ji}^2 D(t))].$$

Consumers who have been aware of the product for the past three periods become people who try the product during the period or have a negligible probability of trial thereafter. This group remains in this state for the study's duration. The trial fraction, $T_3(t)$, is

$$T_3(t) = \sum_{k=1}^{17}\sum_{j=1}^{17}\sum_{i=1}^{17}A_{kji}(3) \cdot \lambda_{kji}^3 * D(t).$$

The lapsed awareness fraction, $L(t)$, may be computed as follows:

$$L(t) = \sum_{k=1}^{17}\sum_{j=1}^{17}\sum_{i=1}^{17}A_{kji}(3) \cdot [1-\lambda_{kji}^3 * D(t)].$$

THE TRIAL-TO-REPEAT PURCHASE PROCESS

The fraction of consumers who are new people who try the product in period t is

$$NT(t) = T_1(t)+T_2(t)+T_3(t).$$

Once a consumer has tried the product, there is an opportunity to make a repeat purchase in each succeeding purchase period. The probability of a repeat purchase increases with the number of prior purchases and decreases whenever a consumer fails to purchase during a period.

Figure 5.7, page 137, shows the repeat purchase process schematically. The nodes represent repeat purchase process states, and the arrows denote the probability of moving from one state to another between purchase cycles.

Primes indicate the number of purchase periods in which a consumer has failed to make a purchase since trying the product. For example,

1 denotes a new trier, one who first tried the product in the time period;

1' denotes a new trier who failed to purchase during last period;

1" denotes a new trier who has failed to purchase in the preceding two periods;

2 denotes a consumer who made a second purchase in the preceding time period;

2' denotes a consumer who has made two purchases, but has failed to purchase in one purchase cycle;

r_1 is the trial-to-repeat purchase probability; and

r_2 is the loyalty factor where $r_2 > r_1$.

For $k = 1, \ldots$, the kth repeat purchase probability is

$$r_k = r_{max} - [((r_{max} - r_2)^{k-1})/((r_{max} - r_1)^{k-2})].$$

Therefore, $r_1 \leq r_2 \leq r_k \leq r_{max}$. The repeat purchase probabilities increase and approach maximum repeat, r_{max}, asymptotically, continually increasing until it reaches the limit.

The consumer who fails to repurchase during a period is less probable to repurchase in the next time period than the consumer who does repurchase.

The first failure reduces the probability of repeat purchase from r_1 to $(r_1)^2$ and the second missed purchase reduces it by another factor of r_1.

After three purchase periods without a repurchase, a consumer's repurchase probability drops to 0; these consumers move into the lapsed purchaser state.

CALCULATING UNIT SALES

Symbolize the volume of an initial purchase in a given package size as VF. Index the product category's most common package size at 1.0. If the average package size is 16 ounces, a 16-ounce purchase VF equals 1.0; an 8-ounce package in this category has a VF equal to 0.5.

Therefore, the standardized fraction of units purchased by people who try the product in a period is NT(t) * VF, where NT(t) denotes the fraction of people who try the product in period t.

Similarly, repeat purchasers may buy the product in the same or a different size. VS indicates this repeat purchase's size or volume. Thus, the standardized fraction of units purchased by a repeat purchaser in a period is R(t)*VS. The total fraction of buyers in the period is NT(t)+R(t), and the total fraction of units sold (the market share in units, or U) gives

$$U = NT(t) * VF + R(t) * VS.$$

Index

About the Authors

Kevin J. Clancy, Ph. D., is cofounder, chairman, and CEO of Copernicus Marketing Consulting and Research, a firm that helps Fortune 500 and other leading companies around the world make better marketing decisions. He is coauthor of six business books including *The Marketing Revolution, Marketing Myths That Are Killing Business,* and *Counterintuitive Marketing.*

Peter C. Krieg is cofounder, chairman, and CEO of Copernicus Marketing Consulting and Research. One of America's leading marketing consultants, Krieg is spearheading Copernicus' expansion in Latin America and the Middle East. He is the coauthor of *Counterintuitive Marketing.*

Marianne McGarry Wolf, Ph. D., is professor of agribusiness at California Polytechnic State University. She has consulted for decades to companies on domestic and international marketing research studies and is a recognized expert on simulated test marketing.